ACTORS
TURNED
DIRECTORS

ACTORS
TURNED
DIRECTORS

ON ELICITING THE BEST
PERFORMANCE FROM AN ACTOR
AND OTHER SECRETS OF SUCCESSFUL DIRECTING

JON STEVENS

SILMAN-JAMES PRESS   **LOS ANGELES**

First Edition
10 9 8 7 6 5 4 3 2 1

Library of Congress Cataloging-in-Publication Data

Stevens, Jon, 1943–
Actors turned directors : on eliciting the best performance from an actor
and other secrets of successful directing / by Jon Stevens. —1st ed.
p.   cm.
1. Motion pictures—Production and direction. 2. Motion picture
producers and directors—Interviews. I. Title.
PN1995.9.P7S72   1997
791.43'0233—dc21   97-34220
                                                   CIP

ISBN: 1-879505-34-7

The publishers wish to thank the Directors Guild of America
for their assistance in bringing this project to fruition.

Cover design by Wade Lageose, Art Hotel

Printed and Bound in the United States of America

Silman-James Press
1181 Angelo Drive
Beverly Hills, CA 90210

CONTENTS

FOREWORD
BY TONY BARR

Reading the excellent interviews in this book, it's pretty clear to me that there is no single approach directors take in eliciting the best performance from an actor. Every actor is different, every director is different. Some directors stroke actors, talk quietly with them, gently coax them to where they need to be. Some like to browbeat actors, insult them, humiliate them in front of the cast and crew. Some get the performances they seek by holding intellectual discussions about the story, the characters, and motivations, while other directors do take after take until something that they like happens, without giving the actor much, if anything, between takes. Some directors like to get there with abstractions, such as "You're a trumpet!" or "It isn't magenta enough!" (Really. An actor told me a director once said that to him.) Then, of course, there are those directors who show actors how to play the scenes or moments.

I believe there's one goal that is common to all directors: get a performance that is real; give the audience the feeling that they are watching a person having an experience, not an actor giving a performance.

On stage, an actor can get away with a lot, because the audience is distanced from him. The camera, on the other hand, is a very intimate thing. The actor can't lie to it. Dishonesty in performance shrieks at the audience. On a stage, the actor communicates through the other actor to the back row of the theater—across theatrical, or unreal, space.

With the camera, the back row is whatever the lens is. The actor need only communicate *to the other actor—across real space*—because the camera puts the back row of the theater on the other actor's shoulder in a close-up, for example. Therefore the actor must be simple, and must be honest.

Not long ago, Sidney Lumet, one of America's most distinguished film directors, appeared on a talk show in Los Angeles. I was in my car listening, and I did something I'd never done before: I stopped at a service station and called the radio station. To my astonishment, I got right through. Without identifying myself, I asked Lumet what he thought about the following acting approach: "Stop acting, start listening; keep it simple, without loss of passion." He thought for a second, then said, "Great. I couldn't have said it better myself."

Sydney Pollack, certainly one of the best actors' directors in the business, said in an interview, "I tell actors, 'Watch *Candid Camera*, then flick the channel to something else, then turn back. You'll see how phony the acting looks because real reaction so often means doing nothing. It's always simple.' The tendency with actors is to think that if you're doing more, you're doing more."

Don't forget that much is added to enhance a film performance: sound effects, good lighting, careful editing for dramatic impact, exciting camera angles, and eighty-seven violins. So what's left for the actor to do? Just be simple and honest. Be "in the moment": listen, absorb, hear, and sense the stimuli hitting him, and then respond to them honestly—therein lies the combination of ingredients that serves as the foundation for great performance. It is the job of the director to be as aware as the actor of those elements, and to provide the actor with an atmosphere and freedom that allows for this simplicity, passion, and honesty to be experienced and expressed.

To me, what it seems to come down to is however a director goes about getting the performance he wants, he's trying to help the actor have an experience, instead of give a performance. Simplicity is beautiful; passion is exciting. What a combination!

Tony Barr, who founded the Film Actors Workshop in Hollywood in 1960, is the author of Acting for the Camera. *He teaches on a limited basis in Los Angeles and conducts seminars on acting for the camera throughout the United States and Canada.*

×

INTRODUCTION

Several years ago, I directed my first feature film, *Out 2 Lunch*. The film dealt with relationships among students in a junior high school, and was entirely cast with students who were non-professional actors. While I did a good job of eliciting performances from my non-professional cast, I felt I could have done better if I had simply known more.

About a year and a half ago, I embarked on directing a feature film, *Irish Whiskey*. Because of my insecurities about my ability to communicate exactly what I wanted from the actors, I decided that my directorial homework should include seeking out a mentor—an experienced director willing to guide me through the process of casting and eliciting excellent performances from my cast. While there have been many fine directors who've elicited excellent performances from actors without themselves having been actors, I believed that an actor-turned-director would have an edge over his or her non-actor colleagues. Therefore, I decided to seek out an actor-turned-director whose wisdom would help me achieve my goal of becoming an excellent actors' director.

For various reasons, my efforts to find such a mentor proved unsuccessful, and for a while, I shelved the idea, as I was consumed with rewrites of the *Irish Whiskey* script.

A year ago, I was offered the opportunity to become a member of the Publication Committee of the *DGA Magazine*, a publication of the

Directors Guild of America that primarily deals with the art and craft of directing. After becoming a member of this committee, I one day found myself in a conversation with Tomm Carroll, editor and publisher of the magazine, who asked me if I had any fresh ideas for articles. I immediately pitched a series of articles entitled *Actors Turned Directors*. Tomm responded with enthusiasm and approved my proposal. I, of course, was elated, because now I had the prospect of having *several* "mentors" who would share with me their wisdom about directing actors.

My first interview, with Richard Benjamin, was successful, and when it was published in the *DGA Magazine*, was greeted with a request from the Screen Actors Guild to reprint it in their in-house magazine. A few months later, I met Gwen Feldman and Jim Fox, partners in Silman-James Press, who thought that the long versions of my interviews would make a wonderful book.

Embarking on my research for the interviews, I read extensively about the process of acting. And the most helpful book I encountered was Tony Barr's *Acting for the Camera*, which went directly to the heart of the actor's process without too much intellectualizing and offered great knowledge about communicating with actors.

Prior to interviewing each of the actors-turned-directors included in this book, I reviewed both the films that they had directed and the films that they had acted in. While some of the questions I then prepared related specifically to how actors were directed in particular scenes, I also designed a general line of questions that I felt all aspiring directors would want answered. Several of these general questions were repeated in most of the interviews in the hope of arriving at a consensus of opinion that could serve as *suggested* guidelines to what directors should and shouldn't do when casting, rehearsing, and shooting their films.

Following my interview with Richard Benjamin, I had the good fortune to interview actors-turned-directors Leonard Nimoy, Jodie Foster, Mel Gibson, Kevin Bacon, Sydney Pollack, Paul Mazursky, Melanie Mayron, Ron Maxwell, and Kevin Hooks, all of whom generously shared their experiences and offered priceless wisdom about eliciting excellent performances from actors and other related directorial chores.

The insights I gained from these interviews helped me tremendously in casting and eliciting marvelous performances from my actors during the rehearsing and shooting of *Irish Whiskey* in the spring of 1996.

I want to take this opportunity to acknowledge my heartfelt gratitude and appreciation to the master actors-turned-directors mentioned above for their patience and magnificent contribution to my growth as a director. Many thanks are also due to Jim Fox, for his splendid editing of my manuscript, Tony Barr, Tomm Carroll, and Gwen Feldman, for their support of this project, and Yolenda Juarez and Ori Seron, for their excellent transcriptions of the interviews.

SYDNEY POLLACK

Sydney Pollack, the versatile and distinguished director, producer, and actor, was born in Lafayette, Indiana, in 1934. Following his high school graduation, he moved to New York, where he studied acting with Sanford Meisner at The Neighborhood Playhouse, eventually becoming Meisner's assistant.

In the late fifties, Pollack began acting in television plays. This work eventually led to his becoming a director of teleplays and episodes of such series as *The Fugitive*, *The Defenders*, *Naked City*, and *Dr. Kildare*. He made his feature film directorial debut in 1965 with *The Slender Thread*. He went on to direct such important and popular films as *This Property is Condemned* (1966), *The Scalphunters* (1968), *Castle Keep* (1969), *They Shoot Horses, Don't They?* (1969), *Jeremiah Johnson* (1972), *The Way We Were* (1973), *The Yakuza* (1975), *Three Days of the Condor* (1975), *Bobby Deerfield* (1977), *The Electric Horseman* (1979), *Absence of Malice* (1981), *Tootsie* (1982), *Out of Africa* (1985), *Havana* (1990), *The Firm* (1993), and *Sabrina* (1995).

Pollack won an Academy Award as Best Director for *Out of Africa*, which also received the Best Picture Award, and was nominated by the Academy for *They Shoot Horses, Don't They?* and *Tootsie*. Among his other honors are a New York Film Critics Award, a Golden Globe, a National Society of Film Critics Award, a NATO Director of the Year Award, and prizes at the Moscow, Taormina, Brussels, Belgrade, and

San Sebastian Film Festivals.

His producing credits include *The Fabulous Baker Boys*, *White Palace*, *Presumed Innocent*, *Searching for Bobby Fischer*, and *Sense and Sensibility*.

As an actor, Pollack has given memorable performances in such films as *Tootsie* and Woody Allen's *Husbands and Wives*.

The following interview took place December 19, 1995.

• • • • •

Why did you become an actor?

Acting was a pipe dream of mine when I was a kid in the Midwest. I didn't expect to literally make a living as an actor. I thought it would be wonderful if I could spend a couple of years studying in New York, because that seemed to me to be a very exciting and glamorous thing to do. I don't think I ever believed I would actually get to be an actor, but I was able to talk my parents into giving me two years' leeway before going to a "real" college to make something of myself.

So, I went to an acting school in New York known as The Neighborhood Playhouse, which in the late fifties was a great, great school. Dance was taught by Martha Graham, and the acting department was presided over by Sandy Meisner, who was a great acting teacher. I became Meisner's assistant and remained there for four or five years, teaching. Through teaching, I slowly segued into directing.

When and how did you make the transition from acting and teaching to directing feature films?

I didn't really decide to become a director. The decision was made for me more by opportunity and other people.

I had the chance to work on several television shows and, subsequently, a film version of Henry James' novel *The Turn of the Screw*, which was Ingrid Bergman's first television show in the United States. I was officially called a "dialogue coach." Ostensibly, my job was to help teach actors their dialogue, but I was really hired by John Frankenheimer to coach the two young kids who were in it.

It was an interesting and difficult job because, although I had to talk to the children about acting, it was very important that I not interfere with the actual directing that Frankenheimer was doing. I was able to be of some help to John and the kids without getting in his way. And as a result of that experience, which went well, he hired me to come to Hollywood in 1960 and work in the same capacity with some teenagers who were in a film of his called *The Young Savages*, which starred Burt Lancaster, Shelley Winters, Telly Savalas, and these teenagers who played Italian and Puerto Rican juvenile delinquents involved in a murder.

I worked with the actors who played the delinquents, and in the process, Burt Lancaster got interested in what I was doing. In a rather joking way at first, which was his way, he began to kid me about it, calling me "the New York acting coach."

He got genuinely interested in what I was doing and began to talk to me about it. And by the time that picture ended, Burt asked me to come over and see him in his office, which I did. He said I should be a director. At first I thought it was an insult—Burt saying I was never going to be a great actor, so why not just become a director. Frankenheimer had also been pushing me in that direction, and even though I had no aspiration to be a director, it seemed like an interesting possibility.

Burt called Lew Wasserman and asked him to meet with me. And Wasserman, trying to do a favor for Burt, I guess, or trusting Burt's judgment, which is less likely, let me observe television shows at Universal Studios for a period of six months. That was my initiation into directing. I watched for six months, and then they let me direct.

I spent four or five years directing television. And I stayed in touch with Burt. In the middle of that period, Burt went off to make *The Leopard*, directed by Visconte, and asked me to come over and watch a bit of it so that I could help him post-record his dialogue. They didn't record with live sound. Most of the picture was dubbed in Italian—Burt was dubbed in Italian. But in the American release, he had to post-sync his voice into the picture and hired me to help him do that.

After that, I did another couple of years of television work. And then I did my first feature film, *A Slender Thread*, with Sidney Poitier and Anne Bancroft, and *This Property's Condemned*, with Natalie Wood and Robert Redford. Then Burt asked me to direct a film initiated by him—*The Scalphunters*.

In essence, Burt was responsible for my becoming a director. He was truly a great actor, a great man. I felt terrific respect, obligation, and gratitude toward him. I was honored and glad to be asked to direct him.

It strikes me that there's a common thread that connects your films. You do romantic stories and your heroes are rebels or outsiders challenging the system. Would you agree?

I always have difficulty talking about my own work on a thematic level, because I don't know that I'm the most accurate observer of my work. But it is true that, when I read observations about it, those seem to be some of the things that are said over and over.

I know for sure that I do romantic stories, because that's what interests me. Even though the genres may change—they may be thrillers or Westerns or whatever—my films usually contain love stories. As to the precise psychological profiles of the males and females, I'm a little bit lost, because they all seem a bit different to me. But I'm sure they share certain properties. After all, I make the choices, so I'm sure that I reveal myself more than I intend to.

You seem to like Westerns. Is there a particular reason for this?

I think that the Western, in a certain way, is the most emblematic American film form. It's the most primitive, and it's the most elegant in its simplicity. It's an extremely versatile and powerful art form that Americans specifically created, and then moved into modern dress, in a way, with the detective. Raymond Chandler's Philip Marlowe is really the gunman who rides into town and cleans up the corruption, and rides off alone again.

I lament the fact that the Western is a form that isn't looked upon with a lot of favor now. It's very tough to make a Western work today. In the past couple of years, we've seen several attempts that unfortunately have not been enormously successful, other than *Unforgiven* and *Dances with Wolves*, which were exceptional cases.

I read that Paramount's President, John Goldwyn, discussing *Sabrina*, said that you are "one of the very few filmmakers who really works on the script." How involved are you in the development of the script?

I work very, very hard on the script. But it's difficult to assess precisely what it is I do. It's a difficult question because I work with very, very good, gifted writers.

It isn't that they're not able to write it; they are. It's that we do a lot of collaborative work, both in the area of concept and in the area of execution. Moment by moment, line by line, beat by beat.

I spend a lot of time in a room with the writer or writers, crawling through and over every page and every line. I give them specific notes, which I'm sure every director does. We talk first in general terms. Then we get more and more specific as the work progresses until it's actually as though I'm directing the scene.

You come across a moment that "bumps" for you, and you say, "Well, this isn't quite working, we have to change something here" or "let's fix this" or "suppose he does this" or "suppose she does that."

Sometimes we work together on scenes. Sometimes we'll develop a concept and then the writers will go away, do a draft of a scene and bring it back, and then we'll work some more on it.

I usually end up typing the script myself. I don't know why. I think it's a way for me to literally ingest it in some way. Once I've typed it, through, I feel like I know it on a much more intimate level. Eventually, I've done all the drafts of the script—every single one—by hand.

For example, take the *Sabrina* file here. [Pollack refers to his computer.] Everything in here is *Sabrina*—drafts in progress or final, final, final. Sixty-four files. Let's open one.

My note here says, "It feels awkward to try to establish Sabrina in the tree then continue to establish the break. Seems as though we ought to end with Sabrina in the tree rather than break it in two. Page two: I lose the thread of the girl . . . shall we use the moon images? Page seven . . . " so on and so on. Thirteen notes on the first five pages.

Here, let's try something else. Under the "Still to do" file: "They're doing real work in the real world, while David watches from the North Shore." A line of dialogue: "I know, and you're awfully good at it. Making money's easy."

You get specific about lines of dialogue?

Oh, yeah, very much so. We also do biographies, little backstories of the characters. It takes a long time.

How long does it take to develop a script like *Sabrina*?

It varies. *Sabrina* took over a year. The main problems for me had to do with moving this story into the nineties without losing the sense that it's a fairy tale. I think that required us to be tougher on some of the logic that comes from the original. I was worried that today's audiences wouldn't accept the lightning bolts of emotional swings that the original had.

I noticed that you brought in David Rayfiel. You work with him a lot. You must have a good rapport with him.

I have worked with him for thirty years. I brought David in to work with Barbara Benedek, and the three of us worked very much in concert. They would go off and write in the evenings and the mornings, and then we would meet in the afternoon and go over it, blending what each had done. And sometimes we would write together in the room.

So each would write the same scene?

Sometimes, but very rarely. They worked together a lot. Sometimes one would try a version, and then the other would rewrite it. And then the first person would rewrite it again, a third time.

The kind of discussion that you and I are having is difficult, because it sounds like I'm taking writing credit here, and I'm not. These are very good writers. I'm not a writer. They wrote a beautiful script. But we did work closely together on it.

Do you encourage the writer's involvement in creative decisions once a script is completed?

Yes. I often will call the writer and discuss things like sets and wardrobe.

What about casting?

I'll talk to the writers, but I feel more strongly independent about that.

Was your television work useful training for directing your first feature film, *The Slender Thread*?

It was very useful. It was the only form of film school that I had, really. In fact, I think of that movie as a big television show. It wasn't a very good movie. I had nice performances in it, but it was all shot a bit like a television show. I was frantically trying to keep the viewer's attention, like you do in short acts, segments of a television show.

How did that project come about?

In 1963, 1964, and 1965, I was nominated for Emmys. Once that started to happen, I would occasionally get a film offer. In those days, the film industry drafted a lot of its directors from the ranks of television. I was part of what I would call the "second wave" of those directors. The "first wave" came out of live television—Frankenheimer, George Roy Hill, Frank Schaffner, Sidney Lumet. They were red-hot, New York television directors. The second wave included Robert Altman, Mark Rydell, Norman Jewison, and myself. We all were directing television at that time. And once you began to get a reputation in television, you would get film offers.

The Slender Thread was a character piece. It wasn't a big, complicated production; it was a lot of long scenes. It seemed an ideal way to jump from the little tube to the big screen without stretching too hard.

How different is feature film acting from live drama or the television programs that you were directing?

Live television dramas, like *Playhouse 90*, were done much like plays. They were rehearsed fully, and done in continuity on tape. Filmed television was very much like doing a movie: You had very little rehearsal, almost none. You did your rehearsing on the set, and then you shot.

What challenges did you have to overcome as a first-time feature film director? What was your first day of shooting like? Did you set out to prove something?

As I recall, I was pretty scared and nervous. I still am nervous on the first day of a shoot. I don't think you ever get over that. There's a lot at stake, and your decisions are critical at each moment. I don't think I was trying to prove anything, I was just trying to get through the movie—make the movie, and make it entertaining and understandable and good.

Did you shoot fewer pages, simpler scenes on the first day?

Now I work very differently than I did then, because then I didn't have control over anything. I just was lucky to get the job; I didn't have any say about anything except, once I got on the floor, staging the scenes and all that. I didn't have tremendous control over the script. I worked on the script, but I was the novice, the new guy.

Your control grows as your knowledge expands. Now, for example, I try not to start a movie at the beginning of the week. I try to start close to the end of the week—on a Wednesday or a Thursday—so that I can do two, three days of shooting, then stop for a weekend and figure out if I have to make changes. I realized how silly it was to try to shoot for a full week with a brand new crew and a bunch of people who don't know each other.

I always try to start with scenes that allow the actors to begin to know each other a little bit, rather than jump into big, intimate scenes right away. Everybody hopes to shoot in continuity as much as possible. But that's not possible with the economics of moviemaking, so you try to be reasonably sane about not doing something that's so far off.

What about a film with a lot of action—do you save the action for later and focus on your emotional scenes first?

It actually works in the reverse. I don't think action is difficult. It's much more difficult to get to the intangible emotional things. When I say difficult, I'm talking about scenes where the emotions reach fruition, scenes that you planted all through the script to develop the complexity of the characters. It's very hard to start with those kinds of scenes; it's very hard to start where the emotions are full-blown.

Action scenes are technical, and technical problems are solvable, like mathematical puzzles are solvable; emotional problems are not. There are millions of ways to solve an emotional problem, and there's no certainty that you're ever right. They're not provable the way an action sequence can be built up.

For an action sequence, you break down the shots, break down the tricks, and decide a better way or a more clever way to do the trick, or a more interesting way to shoot it. But what's very, very tough, is a scene in which ninety-nine percent of what's going on is buried emotionally in the actors. It cannot be solved by some mathematical formula.

For example, there's a scene in *Sabrina*—almost a ten-minute scene, one of the longest scenes I've ever directed on the screen—with just two people. In the scene, Harrison Ford, playing Linus, tries to close the trap on Sabrina, played by Julie Ormond, supposedly revealing the lie that he's crazy about her. But when he sees her full-blown joy at how happy he's made her, he cannot continue the lie and confesses. I can't begin to direct a movie with a scene like that. I would find it completely impossible. The actors wouldn't have any kind of working relationship with each other, unless they've worked together before, and that's very rare. They will not yet have been inside the characters' skins long enough to know them. So I start with much less complex scenes. I give the actors the opportunity to develop a working relationship with each other and to get a more in-depth understanding of the characters they're playing before I get into intense, emotional scenes like the one I just described. And, believe me, the actors feel better about it, and you, as a director, elicit a better performance out of them. So, if there are any rules, and I don't personally think there are, this is one of them. And this is the way that I like to work. I'm sure it differs from one director to another, and maybe from actor to actor.

What was the first scene you shot in *Sabrina*?

A fairly simple scene with Harrison and his mother inside a car. He's on the telephone to his office, asking them to buy up stock, and saying to his mother that his brother, David, has begun to date the daughter of a very, very wealthy man who runs a big electronics company. It was a scene that didn't require days and days of getting used to relationships. It was a good starting point.

Once you get the green light on a project, where do you begin your directorial homework? How do you break down and analyze the script? What kinds of notes do you do? What kind of technical research do you do?

I do all of those things at once. It's like a chess game. It's a mosaic; it's not linear—you don't *just* work on the script and then *just* work on the casting and then *just* work on the physical preparation and then *just* work on the costumes, you do everything at the same time. But certain things happen in order.

The very first and most important thing is to assemble a creative crew—the cinematographer, the first assistant, the production designer, the costumer, the line producer—because they help you to get on screen what you imagine in your head. Then everything starts to cross-fertilize everything else.

You spend a very, very long time on the script, but while you're working on the script, you begin to think about casting and you begin to scout locations, which sometimes give you new ideas for scenes. Everything interacts. I concentrate very hard on understanding and articulating for myself and everyone else involved what I think the picture's about. By "what it's about" I do not mean story. What a film is about, in my opinion, has nothing to do with story. Quite the opposite. It's everything except the story. It's trying to arrive at a sort of spine, if you will, of the picture—a way of viewing it that directorially instructs you on a way to view each scene.

Tootsie?

Tootsie was about a man who became a better man for having been a woman. If you start to look at every scene and say, "In what way does this scene illustrate the idea of a man becoming a better man for having been a woman?" you see that, in the beginning, Tootsie works very hard to show you that part of him which needs redeeming, because if he's going to be better at something, he has to be worse at it first. The minute I define that as an idea, I can begin to measure every scene against it in some way. That doesn't mean it's going to be a good movie. It just means I know what it's about, and can communicate that to the actors.

Then I can start to chart the improvements in the character—what changes in him? how does it change in him? what is the nature of the experience that he's having?—all the time knowing that the idea is to be funny and entertaining.

Do you hand out scene-by-scene notes to your creative department heads?

I do most of it verbally. I occasionally write memos, but I believe in intuitive things. It's all about feelings, and feelings are communicated in many ways. Sometimes they don't have anything to do with words, don't have anything to do with writing anything down. So I believe very strongly in hanging out.

If I hang out with a production designer long enough, sit and have meals with him and talk about everything—sometimes about the movie, sometimes other things in life—if I make an observation about how pretty the light is here now or about the sound in a room or the way the colors of that tree look against the light, the production designer is going to learn and pick up things. It doesn't mean that we don't have very specific talks about what Linus's office looks like in *Sabrina*, for example. We do, but there are also other things to talk about.

That happens in writing, too. I think that all creative work, on any level, is a kind of controlled free-association. When you say, "I'm going to go home and work on my movie," what does that mean? You can't just clench your fists, screw up your eyes, and say, "I'm working hard, very hard." Sometimes the hardest way to work is to just lay down, close your eyes, and let your mind drift about a scene. Things will happen when you do that. You'll find yourself moving from one topic to another in a way that seems random, but isn't.

When you work with a writer, often it's a process of free-association. You start to talk about the scene, and talking about the scene reminds you of something that happened to you. You tell that story, and that reminds the writer of a similar thing that happened, and he tells you a story. Then the third person in the room says, "Well, a whole different thing happened to me," and tells that story. And that reminds you of a show you saw the other day, and you say, "Did you see that show where . . . ?" At the end of an hour of that, you may have arrived at a piece of illumination for the scene. What I'm saying, I guess, is that there is a mechanical technique that can be applied to anything, and it will help you find your way into it.

But the most important part, the best part, that part which is unique and your own creative impulse, which makes one director's work different from another director's, is not so controllable. That part gets freed by doing all the controllable things, even though you know they may very well be wrong.

How do you determine the look of a film?

You read books and screen films. Research is one of the tools. Sometimes you even hire a research person. On *Out of Africa*, I hired somebody to get me details on coffee plantations: What's the precipitation? When do the rains come? What the traditions are in that part of Africa? What are the tribal recreations?

I read a script, and I just try to make it good. How should this look? Who do I discuss the look with? I discuss the look with the people who contribute to the look. The people who dress the actors contribute to the look. The cinematographer contributes to the look. The production designer contributes to the look. The prop man contributes to the look. Anybody who's got anything that gets in front of the camera contributes to the look. And how do you arrive at it? You talk about it. The cameraman might make suggestions. You might make suggestions back. Sometimes the production designer does a lot of sketches.

Do you personally approve each one of their decisions?

The critical ones, yes. The wardrobe, yes; I look at every outfit. And the same with the extras. Sometimes they don't look right.

I notice that, in your recent films, the camera seems to move much more than it did in your earlier films.

Not necessarily. I think of *Out of Africa* and *Jeremiah Johnson* as having a minimal amount of movement—more letting the landscape alone and moving the people within the frame—as opposed to *They Shoot Horses, Don't They?* or *The Firm* or *Three Days of the Condor*, which had more camera movement in it than anything else I've done.

You try to shoot a scene the way you think it needs to be shot. Sometimes you want the world to have rough edges; sometimes you want the world to have clean, perfect edges. And that's the way you compose your shots. The camera is almost never still. Never. In *The Firm*, sometimes you're not even aware of it, but it's slowly, imperceptibly there—imperceptibly zooming forward so slowly that you can't see it. There's just a feeling of tightness there.

Was this something that you determined in preproduction?

Partially in preproduction, partially as we were shooting, as we would stage scenes. It's a thriller. It seems to me that this kind of kinetic energy keeps it moving. Literally. *Jeremiah Johnson*, on the other hand, has a minimal amount of movement. It's about the landscape, and it's about, if anything, the changing perspective of an innocent man against the big landscape, a man who grows to legend and is now big against the diminished landscape.

During much of the beginning of that film, he was shot so that he was a speck in the landscape. As the myth grew, his size emotionally grew, and he began to loom larger and dominate the landscape, or equal it, in a certain way. In most of that movie, it was important to let the physical world speak for itself. It wasn't a question of going in real close and zooming around and being real tight. Quite the opposite.

Do you make those creative decisions after seeing the locations or as you read the script?

Sometimes you know when a breakthrough idea happens, but sometimes you don't. Sometimes it just accumulates. And when you go to the location, you just start to shoot. Redford and I spent hours and hours and hours talking about the mountains and life and his character and what that world must have been like. Those hours are like fertilizer, they go into your brain and start doing something. Sometimes you don't know what they're doing. Once we started to shoot, we didn't talk a lot anymore. We just shot. And it came out how it came out.

You don't always sit down and say how you're going to do everything. You ask yourself questions, and you try to answer them. You ask yourself: "What is this scene about? What is this moment about?" And when you have the answers to those questions, you ask, "What does that mean in terms of how to shoot it?" "This is a memory," you may say. Well, what makes a memory different from a non-memory? Is it the elimination of some details? Is it the addition of many details? Is it impossible combinations? What are the specifics?

In the end, everything is technical in a movie. Everything. It doesn't matter how intellectual you get, you finally have to ask, "How do I specifically realize this idea?" It doesn't do any good to say, "This is poetic, this is lyrical." What the hell does that mean? So it's lyrical, what are you going to do, put a program note up that says, "Hey, audience, this is lyrical"? How do you shoot lyrical? What do you do technically to make it lyrical? Well, different people may do different things. Different people have different meanings of "lyrical."

What process do you go through to help you determine the right way of shooting a film or a scene?

If it is necessary to discuss it with your DP and other creative department heads, you do. If it isn't necessary, and sometimes it isn't, then you don't say anything. You do as much as is required to get the result that you dream about, that you see in your mind.

Sometimes you're just on the same wavelength. One of the reasons I've worked so often with Redford is that there comes a point after all the discussions and the talk and the groaning and moaning, and we both do plenty of groaning and moaning, where we just go to work, and in the process, something happens. On the other hand, with some actors, I have to reiterate an approach every single take and every single day, because we're coming at it from different points of view or it's more difficult for them to understand.

Tell me about your casting process and what you expect from your casting director.

Fresh ideas, a more original approach than I have, I suppose. More than anything, casting begins with an understanding of the material. An understanding of the traps in the material.

For example, in *Sabrina*, if I had cast Greg Kinnear, who played David Larrabee, as a more mature or a slightly more dangerous or challenging person, you would never have forgiven him for his behavior. It's not funny when someone is engaged and then immediately makes a pass at somebody else. It's not funny when someone doesn't ever go to work, drives Ferraris, and spends the family's money irresponsibly. It either puts a smile on your face or it makes you hate them. It depends on who the person is, it depends on their forgivability. The understanding of that is essential to making the part work.

In *Out of Africa*, Klaus Brandauer, who played Meryl Streep's husband, was the worst bastard who ever lived. He gave her syphilis and stole her money, but you forgave him, and she forgave him, because Brandauer had real charm. I saw that in the Bond film where he played a horrible villain who had real charm, which made me desperate to get him to play that role.

Is it difficult for you to adjust your vision if a particular star is unavailable or doesn't want to do the script? How do you take a rejection from an actor? Do you ever take it personally?

Sometimes I take it personally, but most of the time I don't. We all have to do what we think is right for us. Sometimes actors don't feel an identification with the material, and they say no. And sometimes I do have to make changes.

Absence of Malice, for example, was a movie about a man who was Italian, not Irish. He was a dark guy who had a string of laundries, and he was supposed to have all the appearances of a mafia guy. The whole point to that story was that appearances are deceiving. I spent a long, long time rehearsing with Al Pacino. I read through the scenes with him, and at the last minute, he didn't feel comfortable doing it. So we went to Paul Newman. Now that's a pretty radical change. We reinvented the character and made him Irish. We restructured it quickly, within a week. The only thing we didn't change was the character's job—the job of a man who has all the appearances of one thing, but who's really not that thing.

Sometimes you can't make a change like that. The roles that Brandauer and Kinnear played have more restrictive demands. You don't have a lot flexibility. In *Sabrina*, for example, Kinnear had to be believable as Harrison Ford's brother. There were physical requirements he had to have. And, as I've said, he had to possess a kind of forgivability. You also had to believe that he was capable of growing up, taking responsibility, taking over the company.

Who has control over casting your pictures?

There's a myth here that studios are these terrible ogres who are out to crush you. The truth is that they are trying to do the same thing you're trying to do. Most of the time, a director has control over casting. But, if there's somebody that the studio hates, or has had bad luck with consistently, you might have a fight on your hands.

When casting newcomers, what qualities do you look for?

Sometimes you have to hire them without seeing them on film. You're taking a chance with somebody brand new, like Greg Kinnear. I never saw him act. I saw him do his talk show, and because I had an instinct that he could do the movie, I worked with him. I sat here and rehearsed with him, and then shot a video of him. It's a gamble, and sometimes you must take that risk. The whole movie is a gamble.

Do you try to do screen tests with new actors?

I haven't done that many screen tests. I cast on instinct.

Do you believe that reading actors is the best method to find the ones you're looking for?

No. I'd rather see them work. See them in something. If they don't have anything I can see, then I have to read them.

Some directors sit down and just talk to the actor.

That's if they know the actor can act. I don't think there's any director who would cast somebody that they've either never seen work or never seen read for them, but there are exceptions.

Look at the guy who played the Paris photographer in *Sabrina*, Patrick Bruel. He came into my office just like you, sat down there for two seconds, and I cast him. I'd never seen him work, I'd never seen him in anything. It wasn't that big of a part. I felt comfortable from his attitude.

It depends on what you're talking about. If you're talking about the lead in a movie, no, you have to know what they're going to do. If you're talking about somebody playing a reasonably simple part, you can do it. Like that photographer. I had a feeling that you would like him. I knew he was a singer. I saw a lot of personality in him, and I felt comfortable in my own ability to relax him enough on the set to get what I needed from him.

When new actors read for you, do they just read and leave or do you direct them a little bit?

I direct them a little bit to see how well they take direction, to move them closer to the role if I see an interesting quality of work. If they've completely misinterpreted the role, but they've executed it well, if the quality of their acting has reality and truth in it, but they've played the wrong character because they've made the wrong choices, I change the choices.

What are the most important things you want to know about actors you're considering?

All I care about is how well they act.

Your casting always seems so right on. What do you look for in an actor? Do you rely strictly on your instincts? Is there a mechanical thing, a technical thing, that one can do to assure oneself of casting the right people?

You can feel confident and still be wrong. Is there a positive way to identify who is or isn't right for a picture? The answer is, of course, no. Everything is an opinion in this business. *Everything.* *Variety* hated *Sabrina* and *The Reporter* loved it. Everything is an opinion. You can't say one is absolutely right and the other is absolutely wrong. That's just not the way the world works.

When you come to something as personal as a film, you make choices that you trust or believe in. Sometimes you're right and sometimes you're wrong. But you'd better be right more often than you're wrong or you're not going to have a career. It's as simple as that. There's no formula for it.

You try to follow what you like as a director. It's a kind of absolutely necessary egotism, because there isn't any other way to do it. Sometimes, happily, you're right, and other people agree with you. Sometimes, unhappily, nobody agrees with you. There are some people who think that Greg Kinnear is absolutely marvelous, and there are some people who think he's not. Luckily, more people think he's good than not. He's getting wonderful reviews, but am I a genius or a bum? Well, neither, and that's the truth. I made a choice that I thought was right, and I've pleased some people but I haven't pleased everybody. And that's the case with every movie I've ever made. You're dead in the water if you just try to make movies to please other people.

When casting major stars you haven't worked with before, how can you tell if they're going to have good chemistry? Do you bring them together to at least talk?

Sometimes. If they have to play love scenes, I like to see them together. When we were looking for somebody to play Sabrina, I tested her with Harrison Ford. I did a screen test. But sometimes you don't. I didn't screen test Meryl Streep with Redford. This business of chemistry, it's just hard to know. Sometimes people have it together and sometimes they don't. I just try to get somebody who's great for the part. Chemistry takes care of itself.

I remember a little controversy about Lena Olin and Redford in *Havana*. Personally, I thought they had great chemistry.

I did, too. What you mistake for chemistry sometimes is your own chemistry. I really think Redford is terrific in movies and on screen, and like him. And I really think Lena Olin is terrific and beautiful on screen. I assumed they had chemistry. As I watched them, they both worked for me. But that's not necessarily true for an audience. It wasn't on that picture.

Do you ever cast non-actors?

Very rarely. There must be a reason to use a non-actor. Why would I use a non-actor when there are professionals out there whose life and job it is to act? I would rather go with a professional. Sometimes if you're just looking for a fresh face, you'll take a chance with somebody. But I wouldn't go looking for non-actors unless I were doing cinema vérité, a Cassavetes kind of film.

Do you have any keys to successful casting?

I think everything in the film business is about recognizing the traps beforehand and avoiding them, trying to understand what is the wrong casting for a role, and then avoiding that. If you start by saying, "This picture is not going to work if such and such a person plays such and such a role," then you at least know what you're avoiding.

Sometimes you define what to do by defining what not to do. If you have an actor whose meanness you believe playing Linus Larrabee, you're dead. So you have to have a very strong, tough man whose meanness you are willing to overlook because you sense decency in him above all, somebody that the audience would give the benefit of the doubt to.

What's your philosophy on rehearsals?

Some actors like rehearsals, and some actors don't. I personally do not like a lot of rehearsal. I get what I get out of not rehearsing most of the time, because rehearsing, for me, tends to freeze the actors, tends to preview the experience. Now, I've seen the work of terrific directors who rehearse like crazy. This is not a question of what's right or wrong. It's a question of just what works for me. Sometimes, if an actor needs it, I rehearse.

How do you recognize an actor's wrong choices? What do you say to him or her? Any guidelines?

It's different for every actor. If an actor is having trouble, then I have to work very hard. If an actor is not having trouble, then I don't have to do any more than I have to do. There's no sense in directing when it isn't required. If somebody is doing a great job because I cast them so brilliantly that they have an immediate identification with the character, and the script works, then I just sit there and say, "Action! Cut!"

If, on the other hand, the actor is very right for the part, but is having difficulty with a scene, maybe the scene isn't right. Maybe I have to adjust the scene. If the scene is right, and I'm convinced it's right, and the actor's still having trouble, then I have to help the actor.

I do what the situation requires me to do. But there isn't any rule; I can't give you ten commandments about working with an actor. My job is to make the actor as comfortable and free and confident as possible in each scene. It's also my job, my responsibility to the people who are paying for the film, to be ultimately responsible for the choices that are made. So if I disagree with the choice that an actor is making, it's partially my job to try to correct that choice.

My goal is to get exactly what I see in my head on screen. Sometimes it's easy and sometimes it's hard, and sometimes when it's hard, I don't get exactly what I see, but I get close to it or halfway to it.

Does your approach to working with actors differ from actor to actor, scene to scene, rehearsal to actual shooting?

I don't ever work with any two actors in exactly the same way. The differences between Harrison and Julia and Greg were enormous. The differences between Redford and Brandauer and Meryl Streep were like night and day. They all are very, very good actors, but they each have their own personal way to work. Each one has to be approached in a way tailored to them. They can't be forced to adapt to me.

I try very hard to recognize what works for some people, and what doesn't work. Some people need to have something explained in a way that creates behavior immediately, as you explain it. Some people can have it explained intellectually, and they can then translate that into behavior.

Most of the actors I've worked with respond to my approach, although I've had a few who didn't. Sometimes the actor overcomplicates something, and then I have to be very forceful about simplifying it. Sometimes the actor underestimates the lengths that they'll have to go to reach the scene, and then my job is to try to create the size of the experience for them in some way.

All of this is about communication, and people communicate in very different ways. I get very verbal, as you can see in this interview; I talk a lot. That's my way. Another director might use few words, and by waiting for just the right take, get just as good, if not better, results than I get. There just isn't any rule.

As an actor, I worked with Woody Allen, and he didn't do anything the way I do it. He's got his own way of working, and it works. It's great. He didn't tell me how to do it. I kept waiting for him to say what to do or how to do it, but that's not what he does. He does it in the writing and in the casting, and then he watches for when it's right, and says, "Okay, print that."

How can you tell if an actor is pretending?

If a director cannot tell the difference between a fake bit of behavior and a true bit of behavior, they have no business directing. It's not something that can be learned. You have to know the difference between truth and fiction. How do you teach somebody the difference? You can't. It's something intuitive, you just know it. It's called perception. Somebody is or isn't perceptive. That's all you have, as a director, the ability to recognize reality in behavior.

Is there a defined difference between theater acting and film acting?

Theater acting is exactly the opposite of film acting. In a theater performance, the object of the actor is to understand everything so he can repeat it. He has no director around, once it really counts. In theater acting, you have the moment, you have the scene before as a springboard and the scene after as a follow-through. If you don't understand how you did what you did, you're dead. You can't work. In film acting, you don't have to understand how or why you did it, because you're doing it all out of sequence. It's a completely different approach. You're much more dependent on a director in film.

When you work with your DP, do you specifically tell him what kind of lenses you want to use and how you want the camera to move?

I used to do it in terms of lenses. Now they have such marvelous multiple-focal lenses—zooms, as we say, but we don't use them as zooms, we just use them for any focal length we want. We leave one lens on the camera most of the time now, and compose each shot by going to the size that we want. I don't like to mix radical focal-length changes within a given scene, because the cuts become jarring.

The films that I do depend heavily on performances, on actors. The attention has to go to them, I don't like it when, in the middle of a scene, we get radical focal-length changes.

Do you do an extensive shot list?

Yeah. Before I even get to the set.

Do you use storyboards?

Not much. If I need it, I do. If it's a complicated scene that needs storyboarding, then I do it. If it's a scene with a lot of people, if it's going to require a lot of coverage, then I might draw it out.

Do you rehearse on the set with the actors alone?

I would never rehearse in front of anybody. Not even in front of a dog.

Do you have preconceived ideas about how you're going to block a scene before you get on the set?

Always. But I never start by pushing the actors into a position, even though I know that's where I'm going to end up. I always let the actors do pretty much what they want to do, have a lot of freedom, and as quickly as I can, I begin to move that into focus. And I usually try to get what I had planned on before I came in, without making the actors feel like they're being pushed around like puppets. But sometimes, in the rehearsal process, we'll find a way that's better than what I had planned.

Do you have any tips about finding the balance between the emotional needs and the pacing of a scene?

The emotional needs are the emotional needs. If you're talking about a scene where, in order to find the truth of it, the actors are taking a long, long time and you needed to go faster, at some point you have to say to them, "Go faster." Sometimes I will let them take all the time they need, but I cover it so that I can change the pacing in the editing, if I have to.

In *Tootsie*, did Dustin Hoffman do extensive rewrites? Do you ever encourage actors to do that?

I didn't use his rewrites. He came in almost every day with pieces of paper, but I didn't use them. I had a very highly paid, brilliantly talented pair of writers—Larry Gelbart and Elaine May. I don't encourage actors to do rewrites. I have too much respect for the writer.

In this book, Sidney Lumet said he once slapped an actress to get her to express a certain emotion. Do you ever have to go that far?

I almost never have to do tricks. I've never slapped an actress. I've scared an actress. I didn't do anything cruel to her, I just tried to intimidate her a little bit, so that she played the scene right. She knew that was my job.

Does it throw off your actors if you shoot a take one way and then have them try it in a totally different way on the next take? What does it accomplish for you as a director?

It gives me more choices. Sometimes I do that. Sometimes I have an actor do something that I call "bracketing." You know you're aiming for the middle here, but you have them go too far this way and then too far that way, and then try to bracket it. It's just like trying to zero in on the bull's eye. You might start a little to the right of it, and then try a little to the left, a little to the right, a little to the left, and then you can make it just right in the editing.

If the actor thinks he's giving you his best, and you think it's not good enough, is there a way that you can bring more out of him?

You can always work with actors and try to get more from them. It depends on what you need more of. If I want the actor to be shakier, or more upset, I can get that by just doing it over and over and over, until I've got the actor upset. If I want the actor more charming, then I have to create some sort of a mood that lets the actor be more charming.

There are no set rules. Everyone is different. Every scene has a different demand. And you don't get somebody to be more charming the same way you get somebody to cry or to be more intimidating or meaner. You do a different thing in each case. The thing you're always trying to do is create an activity which, when the actor does it, will produce emotion. I might say to an actor, "Check and see whether this guy is kidding you. At every moment that he talks to you, look in his eyes and see whether he's kidding. When he nods his head up and down, does he think you're a fool or does he really understand what you're saying?" Now that's something to do. You give actors a million things to do.

Do you ever play tricks on actors, like confidentially telling one actor to do it one way and the other actor to do it another way?

Sometimes. I do what it takes to get it done. When one engine goes out on a twin-engine airplane, the thrust is asymmetrical and the plane wants to roll over. You control it with a lever. And people invent all sorts of rules to deal with this—the good engine, the good foot, the foot that you're pushing is the good engine, the bad foot is the bad engine. The truth is, if you have to think like that, you're never going to become a good pilot. The answer is, Do what it takes to keep the airplane straight. Don't think about it. The same thing is true here.

Do you talk to an actor beforehand?

I don't have any idea what he's going to do. Why am I going to talk to him? Let's see what he's going to do. Suppose I say, "Let's rehearse. Action!" And then I cry, "Holy shit," and sob because it's so good. What am I going to say? "Stop, I have to direct you now?" Bullshit. Sometimes I've sobbed at the first rehearsal. "Shoot!"

You're looking for some kind of ridiculous rule here. It's not like using a computer: push this special thing down here, get the menu, do the thing. It doesn't work that way. If it's great, why talk? Just get it on film.

Do you think an aspiring director should study acting to enable him or her to better communicate with actors?

I think it's got to help in communication, but I don't think it's essential.

Do you shoot your set rehearsals?

Sometimes. Sometimes I rehearse up to a point, but don't rehearse the really delicate part; I want to just shoot and see what happens with the delicate part. I want it on film the very first time the actors ever get to it. I want them to live that moment for the first time on film.

What are you more prone to do when shooting a scene, listen to the performance quality or watch the action?

It's all the same thing. You watch the camera, watch it move. If it's not a camera move, you're not worried about anything technical, you just watch.

Do you use video assists?

They're there, but I don't watch them. I watch the actors. I'm always by the camera. I only look at the video during the rehearsal and when setting up the shot, unless there's a tricky move that I have to watch out of the corner of my eye.

I think actors need to feel that you're watching them. They're doing it for you. You're the audience. I think you hurt them when you're off somewhere else, looking at the video screen.

Is it more challenging to direct less experienced actors than it is to direct veterans?

Not necessarily more challenging. What determines the difficulty is not the experience of the actor. The real difficulty in realizing a performance is the ambition of the choice you've made, what you want to achieve.

JODIE FOSTER

Jodie Foster's brilliant acting career began at age three, when she began appearing in television commercials as The Coppertone Girl. And after becoming a regular on a number of television series, including *Mayberry RFD*, *The Courtship of Eddie's Father*, *My Three Sons*, and *Paper Moon*, she made her feature film debut in *Napoleon and Samantha* when she was eight years old.

By the age of twelve, Foster had acted in nine movies, including *Alice Doesn't Live Here Anymore* (1975) and was nominated for an Academy Award for her powerful performance as a streetwise teenager in *Taxi Driver* (1976). At the time of this writing, she has appeared in thirty-two films, including *Tom Sawyer* (1973), *Echoes of Summer* (1975), *Bugsy Malone* (1976), *The Little Girl Who Lived Down the Lane* (1977), *Freaky Friday* (1977), *Foxes* (1980), *The Hotel New Hampshire* (1984), *The Blood of Others* (1984), *Siesta* (1987), *Stealing Home* (1988), *Five Corners* (1988), *Shadows and Fog* (1992), *Sommersby* (1993), and *Maverick* (1994).

Jodie is the only American actress to win two separate awards in the same year from the British Academy of Film and Television Arts—Best Supporting Actress and Best Newcomer—for her performances in *Taxi Driver* and *Bugsy Malone*. She has won Academy Awards for Best Actress for her work as a rape survivor in *The Accused* (1988) and for her portrayal of FBI Special Agent Clarice Starling in *Silence of the Lambs*

(1991), for which she was also received a Golden Globe Award, a British Academy Award, a New York Film Critics Award, and a Chicago Film Critics Award.

The first feature film produced by Foster's production company, Egg Pictures, *Nell* (1994), earned her an Academy Award nomination.

It seemed only a natural progression for Jodie Foster to evolve into a first-rate director, making her feature film debut with the extraordinary *Little Man Tate* (1991), which she followed with *Home for the Holidays* (1995).

The following interview took place October 10, 1995.

• • • • •

You've worked with such awesome directors as Martin Scorsese, Jonathan Demme, Jonathan Kaplan, and Michael Apted. What influence did they exert on your desire to become a director?

As a child, I knew I wanted to be a director. I remember being on the TV series *The Courtship of Eddie's Father* when I was six-and-a-half years old, and Bill Bixby did a couple of episodes where he both acted and directed. I thought that was the most amazing thing. I said, "Someday, that's what I want to do." Then I sort of forgot about it and wanted to be President for a while. But ultimately, if you are somebody who loves to make decisions and enjoys the process of being decisive, being at the helm, in control—the leader of a set—it's probably the most enticing job you could ever do. I was fortunate as an actress to work with some excellent directors, and watching them work both inspired and educated me.

What did you learn from them?

The most valuable lesson I've learned from the directors I've worked with is that your style of directing should be about being yourself, listening to your own voice as a filmmaker.

I worked with Jonathan Demme on *Silence of the Lambs*. One of the things that I love about him is that he's like a great parent. He's absolutely prepared from A to Z. He knows exactly where the film is heading, and within those boundaries, he allows people to fly and do incredibly wild, crazy, risky things. And you know that he'll never laugh at you, that he just enjoys encouraging you to take gigantic and perhaps sometimes absurd risks. I felt secure in doing what he wanted, because I knew he had a clear vision of the whole picture in his head. I felt comfortable talking with him about ideas I had.

I never liked the original opening to *Silence*. So when I was training at the FBI Academy in Quantico, running a kind of a Marine-training obstacle course in the beautiful woods, I called Jonathan up all sweaty from a pay phone and told him I had this great idea for the beginning: Clarice running in a forest, not really knowing if she's pursuing or being pursued, not knowing if she's personally a victim, which I thought was true to the movie. The FBI training part was true to the myth itself, the way the heroine makes her journey, discovering who she is, a past she's ashamed of, her fragility, and that she could've been a victim. Jonathan used my idea to open the film.

How did you pursue your goal of directing?

When I was about fourteen years old, I did a short-subject film for the BBC, which was all set to music, with no dialogue, just visuals. It was a great experience, and for many years I kept looking for a story I could commit three, if not ten, years of my life to. For a long time, I didn't feel I was mature enough—there was nothing in the world that I loved enough or knew intimately enough to be able to make that kind of a commitment. But the minute I read *Little Man Tate*, I knew that I could spend my whole life making it.

What special identification did you have with the script that made you decide that this is it, this is the film that will qualify as my debut feature film?

It had a lot to say about my own life and my questions about myself. Like that character, I was definitely a different child. Growing up, I too experienced the world in some ways as a freak, because I had made nine movies by the time I was twelve, and had been nominated for an Academy Award. Based on that kind of excellence, I was pretty much an outsider.

Both *Little Man Tate* and *Home for the Holidays* are character driven. Is that something that you consciously look for in a script?

What moves me and gets me excited will always have a basis in character. My films will always be about somebody desperately trying to make sense of this world. I find that the atoms that connect people and pieces of misunderstanding and how people lie to each other and all of that is a huge universe that is far more interesting to me than Mars or Venus. My impetus for directing is to try and understand people more—to be more communicative and more intimate and in touch with examining perhaps the imbalanced sides of ourselves and the process of working things out. That's the essence of everything that interests me.

How deeply involved were you in the development of your scripts?

Completely. Both *Tate* and *Holidays* went through many rewrites—but always with the same writer. I feel very strongly about that.

I work very closely with writers because I need to make the script mine, so there isn't a color, a prop, a piece of dialogue that I can't talk about and relate to personally. That's what makes the process fascinating. To understand the material and be decisive and be able to answer questions that come up on the set, I have to have a clear and linear idea about the story and the characters. Otherwise, I don't know how to make decisions.

With *Holidays*, we—my production company, Egg Pictures—took the script, which had been adapted from a short story, in turnaround from Castle Rock. We developed it for a year and a half. We changed things, moved things around, and brought in new characters and a stronger plot.

Both *Tate* and *Holidays* are very personal films. Did you have difficulties getting them made?

Before *Little Man Tate* was brought to me, it had spent ten years trying to get made. When I came in, we made an offer Orion couldn't refuse—we told them I would be steadfastly involved in the rewrites, I would star, and I would like to direct it on a modest budget. With me attached as an actress, I think they were pretty much covered. It was a risk worth taking.

What attracted you to playing Dede in *Little Man Tate*?

Well, I was originally introduced to it as an actress, and immediately said, "Yeah, but I'd really like to direct it."

Why did you decide not to play Claudia in *Home for the Holidays*?

I didn't really have an interest in simultaneously directing and acting again. Even though I am very proud of *Little Man Tate*, and feel that the tone was very appropriate and my performance didn't hurt the film, I think there's a very plodding quality to it, which has to do with the fact that I was directing and also acting in it. I would get up at five o'clock in the morning, go in for hair and makeup, stand behind the eye piece, then get in front of the camera, then back behind the camera, and then go back again into makeup, which didn't allow me any time for spontaneity. I feel I didn't get the best performance out of myself; I got exactly what I wanted, but nothing that really surprised me.

Are you in favor of your writers' participation in the film beyond the delivery of the final draft of the script? In casting? On the set?

I like collaboration. If somebody's got a great idea, I want it. At the same time, the movie is ultimately the director's movie. That has to be very clear. You want to have one voice on the film, not ten.

Recently I came across one of the most insane comments that I've ever read: A writer said, "Making a movie, for a writer, is a little bit like designing a fabulous, incredible building and then having some contractor come in and put up something else." I thought that was the biggest piece of bullshit I'd ever heard. The director is the visionary, and the quicker you realize that you are here to serve the director, the better film you will make as a collaborator.

Stephen Spielberg has said that if you are going to direct, you'd better be in shape physically, since it's such hard work.

I don't believe in those crazy eighteen-hour days; I don't think people do their best work in eighteen-hour days. I believe in people having breakfast and going to work, then having lunch and going back to work and getting home at a reasonable hour so they can be fresh for the next morning. In the same way, I really love five-day workweeks.

I would rather have choices made intelligently, and know that the crew's happy, because they will perform better and things won't get by them. I feel the best thing I can do in terms of getting in shape for a movie is to have it incredibly well prepared before any single roll of film is ever fired.

Tell me a bit about your first day on the *Little Man Tate* set. Did you have any fears or doubts that you had to overcome?

Oh sure, my God, a myriad of them. It definitely was a very stressful situation. It's something that you can never be totally prepared for. You have to make instinctive decisions which carry a lot of responsibility—the beginning and end of everything—and that's very stressful.

As a woman, did you feel you had to overcompensate and do something spectacular on your first day to assert yourself as the commander?

No. The truth is that I've been making movies for thirty years. I probably have made more films than virtually anybody else who's on the movies that I make, so I don't know why I would have to assert more authority.

I think you just have to be yourself. Being yourself is probably the key to everything. I also think a sense of humor is terribly important.

Did your actors feel comfortable with you as actor-turned-director?

I would imagine they did. I think *Home for the Holidays* is an extraordinary example of how to make an actor's film and get the most out of actors. It's an extraordinary example of a screenplay that's peopled by actors who love what they are doing and love each other. It was a truly magnificent thing to watch them come up with stuff and surprise me— to watch us work together.

What do you try to achieve in your rehearsals?

I feel the last revisions of the screenplay should happen in rehearsals. It's very helpful to have a group of actors get together around a table and read the script, especially for a film like *Home for the Holidays*. It gives a good insight into what works and what doesn't. And there are certain scenes in films that I've worked on that you really do need to block, so that the crew can do their jobs, so that the prop people and set dressers know where things need to be.

Who do you have with you in your preproduction rehearsals? Do you have your DP and some of your key crew people there?

No, never. Just the script supervisor, the actors, and the writer. It's important for the writer to be there at certain points, because then we can send him away to work on things that didn't work.

Can an actor-turned-director help actors make the right choices in any special way?

Well, yes and no. There are certain areas that you just shouldn't butt into. And there are others where you need to stop an actor. It's like kids with paintings: at a certain point you need to stop them because they'll just keep adding colors until they obscure something that's already good.

I like to be very involved in the actors' process, to be in there and have them do their lines for me. I'll say, "Well, what if he said that?" and "How did that feel?"

Geraldine Chaplin came up with wonderful choices in *Holidays*. She was the most eccentric character of the bunch, so I allowed her to push a little bit more some of those strange behaviors. But I didn't want to push the other actors into wacky, idiosyncratic levels, because these are real people—they're complicated, but they are very real.

Was stepping onto the set of *Holidays* different than stepping onto the set of *Tate*? Did you do things differently because of your experiences on *Tate*?

I just wanted to be freer. I wanted *Holidays* to be more spontaneous. I wanted the people I was working with to know that I would be there to protect them from being foolish, so they could go out there and be as crazy as possible, knowing that I would bring them back if they went too far.

Holidays is a film about chaos, about people having questions about pointlessness and meaninglessness. It's a film that basically feels like you're in a giant washing machine, so you have to have a very technically proficient laser beam of focus, a moral that permeates the whole story and resolves itself in the end. I think that that's a way of combining a studio film and a Cassavetes movie, a way of having all of those chaotic feelings be as real and rare and raw as possible, yet not losing sight that there's a story you have to tell, which should be compelling and moving and understandable.

What was your homework on *Little Man Tate*? Did you have a technical consultant?

Oh, sure. Anything you need to know, you have to know. I certainly spent a lot of time with young piano prodigies, and I listened to a lot of music and talked to professors and musicologists and read a lot of books.

Do you think it's best to do an extensive shot list before you report to the set or after your set rehearsals? And once you set your shot list, do you stick with your plan?

It depends on whether we've had rehearsals. We had two weeks of rehearsals on *Home for the Holidays*, so it was much easier to know what the actors' needs would be.

I always have some type of a shot list in my head, unless we are on a stage, where we have the luxury of knowing it's not going to rain or snow and that there aren't many barriers. I always have a plan, but I'm perfectly happy to change it if somebody comes up with something better.

How much time did you have for rehearsals on *Little Man Tate*?

No rehearsals on *Little Man Tate*. I chose not to rehearse because I felt that young actors become wooden and unspontaneous the minute they have to do something more than twice. I didn't want them learning their lines and not feeling the feelings anymore. Having been a child actor, I know that happens. You have five minutes of sincere attention span with children, and after that they get bored.

Can you share some insights into your casting process? How did you go about casting the Fred character in *Tate*?

We were just trying to find somebody who was really appropriate for the character. We couldn't find that person in the acting community, so we looked to schools. My casting director, Avy Kaufman, found Adam Hann-Byrd in a little elementary school in New York City. She simply asked if anybody had been in school plays, and he raised his hand. And he looked a lot like me, which was one of the most compelling things.

Avy also found Max Pomeranc from *Searching for Bobby Fischer*. Avy's just an amazing person, and we have an intimate and productive working relationship. We sit around, saying, "Why would this person be right?" And then we start defining the characters—what it is we want, what it is we don't want—and learning our movie, little by little. My collaboration with my casting director is a very important to me.

How did you happen to select her as your casting director?

Peggy Rajski, my co-producer, had worked with Avy many times before. They knew each other from when they had both worked with John Sayles. Avy had done a movie that I thought had some of the best casting I'd ever seen, which was *Miss Firecracker*, with Alfre Woodard, Holly Hunter, Mary Steenburgen, Tim Robbins, and Scott Glenn—

none of whom were particularly well-known at the time.

I was looking for great naturalistic acting that could also be comedic, which is a very tricky thing to find. Either you find people who are very comedic and exaggerated and feel like clichés or you find people who are very dramatic and don't really have the timing for comedy. It's hard to do both.

What about the casting of Harry Connick, Jr. as Eddie in _Tate_?

That was a long process. I really wanted something very specific. We must have gone through a hundred guys, from the biggest to the smallest. And finally, Avy and I were sitting around one day, looking through the newspaper, when I saw that Harry Connick, Jr. was playing somewhere. I said, "What about Harry?" And she said, "Yeah, what about Harry?" So we called him up, and he just blew us away. He was exactly what we were looking for, which we couldn't find in a young actor. But the studio was a little resistant and our producer was a little resistant, because at the time, neither Harry nor Adam had ever made a movie before. But once they saw Harry's screen test, their fears were certainly allayed.

What about Dianne Wiest?

She was brought on fairly early. She asked for a lot of script changes, and we rewrote the character for her.

The first screenplay was very promising, but it was very much a black comedy in the spirit of _Dead Again_, another of Scott Frank's original screenplays. I love that side of him, but I don't know how to make camp films. I only know how to make very sincere movies. And if there's humor, there's humor, but I'm not interested in black humor at all. So the rewriting was done to change the tone of the film from an edgy, dark, black-humored fraternity house movie to a movie about a child who's torn between two women, which gave it the human conflict it needed. It became a much more feminine story than it was before.

Tell me about the impressive ensemble casting in *Home for the Holidays*.

Our focus first centered on casting the family members. The producer, Peggy Rajski, Avy, and myself sat down and said, "Let's make a wish list of people who are not necessarily big stars, but actors we love who are absolutely right for the film. Then let's use a Woody Allen approach—call up the actors, send them the script, and say, 'This is our movie. We love you. We cannot imagine anybody else. Please make it.'"

We always wanted Holly Hunter, and never imagined anyone else in her role. So I just sent her the screenplay before we had a finalized draft and said, "I hope you are available in November." And she called me back the next day and said, "When do we start?"

Once we had Holly, it was much easier for the other actors to realize that it was going to be a real ensemble film. We then cast Anne Bancroft, Charlie Durning, and Robert Downey, Jr.

How did you choose Geraldine Chaplin? She was tremendous.

Yeah. She was an odd choice, because Geraldine is the least like her character of any of the people in the film. When her name came up, I thought it would be interesting off-the-wall casting, so we went for her. And I'm glad we did. She brought many surprises to the role.

With the Steve Guttenberg character, on the other hand, we never thought of anybody but Steve Guttenberg. Yet we just never thought he'd do it. But we called him up, and he said, "Sure."

We thought Dylan McDermott was great looking and really had a great leading-man presence, but he was one of the last people brought on, because he wasn't a member of the family. I was very pleased with his performance. He served a different purpose than the rest of the family. He had a different tone—smoother, saner, and more balanced. He wasn't a part of their world, so he didn't have to get all stressed and weirded out about the family's little eccentricities. He was exactly what Claudia, played by Holly Hunter, needed—somebody fearless, sane, and easy.

Do you videotape actors?

Sometimes, although I don't really like to tape them, because people look different on film from the way they look on video and in real life. Video can be misleading if you're looking at it to see what somebody will look like on film. But in the absence of film, video gives you some idea.

Do you use video assist while shooting?

I find video monitors distracting and offensive. They work for framing, but I like to be by the camera for my actors. So other than for absolutely technical issues, I think video assist is really destructive.

On the average, how many actors do you see for a part before casting it?

It just depends. When someone's right, you know it instinctively. Sometimes it's the first actor who walks through the door, sometimes it's number one hundred on the list. Claire Danes, for example, was the only actor we saw for the role of Kitt; we never considered anyone else. She came in, we met her and said, "That's it." For the part of Russell Terziak, which ended up being played by David Strathairn, we saw many people, because it was a very hard role. You don't know whether to play the drama or the comedy, and it takes a very astute actor to be able to do both and not betray one or the other. Finally we threw our hands up in the air and said, "You know, we've always wanted David Strathairn, why don't we go for him?"

Do you cast your extras personally?

We have an extra casting person, but I'm very concerned about who they are. I'm pretty much involved in everything.

Do you have any keys to successful casting?

It is so difficult to be an actor—to wear your best outfit, to wait in a room with all of these other people who are up for the same job, wondering if you're good enough, and then you have to go in front of the casting director, the producer, and the director and bare your soul. So, to me, it's very important that actors be given respect, so they can carry on with dignity. I spend a lot of my time talking to them about other things, making them feel comfortable no matter who they are, because I've been on the other side and find it very offensive not to be treated well in a casting session.

Do you check out actors with other directors to see what sort of experiences those directors may have had with them?

Sometimes, but for the most part an actor's reputation is sort of a matter of record. I'm much more concerned with technicians. I definitely research technicians' references ad nauseam.

As an actress, how did you prepare for your roles? Did you create extensive backstories for your characters?

No, not extensive, just what was pertinent to the movie. Certainly not on *Taxi Driver*. I mean, I was young and it was all pretty much spelled out in the screenplay. Basically, I do as much research as I absolutely need to, because I feel that you need to be singular about what you are trying to say and about how you communicate that. Sometimes you can get bogged down by too much information, which can cloud the sparseness and the classical quality of what you are trying to accomplish.

Do you feel that theatrical stage training is important to a film actor?

Absolutely not. It's not insignificant or unimportant, but it's no more important than loving to cook or reading a lot of art history or listening to rock music. I am not being disparaging. I'm not a trained actress. I just feel that training your common sense is more important.

How involved are you in the look of your films?

I think my films will always be real. I'm not interested in flashy, over-the-top visual choices. I'm not very operatic in that way. That's not what moves me when I go to movies. But chances are that every movie I make will have the tone that's appropriate to it and the style that's appropriate to it and probably the visuals that are appropriate to it, because obviously there's some continuum there in the voice.

You had a very clouded look in *Holidays*.

Yes. *Holidays* was all about chaos, about certain people moving in and certain people moving out, about people changing directions, and about the strange rhythm that people get in groups.

So you make statements in the way your films look?

Yes, absolutely, as it relates obviously to the story and characters. I think that every department gives you a different piece of language—the language of sound, of music, of visual design, of lighting, as well as the language of acting. And all of those have to be working in unison. In every film there will always be a particular style.

Can you tell me more about your creative directorial thought and technical preparation process? Do you go through the whole script with your key department heads?

I have one of these computer memo lists that goes through every single scene for every single department, and is distributed to every department head, so that every department has a log of everything that has ever been discussed about why we are doing what we are doing. A lot of people probably find that very unspontaneous. It's not like anything is etched in stone, but it gives everyone on the production staff an anchor, a sense of organization, so that when surprises do come up, we're prepared to deal with them.

I go through the entire script, scene by scene, and write these incredibly long memos to myself about the full vision of the film, and each department gets one. I'm really meticulous about this. It's about more than production logistics, it's about communication. It makes everyone a part of the big picture, so that they all understand the choices that I'm making in terms of composition, lighting, staging, even music. Each department will have a step-by-step idea of where the character starts, what the character's point of view is, how that point of view evolves, and what the conclusion is. These are a part of the choices that you make as a director, and composition, lighting, and staging grow out of your overall vision for the film—both what you see and the subtext. So when a prop guy asks, "What kind of a drinking glass should I get? Should I get the one with Miss Piggy on it? Should I get the Pyrex kind?" he has been let in on the bigger picture of the film, which helps him make a choice in a way that is artistic and realistic in relation to who the character is, what that character is feeling, and what the scene expresses.

So, for example, was that wide shot of Tate and his mom on his birthday something that you specifically preplanned and told the DP to do?

We knew the movie really well, and we had talked about doing that scene with close-ups, but when we got on the set, we looked at each other and the DP said, "Are you thinking what I'm thinking?" And I said, "Yeah, it looks like it's one shot," which conveyed the sadness better than anything else. Being prepared and really knowing what you want gives you the opportunity to be flexible and open to those magic moments that come up on the set. So that's the way we shot it. We then got a call from the studio the next day. They said, "Wait. Where's the coverage? Why didn't you get a close-up of that?" They didn't get it.

You must know a great deal about lenses and what they can accomplish.

Not as much as I need to know. I don't pretend to be as good a technician with that instrument as the DP, but I have been an actor for many, many years, and have been watching movies for many years, so I pretty much know what I need to know.

Do you tell the DP how to light the actors, or do you just describe the mood you wish to evoke and trust the technicians to accomplish what you want?

Obviously I never tell the DP how to do his or her job, and certainly not regarding lighting. But we do discuss the kind of richness I'm looking for—should it be warmer or cooler?—and talk about the actors' faces: "I think she looks better like this" or "If we moved in tighter on her, we'd know that the experience was important to her," things like that.

It all depends on what I'm trying to achieve; sometimes I may want to be more distant to create a sense of loneliness. For example, in *Tate*, Fred remains alone in the schoolyard, the birthday invitations he just handed out scattered in the wind all around him, so I shot that wide and from a high angle to convey his sense of isolation.

Something in *Tate* that stood out in my mind was Dede's Fourth-of-July telephone call, which was very visceral. Was it scripted that way or was this something that you decided to create?

It was scripted that way. It was all about subtext, which I love more than anything else.

I would say that one of the reasons actors are so well equipped to move into the directing seat is that they are the only people on a movie who understand why a scene works emotionally. So instead of perhaps focusing on a flashier crane shot or a bigger stunt, they work from an inner level, because if you have performances that move you, so what if the film was shot in grainy 16mm.

In *Home for the Holidays*, I said to Lajos Koltai, the DP, "I don't like the ending of the film. I feel like it's cheating; it's not right. I really just want something that's more inclusive, more about Americans in some way that reunites all the ideas. Have you ever seen a home movie and cried about the lives of people you don't even know? You don't know why you cried, you just know that there's some loss somewhere. You think about moments that nobody ever got on film, moments that aren't documented, moments in your life when you were unself-conscious, moments that other people will never understand. And the weird thing about home movies is that they're so self-conscious—everybody is looking at the camera, but they're also so raw, so real."

Lajos had done a lot of documentaries back in Hungary, and he said, "Oh, yeah, we'll get out the 16mm Arriflex." And we started building this sequence of moments that shaped and defined each character's life, moments that no one else will ever understand. We had no script. I was pretty sure about what I wanted, but I acted like I wasn't. We didn't tell the actors what they were going to be doing. We just kind of threw them out there. Here we were with this little Arri, Lajos operating with a reduced crew, and in some ways it was more fun than any of the stuff we'd done on the film. And emotionally, it worked just beautifully.

You mentioned that you love working with the subtext. How important is it, for example, when working with a child actor? How do you get them to achieve that level of performance?

Any language is good language, anything that gets through. Sometimes with young actors under six years old, you just say, "Hey, do it like this!"

And with a veteran like Charles Durning?

Charles is always so right on that sometimes it will be just one word, or "bring it down" or "bring it inside and don't let me see so much on the outside." Because he is so intelligent and can be so articulate and witty, I wanted his character to be somebody who didn't know how to talk, and every time he tries to talk, he stumbles and says the wrong thing. So I had to keep making him less articulate, keep making his choices less conscious to himself. His challenge was to be a little less intelligent than he is.

Anne Bancroft is somebody who is meticulously planned—every fork, every knife, every table cloth, every line of diction, everything. So I would just play with her when she'd ask me a question about where was the fork was going to be, for example. Even if I knew the answer, I'd say, "Oh, I don't know," just to make her nervous, shake her up a little bit.

What sort of character-development direction did you give Holly Hunter in *Holidays*?

Her character was the most difficult character in the movie, because she reacts. She's a character who is going through an identity crisis, and, boy, it's really hard to play that without being a whiny victim. I think Holly did it brilliantly. I think you get a really good sense of Claudia, yet she is somebody who changes with every person she meets. Her tone changes every time somebody new comes into the room— she speaks their language.

When you read a script, do you look for the setups and make sure that if you have a setup, there's a payoff somewhere down the line?

Sometimes when you think of things that way, and it's a little bit too didactic, what you end up getting is a perfectly drawn screenplay that nobody cares about. A really good example of that is the scene between Joanne and Claudia, when Joanne says, "If I met you on the street and you gave me your phone number, I'd throw it away." And Claudia says, "I'll let myself out." Just because it's the end of the movie and just because it's the last time you see Joanne doesn't mean that she has to have some big make-up scene.

You lingered on Joanne for a while after Claudia left, which was very symbolic because first you had the camera moving in kind of a medium shot on her and then you went to the wide shot of her to end the scene. Was that something that you decided during editing?

To tell you the truth, that was the only reshoot of the movie.

Why?

Because I felt like I needed it. I felt like it was cheap to leave her there and say, "Oh, well, she's the enemy. We're not going to pay any attention to her anymore." The truth is that she has a very rich and complicated relationship, and she probably is the only true victim of the movie. This is a woman you should feel sorry for, because she has given up her whole life and she's a good person—she's followed all the rules and she's just gotten shit on. I wanted her to be featured and to have an arc. So we went back and shot her close-up.

One of the nice things about being an independent company is that when you are producing and directing, you can look at yourself and say, "Should I reshoot that?" and I say, "Yeah, I think so."

It's very important for the financiers to keep in mind that sometimes you do need to reshoot.

Absolutely. It's not just about test audiences, it's about the integrity of the movie. I also did quite a few reshoots on *Little Man Tate*, because as a young director, I just didn't know what I was going to need.

Do you pre-budget for these things?

Yeah. I think everybody does these days.

Do you communicate differently with less experienced actors than you do with those who are more seasoned?

You take each one individually, and you talk to them in a different way. You figure out what people need.

Do you like using multiple cameras when you do certain highly emotional scenes?

Not really. Not for the emotional stuff. But definitely for the Thanksgiving dinner in *Holiday*, when the turkey flew and landed on the actress's lap. I didn't want to drag that actress through it too many times. Also, I knew there was going to be a mess and a lot of weird things happening. I just wanted to make sure I could cut it together.

What techniques do you use to stimulate actors to tap their emotions and give you what you want? Do you walk them through it moment by moment or do you pretty much give them their freedom?

I let them tell me what works for them. Everybody is different. Some actors really get sick and tired of you talking to them. They just want to do it, and the more you talk to them, the more confused they get. And then other actors, like me, for example, love talking. I love hearing everything that's on the director's mind. I want to know everything he's thinking, and then I'll make choices about what's important for me to play.

How do you handle the temperamental actor who disagrees with your concepts and your interpretation of the character?

Fortunately, I haven't had too many of those. You try to strike a balance, but ultimately it's your movie. You don't want to be a hero on the day and then get into the cutting room and not have what you want. So that's when you need patience. Patience is probably the best way to deal with people like that. I don't believe in tempers on a movie. I don't ever believe in people yelling on the set. I don't think you get anywhere by that, and it ends up being very destructive to the whole process.

What type of environment do you try to create on the set?

I like a happy set. Everybody should be having a great day; they just happen to be working at the same time.

Who sets the tone on the set, you or the AD?

Ultimately it's the director's responsibility. My AD is great, he never yells. And more importantly, he is one of the funniest people I have ever met. We are always making jokes, nothing is that serious. And I think that what ends up happening is that the crew loosens up, they're not so intense—they do their job, but they don't get burned out by an incredibly stressful, horrible day.

How closely do you stick to the scripted dialogue once you lock your script? Do you allow your actors to rewrite dialogue on the set?

It depends. In a movie like *Home for the Holidays*, there was always a certain amount of improvisation. But in general, the actors stuck to the script once we had honed it down. The only person who I really just let make up whatever he wanted was Downey. I would guide him, and say, "You know that thing you just said? Don't say that" or "Make it shorter in the first part and, you know, mention something about her hair."

Why only with him?

He has an incredibly fertile creative mind. He basically comes up with better things than most writers do. He is really one of the most gifted actors I've ever worked with.

What happens when you realize that you got the best performance you are going to get from an actor but you still need more? Is there a technique to stimulate an actor to give you still more?

You try the traditional method of talking about the screenplay and telling the actor what you want, but sometimes you have to come up with another plan, because the actor still may not get there. You may have to say, "Okay, maybe he isn't having an enraged moment in this scene, because he looks phony when he's enraged." Maybe he's really approaching it in a more subtle way or with a sense of humor. Sometimes you have to change your ideas based on the limitations of an actor. Sometimes making movies is about compromise.

How do you deal with an actor who needs more takes than another actor who's in the same scene?

That's a really tough one. Spontaneity pretty much always rules. If there's an actor who really needs a lot of takes, I'll do a ton of rehearsals, and tell the actor who doesn't need as many takes just to not give anything.

What if you've got one actor who works by gut instinct and another who is very cerebral?

It's really up to them to work it out. I've worked with a lot of actors with a lot of different techniques, and I don't care what they do to get there as long as they get there when we start shooting. I don't care if they have to wear a funny red nose or make weird noises, it doesn't really matter.

Do you ever speak to your actors while the camera is rolling?

It's a really annoying habit, but sometimes I do. Dick Donner does this amazing thing: While you're actually talking during a scene, he yells at you things to do. In comedy, it's funny, because it makes the comedy very chaotic, and of course you have to loop everything. But some actors just can't stand it.

But you, as a director?

I never talk during the takes, unless I just have to say, "keep going" or "walk through the door" or something.

Do you talk to your actors privately on the set or in public?

I usually take people aside and give them their notes away from everybody else.

Do you have any specific techniques to get actors to listen and respond to each other?

Usually I'll say, "Hey, listen to her." If the actors don't listen to each other, it's really, really annoying. For example, you'll be doing a scene with somebody and you haven't even finished your line of dialogue, but they are darting their eyes around getting ready to say their line. It makes me want to say the wrong line just to bug them. Sometimes you tell them to listen, and then sometimes you have to make sure that you are going to be able to cut in some listening pauses in the cutting room. I watch out for that while I'm shooting.

Do you ever shoot set rehearsals without the actors knowing?

Oh, no, I never do that.

When you shoot a scene, what is your attention most focused on, the sound or the visual?

I feel like they are all one. You know, I'm an actor, so I focus on the performances. I'll tell you one thing I never notice—I never notice what somebody looks like or what they are wearing. Once we are through prep, I hope that the designer and the makeup person are paying attention, because I just don't see it.

Do you do more rehearsals on emotional scenes or less?

I only rehearse emotional scenes for blocking and for impact and for what we are trying to talk about. I never, ever, blow an emotion on a rehearsal.

Do you shoot close-ups first in a very emotional scene?

It depends. Actors work differently. Some actors work through the scene, and by the last setup, they're really moving. So it just depends on who the actor is. If I'm directing myself, I shoot my close-ups first.

How many takes do you average?

Five or six, but I almost never print more than two takes. And, in fact, I'm famous for printing one take on everything, because I don't like getting into a cutting room and having forty choices, and not remembering why I didn't like them. I don't like too many choices, because I feel they distract me from what I'm going for. I'd rather be really specific, and then, if we run into a problem in the editing room, I can go back and maybe check other takes that were not printed. I always have the script supervisor make notes about why takes weren't printed.

When I worked on *Silence* with Jonathan Demme, I visited his cutting room for a day, because that was really the only part of the process I had never been a part of, and I wanted to learn more about. Editing is truly a great process, and once you understand the mechanics of it, it helps you in terms of what kind of coverage you need to get and what kind you don't really need to get. It's also a process of learning your film, in the same way that rewriting is a process of learning your film. I think they are virtually the same exercise. The only difference between rewriting and editing is that when you are rewriting, you actually don't have anything in front of you—you don't have the material to fool with—you have to imagine it, make it up. If you understand writing and narrative and storytelling, you certainly are that much closer to understanding editing.

Do you think you can improve a performance in the editing?

You can't manufacture something that isn't there. I think you can definitely help performances in the cutting room, by intercutting reaction, maybe re-recording lines, adding lines over reaction shots. And you can help a film's structure by moving sequences about and dropping scenes that hold up pacing. And sometimes you can use bits and pieces from different takes, which also helps a lot. What you can do in the editing room to help a film is amazing.

Who do you think are the best actors from a director's point of view?

From a director's point of view, I'd probably have to include my entire cast of *Home for the Holidays*. And I would say that Mel Gibson and Robert Downey, Jr., are very similar. They do something that I can't do as an actor.

Which is?

They have the ability to completely make up something on the spot. That is absolutely amazing. So I would say that of all the actors I've worked with, the two of them, who are very similar in style, just continually amaze me.

From an actor's point of view, who is the ideal director?

As an actor, my favorite filmmakers are the filmmakers who have a real auteur's hand. Directors who make you feel like all the movies they make, even though they may be about different things and may have different styles and different visuals, are still a part of some personal agenda of theirs that they are working out through their whole life. For me, the director who represents that is Scorsese. As an actor, it's easier for me to serve that kind of director, because I know what he's going for, and I know how to make it personal for him. I love directors who know exactly what they want.

What do you think constitutes an excellent film performance?

As an audience member, an excellent film performance makes me feel like I am inside the actor's face. I know that's a silly thing to say, but sometimes I get this experience where I feel like I'm inside their face, experiencing what they are experiencing, and that's a very rare thing, that's an amazing performance.

LEONARD NIMOY

Born in Boston, Leonard Nimoy gained worldwide recognition playing the character of Dr. Spock on the popular TV series *Star Trek*, which earned him three Emmy nominations. His other television work includes two years on *Mission Impossible* and numerous appearances on such dramatic series as *Wagon Train*, *The Man From U.N.C.L.E.*, *Rawhide*, *Perry Mason*, and *Combat*. He also has appeared in many television movies, and for his role in *A Woman Named Golda*, he received an Emmy nomination for Best Actor in a Dramatic Special. His co-production of the television movie *Never Forget*, in which he starred, was nominated for a Cable ACE Award.

In addition to his television work, Nimoy has starred in numerous stage productions, including *Fiddler on the Roof*, *Camelot*, *Oliver*, and *Vincent*, a one-man play which he also produced and directed. He played the title role in the Royal Shakespeare Company's *Sherlock Holmes* and starred in Broadway productions of *Equus* and *Full Circle*.

Nimoy made his feature film directorial debut with *Star Trek III: The Search for Spock* (1984), in which he co-starred. He also directed and co-starred in *Star Trek IV: The Voyage Home* (1986), which became the most successful film of the series, and produced *Star Trek VI*.

Exhibiting enormous versatility, Nimoy has moved from science-fiction to comedy and drama with equal excellence, directing such films as *Three Men and a Baby* (1987), *The Good Mother* (1988), *Funny About Love* (1990), and *Holy Matrimony* (1994).

The following interview took place September 12, 1995.

• • • • •

Viewing your films, which range from the *Star Trek* series to *The Good Mother* to *Funny About Love*, made me realize how versatilely you move from adventure to comedy to intense human drama.

Well, it's been an interesting ride. It all happened in a very strange, in-the-back-door kind of way. Much of it by happy circumstances.

What inspired you to become an actor and who were some of the teachers who influenced you?

I was influenced very strongly by two young directors, Boris Sagal and Elliot Silverstein, who were directing in my neighborhood when I was a teenager in Boston. Boris was a very vital, very talented director who did some films and a lot of television. I think that he did one of the early Elvis Presley movies. Elliot Silverstein directed *Cat Ballou* and *A Man Named Horse*. I worked in plays for both of them, and, eventually, when I played a juvenile during a production of the play *Awake and Sing* that Boris directed, I became obsessed with the idea of acting for a living.

Were your parents enthusiastic about it?

No, no. On the contrary, they were very negative about it.

I came out to California when I was eighteen to study and become an actor, and I stumbled a lot along the way; I guess everybody has to. Boris and Elliot arrived here after going to Yale, and I worked for both of them on various projects and, bit by bit, put a career together.

At what point did you decide you wanted to be a director, and how did you make that transition?

I had a strange path toward directing. I was often advised in the early years to be a director, but I was so bent on being an actor that when the advice came, I often rejected it. I was actually somewhat insulted because I thought, "Is this a comment on my acting? Is this a comment on my potential as an actor?" It was as though, if I turned to directing at that time, it would have seemed an abandonment of my immediate goal and an admission of my failure as an actor, and I just couldn't do that. I directed occasionally because opportunities came along that didn't threaten my acting career. So I directed a play here and there, and some radio. I was pretty good, and it was offered to me a lot more frequently than acting work, but I still felt that I had to do this acting thing. So I persisted.

Then I started teaching for Jeff Cory. I was a student of his for a couple of years and, at the end of the blacklist period, when Jeff started working again as an actor, he asked me to teach some of his classes. And that too led to directing offers. People then thought of me again as a teacher/director, but I was still very reticent about the idea.

After I had done the *Star Trek* series, and spent a couple of years on *Mission Impossible*, I signed on for a year at Universal. By now, I was a little bit more relaxed about the idea that maybe I should do some directing. I guess I felt that I had come some distance as an actor and now it was okay for me to broaden my interests.

I did my first DGA job while I was at Universal, directing a *Night Gallery* episode, and I was very happy and pleased with the process. But there were still a lot of things I wanted to do as an actor. So during the seventies, I went back and did a lot of theater—Broadway twice, a lot of regional theater, a national tour, and a couple of plays—all as an actor, with the exception of a one-person show called *Vincent*, in which I played Theo Van Gogh talking about his brother Vincent Van Gogh. Later I directed it for television as well as at the Guthrie Theater in Minneapolis.

Then there was a moment after we had done, I think, the second *Star Trek* movie when producer Harve Bennett, who had a TV series called *The Powers of Matthew Star* on the air briefly, just called me out of the blue and said, "I'd like you to direct an episode for us." And I thought, maybe it's time I got the message here. I was delighted, I thought it was really very refreshing, and I went and did it. I think it was a confidence builder to be called and to go and do the job.

Then, the big turn came when Spock, my character, died in *Star Trek II* and the studio, Paramount, clearly wanted to find some way to reintroduce him into the films.

They called me to a meeting, and the question that was put to me was very interesting. It was very open-ended. In effect, they said, "We'd like to know if you'd like to have anything to do with the making of *Star Trek III*," which was a nice way of saying, "We'd like you in the movie. How do we go about doing this?" So something inside of me said that maybe it's time to stand up and take a position here. And I said, "Yes, I'd like to direct the picture," and I got the job. Spock was reintroduced into the film and it became my feature directorial debut.

It went well, and I was called to Jeff Katzenberg's office even before the picture opened and told that they wanted me to do another one. So I did *Star Trek IV*, which was quite successful and had some comedy in it. By the time that picture opened, Michael Eisner and Jeff Katzenberg had gone to Disney, and they called me to direct *Three Men and a Baby*. And one thing led into another.

How does one elicit the best performance from an actor?

It seems to me a lot of events have to form before you get to the point where the actor can give you a performance of merit. And by that I mean the script has to have some merit, the role has to be playable—it has to have integrity so that it makes sense from the beginning to the middle to the end and can be encompassed by a performance. I think it's vital that the director have a grasp of how the performance should function within the piece, so that if there is any doubt or question in the actor's mind, the director can be solidly supportive.

Does the director have to know as much about the character as the actor does?

Obviously so, but I expect the actor to bring a lot. I hope for surprises from the actor.

What kind of surprises?

I believe good actors, to use the generic term, discover things by immersing themselves in a role. Working from that immersion then touches a flow, moments, thoughts that fleet across the face, a change of attitude, a blink of an eye, a look, a wonderment, a puzzlement, or something that the director can't necessarily anticipate.

It seems to me that the director has to keep an objective overall look because he or she has the overall picture.

Yes. Now you come to the question of whether all the things that the actor brings fit into the overall scheme. It's a question of direction, a question of making choices—saying to the actor, "That's very interesting and very exciting but doesn't necessary fit the larger scheme of things; that's not what this movie is about." If a clever idea doesn't work, let's try something else. That is the directorial process.

As an actor, what sort of preparation do you do for a role?

Well, the preparation would be determined by the demands of the specific role itself. In some cases it would require a certain amount of academic research: Let's find out who these people were in their time and place. What's the geographical setting of the character? What are the sociological constraints surrounding the character? Where does this character come from? What kind of society? What kind of home environment? Family relationships? Married? Single? Father? Childless? Divorced? What is the psychological design of the character? What's the truth about the life of this person? That kind of sociological and geographical research is sometimes very helpful if you need to find an entry into the life of the character, and sometimes the director can be very helpful in pointing out certain aspects that the actor may not be conscious of or in touch with.

The director may educate the actor by perhaps providing literature on the subject or providing a role model for the actor, saying, "This person in some way is like this such-and-such person that we both know."

In some cases, if you feel an immediate grasp of the character as you read the script, you don't have to do all of that, just let your instincts take over and say, "I've been this person" or "I have a person in mind who helps me immediately to get in touch with the life of this person."

At what point do you create the characters' nuances?

That's an interesting question. Sometimes, as an actor, I'm able to best grasp a character through a gesture, a particular character gesture that has been called "the psychological gesture of the character." What is a psychological gesture of a character? Is it a stroking of the chin, a studious kind of thing? An image that comes to mind is Captain Queeg in *The Caine Mutiny*, who was constantly rolling those metal balls in his hand. A gesture that tells you something about the character.

In that particular case, the gesture was written in.

Yes, that's an enormous entry into a character for an actor, and in this particular case, a specific instruction for the actor existed in the source material, the book and the screenplay. Most of the time, however, the actor has to discover one. Does the character stand with his hands behind his back or his hands in his pockets? It makes a big difference. For example, in the movie *Body Heat*, Ted Danson would every once in a while break out into a song and a dance, which was peculiar behavior for an assistant D.A. but which made the character different and memorable.

The movies that you direct seem to have very strong themes.

Well, yeah. I am very much concerned with the thematic center of a piece: why we are doing it, what we are saying, what it is about. Not the plot. When I used to teach classes, this was a favorite concern of mine. I would try to teach actors that they should be concerned about what the piece is about, not the plot.

Don't tell me the plot. I know it's about a guy who holds up a liquor store and gets in trouble, and then he's on probation and his father comes and says there's just this little thing I want you to do for me. Whatever. There's a plot. But what's it about thematically? What does it say about the human condition? What does it say about our human experience or our non-human experience? What does it say about us as a people? What does it say about us as a society? What does it say about family? What does it say about religion? What does it say about commerce? What does it say about art? What does it say?

When a script is submitted to me, I'm concerned about what it's about. Does it touch something in me that's larger than the plot? What does it illuminate for me?

How involved do you get in the scripts that you direct?

It depends on the circumstances. If the script is wonderful, I'm the last to start making changes. The film *Funny About Love*, written by Norman Steinberg, who wrote *My Favorite Year*, and David Frankel, who wrote and directed *Miami Rhapsody*, required a lot of work, essentially because the script was too generous, which is the best way I can describe it. It was a very, very ambitious script. It was extremely full of anecdotes and events and characters. It was a full and rich and large endeavor that needed to be pared away to discover what was at its heart. Most of it was a clarification process—to get to the essence of what it was about and to try to retain those things that helped give it a thematic center.

On the *Star Trek* films, I was involved from scratch in the design of the two films that I directed and the one that I produced, and I worked very closely with the writers, actually laying out the structure for the stories and everything. This was particularly the case on the two that I directed—*Star Trek III* and *IV*. In some cases, I was so specific that I would say, "I need these two characters to go to a place where they do this. And these two characters need to go to a place where they have this kind of experience. And these two characters do this to this person." I was lucky enough that the writers—talented as they were—were able to find creative and wonderful, dramatic, or funny ways of doing it.

What about *The Good Mother*?

The Good Mother script was shot almost verbatim, with only a handful of word changes.

What about *Holy Matrimony*?

Holy Matrimony went through a development process. The two writers who were on the job when it first came to me took it the distance, and we got to the point where I thought it needed a different kind of eye—something a bit more streetwise, a little bit more cynical, a little bit more edgy in contemporary terms. So we brought in another writer.

It was always a dangerous project in concept. It was about this girl who needed to revise her thinking about who she was and what her place was in the world. It was about her transformation, and also her maturation. She had a childish fantasy view about how the world would work for her and she comes across this twelve-year-old child who is very wise. So they kind of switch roles—he becomes the adult for her; she becomes the child to learn from him. I found this interesting.

You learn things from making movies, and I had a fascinating time learning about the Hutterites. I spent time on their farms. The colony set that we built on a working wheat farm—all of those colony buildings were specially constructed by us—was built on a Hutterite pattern. The nature of the buildings and their placement was exactly like the Hutterite farms in the area.

Do you encourage the writer's involvement in the creative process once the script is written?

If I am enjoying my relationship with the writer, I'm very happy to talk to the writer every day—to have conversations about the casting, to have conversations about the way a scene is played or whatever. It is entirely possible that we get into a diversion of vision about the way the thing is going and the way it is supposed to go, in which case, it can become a very unhappy collaboration, which I think is very destructive.

So I'm just simply not ready to say, "I want the writer there" or "I don't want the writer there." I think the director has to make the picture, and if the director feels comfortable with or helped by the presence of the writer and they enjoy a great relationship, then by all means, I encourage the writer's participation. Many great movies were made by great relationships. There's no question about it. But if it comes to a difference of opinion, it's the director who has the final say.

Do you recall what it was like to step on the set for the first time as a feature director?

Yeah, I remember the first day. I had this very peculiar situation, and I was naive about it. I was mistaken about what the nature of the chemistry was going to be when I first started on the job. I was operating on the assumption that there would be a sense of camaraderie that would grow out of the idea that one of us actors is now going to direct the picture, and being one of our guys, he will therefore know us, help us, understand us, listen to us, and be responsive.

That wasn't necessarily the case. I was shocked to discover that the actors were waiting to pass judgment. The attitude was not so much "Oh great, here he comes," the attitude was, "Well, let's see what this is going to be."

How did you deal with that?

By being well prepared, solicitous, professional, and concerned, and by doing my job well. I really appreciate actors a lot, and I think they came to realize that this was not simply: "I'm the boss, and now I'm going to tell you how things are going to be done. For all these years, I've had a difference of opinion about the way you have been playing your character, and now I'm going tell you what I really think should be done with this character." When they discovered that I really was extremely prepared and I really was solicitous and concerned, and made room for their comfort within each scene, things smoothed out.

What do you mean, "room for their comfort"?

Well, for me, as an actor, the worst kind of moment in an actor/director relationship is one where you come onto the set with a certain sense of where the scene is structured, where the heart of the scene is and you discover that because of the way the set has been designed or because of where the camera is or because of the staging of the scene, there's discomfort and you are not able to deliver the tonality of the performance that you are trying to reach. And maybe you even come to agree with the director, but the director may in some way not be aware that he or she has created a design in which you can't deliver those goods. So you get into this thing, saying, "Gee, I'm in this corner for the entire scene. I thought the character that I'm playing should be surrounding this other person. I should literally do circles around him," or whatever it is, or say, "I can't do that" because I'm trapped here because of the schedule or the set or the lights, or because we don't have the room to move the camera . . . whatever.

I'm just giving an extreme example of how I think that a director who has had acting experience and understands the nature of that problem can be helpful to an actor in finding a way out of that dilemma, particularly when you get into a situation where for one reason or another there has not been a rehearsal before the staging of the scene and the actor arrives on the set and it's lit, cameras ready, and the scene has been pre-staged in a way that traps the actor. So whenever it is humanly possible, I think it is extremely advisable to rehearse with your cast and all the key elements present, so the actor has his room for comfort and is not trapped by conditions that stifle his creative impulses and freedom to express his best work.

Any challenges in _Star Trek III_ that you didn't have to go through in _IV_?

There was the challenge of dealing with the actors, winning their confidence. By the time I did the second film, I thought I was in a much better position, but on the contrary, I had the reverse. In the first film, by the nature of story, I had very little to do as an actor. My character didn't show up until the very last moments. To a great extent, I intentionally designed it that way. The story was structured so that Spock would be seen growing from a twelve-year-old to an adult, and I had other people to do the performance, so there was very little of my having to act and also direct. In the next film, however, I had much more presence as an actor. As a result, it got tougher because the Spock character called for two hours of uninterrupted make-up work: I learned very quickly that you cannot come in and sit down in the make-up chair and also go to the set periodically to check this or check that, take a look at this shot, take a look at this lighting, take a look at this paint job—whatever is needed—and then go back into make-up. You would never get finished with the make-up.

To go to work at 7:00 A.M. as a director, I would have to be in the make-up chair at 5:00 A.M., and remain uninterrupted there for two hours. At seven o'clock I could step out of the chair and become the director. So the job got tougher on *Star Trek IV*.

On the other hand, we had a great time making the picture because it was a much more light-hearted film than *Star Trek III*, which was a tough study in character struggles and problems to be dealt with. *Star Trek IV* had a lighter motif to it and more sense of adventure. There was more élan about the whole thing.

If you had your choice, would you rather separate the acting and directing?

Yeah. I have great respect for the people who do it film after film. But I would rather not, particularly if I'm doing a two-hour make-up job.

As a director, what do you do once you get the green light on a project? How do you begin your homework? Do you break down and analyze the script? What kind of notes do you do? What kind of technical research do you do?

Well, in the films that I've made, by the time we got the green light, I'd already done a lot of breakdown work—studying the arc of the adventure or the arc of the story: Where are the internal break structures for the second and third acts? Are there tonal shifts? Are there location issues? These are the kinds of notes I make to discuss with the production people.

Obviously, by now, casting has been in progress. To a certain extent, the green light depends on successful casting, and a lot of that would have already been going on. So, by the time the films that I've directed have been greenlighted, there's already a momentum—already a sense that this is a moving film, this is a moving project. And now, in terms of the simplest, broadest strokes of storytelling, you have to be aware of what are the major events that are turning points and rising action.

You have to be prepared logistically, because in one scene we turn a corner and suddenly discover that there's a whole new city; we play several night scenes and suddenly, bang, we are out into the street in daylight and there's a whole new atmosphere that you want to communicate to the cameramen, the actors, the composer, everybody. We need a shifting of gears here—we're in a whole different mode, things have changed, we have discovered in the last scene that such and such is no longer true, we have new information that must be assimilated and acted upon.

So what sorts of notes do you write down when preparing yourself to go out there and do it? Do you work with extensive shot lists?

It depends on the nature of the scene. If it is, for example, a location situation where there's a particular shot called for that opens a scene, you have to have a design for the shot, because if it calls for a crane and you haven't designed the shot, there's no crane when you arrive to shoot it. So those kind of logistics have to be thought out, and I'm very precise about planning them. I may want to get up there on a ladder or on a lift of some kind with a lens and say, "The first shot will be right here." I will show the cinematographer the specific frame and say, "That's the left side of the frame, that's the right. We start a pan across, and arm in at the same time, and we end up right here." We take measurements and nail that down so that the crane can hit those marks. I am already visualizing it in my head.

And then maybe some changes may occur as a result. There's a helicopter shot in *Funny About Love* when Gene Wilder and Christine Lahti are standing on the bridge outside the cab that's broken down. I feel this is a major turning point in the movie—it's the breakdown of their relationship. The shot was designed to be the end of an act because we are seeing the dissolution of their relationship as they stand there, a couple of isolated figures standing beside this broken-down taxi in this terrible sea of humanity. In the very next scene, we see her moving out, so I wanted a big shift of gears here.

That shot was very carefully designed, as you can imagine, because of the helicopter and all the logistics involved in closing the Queensborough Bridge.

We shot the scene on a Sunday, and it was very difficult, there was a lot to do. As I recall, there were five pages inside the cab as well as this gigantic helicopter shot, and we had control of about 100 cars. But because it was well thought-out and planned, we were able to do it all in one day, one very rough day.

On the other hand, a simple dialogue scene in a controlled environment may not require such a predetermined shot list. In a scene of this nature, I'm more influenced by what the actors do, their usage of the set. Once I see their actions and movements, I can set my shot list to best serve both the technical and the emotional life of the scene.

In the same film, how did you shoot the Madison Square Garden stuff? Was there a real basketball game in progress?

Yes, it was a real game. We got permission to put a camera in that exit hallway off the Garden floor, and the players knew that there would be a camera and lights there, and that our principals, Gene and Mary Stuart Masterson, would mingle with them as they came off the floor. It was a shot where we simply had to roll the camera. We obviously couldn't rehearse, so the success of this shot depended to a large degree on luck. I told Gene and Mary Stuart, "Get in as close with the players as you possibly can and don't let yourself get blocked by them, find the camera and walk past." That's how we got the shot there, and it worked.

When do you start working on your schedule with your first AD?

Around the time we get a go on the movie. Though it may be necessary to get a rough breakdown of the shooting schedule, which can be done earlier with the production manager, so you can create a preliminary budget. You'll say, this picture should be done in forty-five days or fifty-five days or sixty-five days or whatever it's going to take, so you can get a fairly precise budget. Then you sit down and make sure that you can schedule it intelligently. You go through it, scene by scene, and say, I think this scene can be done in a day or I think it can be half a day or I think we need three days for this scene because there's a lot of water or wind or fire or a big crowd or whatever. And there are lighting concerns if it's exterior; maybe we can only work in the morning because by the afternoon the sun is in the wrong place. Sometimes you can't really determine it until you actually see the location, but you can at least estimate it.

Naturally, it helps if your UPM and AD have had previous experience in making the kind of film you're making, have a deep understanding of the logistics and costs involved because they've been there before, although I've found that every film will surprise you with challenges which must be faced and overcome. So no matter how prepared you are, there is always the element of the unknown, which keeps it exciting, but at the same time, can be draining on you physically.

What sort of ADs do you prefer working with?

I like an AD who is extremely precise about detail, who gives me a sense of confidence about the information that I am getting and has a good sense of the political requirements of a set. I like to work quietly; I don't like a lot of noise and yelling and shouting, and I certainly require that everybody be dealt with respectfully in tone and attitude. Everybody is professional and we're all here doing a job. To me, it is important to work calmly. Chaos within the scene when it's called for, but not behind the camera.

I think good assistant directors are also sensitive to the nature of the scene that's being played and can help to create the correct kind of atmosphere to pull it off. I take creative ideas from anybody, at the right time and in the right way, but there comes a point where the AD simply has to help the director do what he or she feels has to be done.

How does the casting process begin for you? How do you hire casting directors? What do you expect from them? And do you visualize the actors as you read your script?

To some extent you can visualize. I'm not always successful at it. What I expect from the casting director is an intelligent and sensitive list of actors or actresses who might be correct for the roles and the money we have to pay them.

I really respect casting directors who have a good feeling for the talent pool out there and some sensibility for what the roles call for. In casting the leads, it gets very complicated because there are so many issues at stake, not just the quality of performance and the correctness for the role, but different people's visions of the role, the economics involved, will this person get this movie made? will this person get this movie opened, as well as give us a wonderful performance?

And then you are presented with, How about this or that person? But, gee, that wasn't the way I saw this picture. So I say, "Wait a minute, am I being closed-minded here? Let's go back and sit down and think about what this picture would be with that person in this role and see if maybe there's another way to approach the telling of this story."

Can you cite any specific examples of casting someone you hadn't thought about before and the casting turned out better than you had originally conceived?

Well, I had seen Patricia Arquette in a film that Diane Keaton directed. It was a wonderfully touching, powerful, and emotional performance, but nothing like the girl that we needed for *Holy Matrimony*. But then my wife and I went to a screening of *True Romance* and there was this *other* Patricia Arquette. We both turned to each other and said, "That's the girl," and immediately started the pursuit.

I find it amazing what you can do with an actor just by changing their looks, the way they dress, their attitudes. One always has to stay open-minded; sometimes an actor who you may not have thought of at all knows what you're looking for and will come in dressed for the part and using the specific accent required by the character. The actor does a screen test for you and you're in for a major surprise. A classic example, of course, is Marlon Brando in *The Godfather*.

When you cast newcomers, what sort of quality do you look for? What do you look for in their reels? Will you hire actors that you've never seen on film? Do you give them a screen test? If so, what do you look for in a screen test? Tell me, for example, about the twelve-year-old kid in *Holy Matrimony*.

He was just so wonderful. We tested a bunch of kids for *Holy Matrimony* and everybody agreed that there was such honesty and intelligence in him. I will test if the actor has nothing on tape or film. What I try to look for in a screen test is a sense of honesty; that's what I looked for in this kid, and he had it. In his case, it wasn't so much a question of a look, it was more a question of an emotional center—a performance.

What about Liam Neeson in *The Good Mother*?

I met Liam when I was in Toronto making *Three Men and a Baby*. He was working on a film called *Suspect*. But he was playing a mute; he had no dialogue. I saw a little bit of that, and I saw him in small pieces of other work. He came in several times, and finally to tape some scenes with Diane Keaton. We put the camera on Liam and I was very excited about it. I thought he brought a lot of interesting elements to the character—an honesty, a kind of integrity—he was a solid, interesting guy. I was very concerned that the guy be not devious in any way, be not undesirable in any way, because it was important that Diane's character would not allow some devious, sneaky, scary guy to be alone with her daughter. We had to trust him as she had come to trust him, and we had to understand why she trusted him. That was important to us.

Did you consider others for this role?

It wasn't so much a question of who was considered; there were a number of people we would have gladly had in the role if they would have accepted it. There were a number of actors who rejected that role because they didn't want to be the person who had abused a small girl. There were a couple of very good actors who said, "I simply can't play this guy." And you tell them, "Well, look, he's a character—you are playing a character here—and the guy is protected by the script in a lot of ways."

The script, in fact, explains what his reasoning was. It was a well-reasoned, well-thought-out, and very, very sensitive script. And yet, these actors rejected the role.

I thought Diane Keaton gave a textured, award-winning performance. How did you work with her to develop it?

We had a lot of conversations before we started shooting the picture. We had a lot of opportunities to work out scenes together. We got to know each other and trust each other. She trusted that I had a sympathetic understanding of what this character was going through and what she was experiencing and who she was. In general, I think everybody in the cast had a really good sense of who they were and what they represented, and that was important.

Tell me about casting her.

We went through lists, and there were some actresses that were considered who quickly removed themselves because they too were concerned about whether or not they were playing a heroic character.

That's not what this movie was about. Thematically this movie was about our society's difficulty in accepting sexuality and motherhood in the same person. It's the old Madonna/whore question. The mother is the Madonna and cannot be sexual. To perceive mothers as sexual is too difficult in our society. So when this woman, who is a great mother, is revealed to have had a sexual life, she's punished by society. That's what this movie is about. It's not about happy endings. It's not about what should she have done; it's not about whether she would rise to the occasion, stand up in court, tell them all to go to hell, and run away with her child. The movie is not about winning; it's a study in integrity. But some of the actresses I interviewed felt that it should be done the other way—there should be the final act where she rises to the occasion and has everybody on their feet cheering for her. That's not the character we were portraying. That's not the way it was in the book, and that's not the movie we set out to make.

But Diane Keaton saw the integrity in the character and was willing to do it. I had meetings with Diane to discuss the role with her before we determined that this was a deal. I mean, she had to find out if she was comfortable, and I had to find out if I was comfortable. She did not audition for the role. I felt very comfortable with her intelligent fix on what the film was all about, and I was delighted that she wanted to do it. I think she is a very talented, bright, courageous lady. Additionally, she agreed to come in and read with various actors, which was very helpful and not something that many actors would do. She felt it was important for her to have a sense of where this was all going.

What is involved in recognizing talent? Is it a gift as a director or is it luck or is it a combination of things? How do you

know whether this is the right person, whether this person will be a star?

I'm not sure that anybody can accurately predict it. I think some people claim that they can sit in a room and say this person is going to be a star, this person will be brilliant in this role. I think there are certain ways to qualify and quantify the nature of a person's craftsmanship, their training, their ability to portray certain qualities within a scene. Their sense of rhythm, their sense of timing, their sense of pace, their sense or degree of sensitivity to what a character is experiencing—those things are craftsmanship and a combination of craftsmanship and talent, but I don't think you can predict that one actor is going to become a star and another is not.

What's your approach to reading actors? As an actor, how did you feel about it?

I understand the concern about that, I've been there and I have felt abused by that process. There are times when an actor reaches a point in his or her career, where he or she says, "I shouldn't have to read for this role. I've done enough work; take a look at my work."

You can take that position if you want to. You are entitled to it. Nobody can put a gun to your head and make you come in and read for a role. My agent might say, "Look, they're reading actors for this role. If you'll read for this role, you'll have a chance of getting it; if you don't read for this role, you will not be considered for it." You make a decision; you say, "Okay, I'll throw my ego and my fears aside" if I really believe that the only way to get this role is to read for it. But if I feel that they are just reading actors for frivolous reasons, and I've been there, then I may say to my agent, "Please let them look at such and such work of mine. I think that might give them an indication of whether I can play this role." In other cases, I have been cast against my own better judgment. I have had people say to me, "You can do this." And I have said, "No, I can't. I'm wrong for this," and taken the role and been successful in it—playing Golda's husband, for example.

I know the actor's fears, the actor's insecurities—the painful process of putting yourself on trial and being judged is very difficult—but I also know that the actor sometimes cannot be the best judge of those things.

Would you prefer actors to come in to a reading with monologues or do you want them to read a scene from the movie you're casting?

I prefer to have actors reading from the movie they are auditioning for, because, as the director, I would like to see if the quality of the actor mates with the material. It's often not a question of talent—often the talent is a given. You say, "I know this is a very talented person, but I really don't have a sense of what this human being will do to this role and this film."

When reading actors, sometimes I have them do it in several different ways, but I don't encourage improvisation much. I think it's extremely difficult, unless you have a lot of time with a person who has been cast in a role; then, if you want to do some exploration, I think it is great. But under the structure of the reading situation, I will give directions for a couple of different reasons: Maybe I think the person has got the wrong slant on the scene; maybe there's some information this person doesn't have that makes the subtext of the scene different than what that person would bring; maybe something this person does is suddenly illuminating the character in a way that I hadn't thought about—I'll say, "Why don't you try a little bit more of that in this other scene," or whatever, to see if maybe that takes me in a new direction, and I start to get excited about what we are discovering. So in cases like that, I will give direction in reading. Sometimes, if I just think, no, this really is not right, I'm not comfortable with this person in this role, then I thank the actor very much for coming in and go to the next actor.

Do you see a lot of actors before you make a decision? Let's say you just started interviewing for a role and somebody walks in—the second person—and is great, would you just stop and say, "This is it"?

I'm perfectly happy doing that, sure. If the person really is right and wonderful, then absolutely, absolutely.

How important is your casting director's input in your final decision? Will you go against their instinct if they have a very strong feeling about someone?

I've never had a case where I said, "I want this person" or "I like this person," and the casting director said, "You're making a mistake." I don't ever remember casting against that kind of a negative feeling. I have had occasions where a casting director felt strongly about a particular person that I didn't want in a role. I might say, "I understand why; I see what it is that you see in that person," or I might say, "I don't get it; this person doesn't touch me in the same way that you are obviously being affected by them."

Do you find the process of making final casting decisions an exhilarating experience?

I find it very, very trying because I sympathize with the actors a lot. I find it very draining to go through the interview and the reading. I sometimes wish that I could sit in the back of a room, unseen, in the dark, and let other people handle the process—just sit back there objectively because I get so subjectively involved in what the actor or actress is going through.

Have you ever made a mistake in casting?

I've have, on occasion, cast a person because there seemed to be an understanding of the role and a proper fit with the orchestration of the cast—all the elements were there—and then, during the course of making the film, discovered that the quality that this person brought to us in that reading was all I was going to get. There was no creativity, no variation on the theme, just this one note being repetitively hit in every scene. And then you start to dig to see if there's some way to awaken some other instincts.

How do you do that?

Well, sometimes it's possible and sometimes it isn't, so you have to find some way around it by putting the emphasis someplace else in the scene, maybe rewriting, if necessary.

Do you re-cast?

I don't think I have ever re-cast. I think I've always worked it through in some other way. But, I have been disappointed at times. On the other hand, I have been very lucky in some casting situations where the person just miraculously rose to the occasion and gave wonderful,

wonderful stuff—not necessarily surprisingly, but certainly pleasingly—by coming to work having done some homework and some thinking about what's going on in a scene or a script, and that's great.

When I arrived on *Three Men and a Baby*, Ted Danson, Steve Guttenberg, and Tom Selleck were already cast. I consider myself a very lucky guy—those three actors were wonderful in that movie.

We did have some time sitting around the table working on the script together, and that was very helpful as part of the development process. They were very clear about what they were playing and who they were. They found a way of making the situation believable, and it paid off handsomely.

And Margaret Colin, who played Tom Selleck's girlfriend, was wonderful. She brought a wonderful kind of intelligence to her character and a way of dealing with Tom's character that was, in effect, not going to let him get away with his childishness.

For me, the movie was a story about three Peter Pans—three men who didn't want to grow up—who suddenly are confronted with this terribly responsible situation of taking care of a baby left at their doorstep.

Also, Paul Guilfoyle brought a lot to the very tricky role of the drug dealer. It was a tricky role because the most dangerous scene in that film was where he arrives and says, "I'm here for the package": He's coming to pick up drugs and they hand him a baby. I was terrified. I thought if we don't cast this right and play it just right, the audience will quit this film right then and there. Guilfoyle had to find a performance that was interesting and a little bit strange, yet was acceptable enough that he could say, "Yeah, I'm here for the package" and walk away with a baby in his arms.

Did you give him a screen test?

I knew his work somewhat, but he came into the office and I felt immediately that he had a lot to bring to this role. It's all about instinct, a feeling that you get. You just know.

What about Nancy Travis, playing the baby's mother? How did you cast her?

I didn't know her work at all. We had to have a lady who could come in and say, "I'm the mother" and not have the audience boo and hiss her off the screen. She also had to be able to play that very difficult final scene where the guys come home and find her with the baby, having changed her mind, saying, "I don't want to go to London, I want to stay here"—a tough scene to pull off. You say, "Come on, lady, why don't you make up your mind? You're driving these guys crazy, you're bouncing this baby from home to home to home." We tested her and she played that scene so wonderfully. She was so touching.

Do you check an actor's references with other directors?

Occasionally I have. I've had conversations with other directors about an actor and said, "What was your experience with this actor?" I've done the same thing with crew. I've called other people and said, "What was your experience with this cinematographer?" I think conversations with other directors can be very helpful on all subjects. On casting, on crew, on production design, on locations.

Would you cast non-actors?

In some cases, that's an ideal situation. On the other hand, if the role calls for the person to in some way rise to the occasion and read dialogue that they are not used to playing or to add some nuance in a scene, it can be deadly. So it would depend on what the demands of the role are and if this person had some kind of experience fulfilling those demands.

Like in *Holy Matrimony*, where you went into a special community?

Well, that's a very interesting question. Hutterites will not perform in a movie. Hutterites won't even go to movies. Now, it happened that we had a couple of people in the movie who had been Hutterites and had left the colony. They did not perform any major role or function— they were in some of the crowd scenes. But the Hutterites that we visited knew that we were making a movie, and some of their elders read our script. They knew that we were treating them respectfully, but they would not have anything to do with the making of the film. We were not welcome to shoot on any of the colonies, but they were very happy to have us come in and visit. They told us all about who they are and how they function and what their life is about. We had some fascinating times with them.

Tell me about casting Christine Lahti in *Funny About Love*.

I saw Christine Lahti in a play and met with her afterward. We talked and she met with Gene Wilder, and they both enjoyed each other. I felt we could have a nice relationship here. I think the chemistry between them was very successful in the movie.

I thought the chemistry between Mary Stuart Masterson and Gene Wilder was right on. I almost wanted him to stay with

her. I said, "Why wouldn't he go back to this girl who brought light into his life?" I was shocked that he'd want to go back to Christine Lahti, with whom he fought a lot, while the character played by Mary Stuart Masterson made him laugh all the time.

You're right, it was the danger in the story. My hope was that we would understand that he had a more mature relationship with Christine, that she offered more stability and there was a real deep love between them. The relationship with Mary Stuart Masterson was fun, it was sexually exciting for a while, but his heart really wasn't there. He had to work at it. It was trying for him, and he felt dishonest in that relationship. I think we captured some of that.

Tell me about casting Gene Wilder?

When I felt that Gene was the guy, I asked the studio for approval to send the script to him with the understanding that if he accepted it, we would hire him. I was really, really interested in casting him, so I called him, on the phone, through his agent, and I said, "I'd like to send you a script. You'll get it tomorrow, and I'll visit with you the next day." I didn't want to wait for a response from the telephone, or whatever, because I wanted to discuss it with him before he could say no. I spent a couple of days with him at his home in Connecticut. He was very warm and friendly and wonderful. He had made endless notes and questions that were all intelligent and in keeping with what we would try to accomplish. Once we realized we had a meeting of minds, we went to work.

Would you share some keys to successful casting?

As a general rule, and this rule is to be broken periodically, I have found that the actors and actresses who reject a role are probably doing you a favor. There are exceptions, of course. I have been talked into doing a role in which I was successful: I didn't want to play Morris Myerson and Ingrid Bergman didn't want to play Golda. Harve Bennett, to his credit, pursued her relentlessly. I saw mail from her that said, "Thank you very much, I'm very flattered. It's a wonderful role, but I don't believe I can play this character because . . . please accept this as a final no, no, no." And still he pursued her and got her to play the role. And she did an amazing job.

I didn't feel for a moment that I could pull off Morris Myerson. I thought I'm totally wrong for this guy, everything about me is not what this guy needs to be, but Harve pursued me and pursued me, and I ended up getting an Emmy nomination for the job and having a very satisfying experience.

How did he pursue you?

Three or four times, I said no. He just kept engaging me in conversation about it. One time he called and said, "I have something I want you to see." I said, "What?" And he said, "It's a photograph of Morris Myerson that you could not have seen. I think you might find something interesting about this." I went to his office and he showed me the photograph, and I said, "Harve, are you saying that I look like this guy?" "No." "Are you saying that there is something about this guy that I should recognize in myself?" "No, not necessarily, but there's something about him . . ."

He just kept pulling on the finest little thread, anything to convince me, and he did a great job of getting me talking about this character until finally I found a point of interest and said, "Maybe I'm beginning to understand what I have to do to play this role. I'll try it." I ended up being extremely happy that I did.

But, when I have been rejected by an actor or actress who I thought was right for a role, I have most often found that the person whom I ended up with was better in the role than the person I went after previously. So, as a general rule, I think intelligent actors and actresses are helpful to you when they say, "You'd better get somebody else." With an occasional exception.

Do you like lengthy preproduction rehearsals? What do you try to accomplish with them?

It depends on the nature of the show. In cases where I am very clear and everybody has got momentum, I think rehearsals can be draining. I tend to want to get on with it, get started and shoot it before I overthink it, overwork it, over-rehearse it, and over-discuss it.

On _The Good Mother_, which is so intense, did you do a lot of rehearsals?

Lots of conversations, very little rehearsal.

Does any experience in working with your actors while filming that movie stand out in your memory?

We had one terrible, terrible experience with Diane; it was an accident, a mechanical accident. It was in this very crucial scene where the court-appointed psychiatrist is asking her questions about what happened with her marriage and why she thinks her husband is trying to take custody of her daughter and so forth. The psychiatrist is very neutral, very Freudian, and she has several pages of monologue where she talks about her life and the love affair that she's having, how she's suddenly come to life, and how she felt it was good for her child to be in that kind of atmosphere. She goes to tears telling this story.

I said to the cinematographer, David Watkin, "I want to do this scene with two cameras on her." He was aghast and said, "What on earth for?" I said, "Because she's going to become extremely vulnerable and emotionally involved, and when she does it, I want to know we have it captured with two sides close up and the looser angle." So we set up two cameras.

When we started to make the film, David Watkin had come to me with a wonderful idea. He said that he would like to shoot two different kinds of film on this movie—Agfa film on the scenes in general and Kodak for the courtroom scenes, because Kodak would give us a grittier quality, a more contrasted, sharper edge. I said, "Fine, let's do that."

So we set out to film this scene with the psychiatrist, which was obviously to be shot with Agfa since it was not a courtroom scene. We set up, put the cameras in place, and Diane sat down and talked her way through the role. I thought this was going to be wonderful. Take one was pretty good; take two was very good. With take three, I'm standing behind the camera in tears when she talked about this crucial experience in her life. We finished the scene, I said, "Wonderful, wonderful, beautiful. Thank you very much. All we have to do is turn the camera around on the guy who is asking the questions. Diane, you will be off camera; take a forty-five-minute break."

She goes to her trailer and I walk out on the street. It's now about 11:30 in the morning, and I know that we've only got about an hour of work left to do; we'll be able to pick up something else or take the afternoon off. I'm exhilarated, I'm thinking that that scene will get her an Academy Award nomination. As I'm on the sidewalk, walking, on the most beautiful spring day in Toronto, I suddenly see two terrified figures running toward me. It's the camera operator and first AD, running with drained faces. They get to me and say, "We have a terrible problem. There was a mistake in the loading of the film in the two cameras. There was an inexperienced loader who put Agfa film in one and Kodak in the other. You cannot use the two together in a scene, cut to cut. There is such a difference in the quality that they won't match. You have to re-shoot with either one of the two cameras." After what she had just done, I was aghast and said, "Well, load it up, get ready, and let's re-shoot. I'll go talk to Diane. I'll have to give her some time."

As an actor, I know that when you are facing that kind of a scene and you do it and it's done, it starts to drain out. It's like you pulled a plug on the bathtub and the water is running out. You say, "I don't have to hold that in me anymore. I've been preparing for that for days or weeks, and I can let it go now because it's done, it's on film."

So before I went to her trailer, I said to them, "Get me a couple hundred dollars' worth of flowers right away." Then I went and knocked on her trailer door and said, "I'm sorry, I have bad news." And she asked, "What's the problem?" I told her and she said, "Well these are the kinds of things that happen when you make movies."

I was so grateful for her professionalism. She could have screamed, cried, got angry. The flowers were unnecessary, but they were delivered to make me feel better. I said, "Take your time and, when you are ready, send me word that you are ready to start shooting again." About a half hour later, she walked in, sat down, and went six takes. On six she hit it again. And it was a beautiful thing to watch a professional person do this terribly difficult, very moving scene, which had to grow and unfold like a blossom.

Did you do much rehearsing on *Three Men and a Baby*?

We did a lot of discussion at the table and a lot of line polishing to make sure that the characters were honed right. The entire script needed a major rewrite. Originally it had been a French movie and we wanted to take a totally different approach to the language and the nature of the characters. The actors were heavily involved. We were all there at the table—the actors, the writers, the producer—discussing what every scene, every line was. It was very much like doing a play. The writers were writing at night and coming in the morning with new pages, and they were extremely professional and generous about it. They did great work.

Did you cast a double for the baby?

We had a set of twins. The casting of the babies was fairly easy for me because there had been a lot of work done before I arrived. There were a lot of videotapes shot all around the country, and when I arrived in Toronto, they showed me tapes of maybe twenty sets of twins. From those I chose four sets of twins that I felt I should see personally. They all came to the studio in Toronto, the parents with their babies. And when we finally agreed on the pair we felt were ideal for the job, lo and behold—a miracle—those twins lived in Toronto.

They were a wonderful pair of kids, not only with great on-camera persona, but they were at precisely the right time in their lives, not a minute too soon, not a minute too late. By the time we were finished, they were changing their personalities. The babies were six months old when we started shooting and eight months old when we finished, so you can say that twenty-five percent of their lives took place during the shooting of this movie. They were getting to be a little bit more concerned about why they were brought in here again. "What is that thing—the microphone? Why is it over my head all the time?

Where is it going? Why do they keep taking me from here to there, then back, and then from here to there again, and back? Why do they keep washing me over and over again? Who are these guys changing my diapers?" They were not quite so willing to take things in stride. I thought to myself on the last day that if we let it go another week, we'll be in trouble.

Did working with the babies affect the schedule in any way?

No, it was a process of working with the parents—the mother particularly, who was there all the time and who was extremely accurate about what we could anticipate with the children. The first AD worked brilliantly with her. A typical conversation would be: "Tomorrow, we need the baby hungry so when she's offered the bottle she'll take it." There were no hitches there.

As a director, how do you guide the actors in making the right choices, or do you leave it pretty much up to the actors themselves?

As a general rule, if we start to rehearse a scene and I sense that the actor is going in the right direction and we have the same concept of what the scene is about, that settles it. It might be just a matter of some fine-tuning here or there. It might be a technical requirement: I need the actor to turn at this point so that I can see a certain object or solve a camera problem. But if the actor is on the track with the character and what the scene is about, then my input becomes very minimal. I may just say, "great" or "a little less" or "a little more, don't be afraid to be a little more."

How can you tell when an actor is faking it, and what do you do about it?

It's a question of a trained instinct. I taught acting classes for five years. I have a pretty good sense of when an actor is really delivering experience and when an actor is indicating an experience. That's a judgment call, an instinct. Either I believe it or I don't. If I don't believe it, then I've got to try to find some way to help this actor get through a reality. I make a suggestion about this or that and then it becomes a question of whether the actor is capable of getting in touch with something more real.

In the emotional kitchen scene in *The Good Mother*, Diane Keaton threw things, broke plates. How did you guide her performance there?

The script indicated that she goes in the kitchen and starts to get violent. The difficult thing for Diane, and for Liam, was that the scene had to move to three different physical areas. And there had to be an emotional line as though the whole scene were played in one fluid move, but it wasn't possible to do that.

The scene starts with them sitting at the far end of the living room, and then they get up and move to opposite sides of a table, where they argue back and forth, and then into the kitchen, where the final eruption takes place.

When they came from their first position to the argument across the table, I had opposing cameras, which presented a lighting challenge. The DP, David Watkin, accommodated us by lighting the sets in such a way that the actors had the freedom to continue this conversation, which builds into an argument across the table, in one continuous piece. Then we cut, and there was a move into the kitchen, which required a re-lighting job. Both Diane and Liam are professionals and they were able to pick up the scene at that emotional level and go into the kitchen and finish the job.

Once we were in the kitchen, I laid out things that Diane could throw—a rack and dishes—and I said, "This is the area you can use; feel free to move from here to here to there. Liam, you are here and then end up on the floor."

When it was over and she slumped to the floor, I thought we had a real vision of a deeply felt experience. They were capable of doing it, they were able to rise to the occasion time and time again and do it right. They had to do it again a few days later because we had a streaking—one of the camera magazines had a loose rivet and some light had leaked in and streaked the film on one side of this two-sided argument. So all the pains we had taken to be able to shoot the two sides of the argument simultaneously went for naught because we couldn't use one side of it.

I think I was able to be helpful to them by not breaking it up into three parts but breaking it up into only two.

In *Funny About Love*, I noticed a lot of long scenes that seemed to require a lot of choreography.

Yeah, scenes like that pretty much have to be thought-out in advance in case you need a certain piece of equipment to get the job done, and that piece of equipment isn't something that you are carrying on the job all the time. I used a crane on one piece where there's a conversation between Gene and Christine in the doorway of the apartment, and then they eventually move into the apartment and up a flight of stairs to the bedroom. That was all done in one piece. Shots like that have to be designed in advance.

I thought the shot when Mary Stuart Masterson tells Gene Wilder good-bye was beautifully choreographed. Is this something that you let the actors create and then set your shot, or is it something that you preplan beforehand?

In the scene where he comes in and finds her packing, and they move to a couch where she sits down, crying, and says, "Why didn't you say that you loved me?" the most important thing for me was the choreography. It seemed to me that the scene needed some fluidity to get from point A to point B—it needed something more than just two people sitting and talking to each other.

I said to the actors, "I'd like to start it here and move there, sit on the couch and end up in this position, and the camera will follow accordingly." The most important thing about that scene was that there's a moment where she becomes the parent in the relationship. She sits Gene Wilder down and teaches him something, tries to focus his thinking. One of Gene's problems in the story was that under ordinary circumstances, if he possibly could, he would avoid this kind of confrontation. So she literally sits him down, starts the conversation with him, and then ends up sitting on his lap, which I thought was kind of touching.

So to answer your question, I have a shot in mind but I give the actors the freedom to be creative, keeping in mind that if I cannot successfully execute the shot I have in mind, I can easily come up with an alternate.

When do you make these decisions? During your rehearsals on the set or before your start?

When I do the staging before rehearsals. Before the actors even arrive, I walk through shots with the cinematographer or the maybe the set dressers or the scene designer, and I say, "I'd like to . . ."

There's another element that we should mention here: making use of the set. In the case of *Three Men and a Baby*, we built an elaborate apartment set, so part of the design of the shots had to do with using that set successfully: How do we get them from the bedroom to the kitchen? Can we do a shot from the kitchen all the way up to the upstairs work area? We reveal and use these spaces in a way that helps the emotional line of the story. Some directors let the actors rehearse first, let them move around, give them all the freedom they want, and then do their shot list. But I'm more precise than that; I'm more preplanned than that.

Are you technically oriented in creating emotion with your camera, or do you leave it all up to the DP?

If the DP comes up with an idea and presents it to me, I understand what he is talking about, and will either say yes or no, depending upon the nature of the film, the style of the film. If it's a family story, if it's a reality-based comedy or drama, chances are I will do very little in the way of in-camera effects.

I try to keep rack focus to a minimum; I try to avoid zooming unless its absolutely vital or really part of the overall tonality of the picture. I try to avoid camera effects because I don't like shots that call attention to themselves. But there were two shots that I remember in *The Good Mother* that were very especially designed shots that had to do with emotional moments that I thought could be helped by the camera.

One was the shot of Diane and Liam and the little girl in bed to-gether—the three of them with the camera pointing straight down on top of them, and then rising away at the end of a dramatic moment. And the other was the scene when Diane has discovered that she has lost custody of her child: She comes into her bedroom and falls on the bed, crying, and we get a light change to show the passage of time—a very intricate and very beautiful move of lamps during the shot to create a change of shadows in the room, to see the sunlight and the sun setting and moonlight rising all in one shot. It was a very carefully rehearsed and choreographed piece of lighting. But that's a very special situation where I think I can get away with it without saying, "Look how clever we are being."

Do you feel that it's necessary to shoot coverage when a master will suffice?

It depends on the scene. I have no qualms about shooting coverage if the scene calls for it. If there is a way to design a scene where it can be played in the flow of a master, sure, why not?

I have noticed it's being used a lot now. Woody Allen, for example, often uses it. Characters move in and out of the frame.

I think you can do that to excess, to the point where the audience becomes conscience of the fact that there is some kind of special trick going on. I am bothered by it if I become conscience of it. I want to be totally absorbed in the story; I don't want my attention to be distracted by clever direction—mine or anybody else's.

What methods do you use to stimulate your actors to tap their emotional triggers on the set?

To me, subtext is terribly important: What's this scene about? What are you really after? What are you really trying to accomplish? What do you want? What are you trying to avoid? What are your looking for?

What are you hoping to discover? What are you frightened of?

These are things I discuss with the actors. For example: "She's try-ing to get you to do blah-blah, and you've got to prevent that because . . ." or "You have got to try to get her to agree to so and so" or "Do you know that she's really planning to do such and such a thing that would really be a big problem for you? So don't let her get out that door." That kind of thing.

Do you discuss things with your actors in front of the whole crew or in private?

I try to keep public directions to a minimum. If it's a question of a little bit more to the right or a little bit to the left—something strictly physical or technical—fine. But if it comes down to the interior life of a performance, I always try to get away from the camera, go to the actor and speak privately.

Do you find it helpful to work with a video assist?

I do, I do. It's very helpful, but treacherous. I don't think you can really watch performances adequately, because you're looking at a small screen and a poor resolution and you are not really seeing the nuances of what's happening on the actors' faces. But, at the same time, it is terribly help-ful in watching the composition of a shot. If there's any question about which way the camera is moving, it can be helpful because you know what you've got and you don't have to be concerned about whether you've communicated successfully to the operator.

What do you focus on when you watch a scene? Do you mostly listen to what the actors are saying to get the sense of the per-

formance or do you watch all the other details that make up a shot?

It depends on the scene. I'd rather be with the actors if it's a performance moment, but if it's an action piece or a tricky camera shot, then the question is what does it look like more than what does it sound like.

What do you try to accomplish during your set rehearsals with the actors?

I think it's a question of understanding what the scene is about, so that we are all—the actors and myself—on the same track.

Do you allow actors to change lines on the set?

It's not a common event. Only rarely do we run into a situation where the line just doesn't seem to play. Maybe it's always bothered me and I can't figure out why and the actor stumbles on it. Maybe the timing of the line doesn't work with the piece of action, so you need to extend it or shorten it in some way. Those are minor events, very rare.

How do you deal with actors who come from different backgrounds? Maybe one studied at the Actors Studio, another studied with Meisner, and they all have different techniques.

I don't think those little nuances become a problem on the set. It seems to me that most actors find enough common ground. Sure, you find actors who are troubled by another actor in a scene occasionally playing some other attitude. When this happens, you just talk to them and make an adjustment. But that's more about the nature of the actor as a human being than the actor and his study process. All actors are different, as they should be, and when you bring two people or a group of actors together, you may find different attitudes and techniques, but that has never been a problem for me.

Do you find there is a big difference in your approach to actors when you are directing comedy versus high drama?

When you're playing comedy, I think it's important that the actors understand that it calls for a certain kind of pace and a certain kind of attitude. There should be an atmosphere of "We've got to find the fun of this piece here. We've got to find out what's entertaining, what's funny about this," and it's got to be played with a certain kind of rhythm, a certain kind of understanding that somewhere there's a joke here. I don't think we should keep it a secret from the actors when we are doing comedy.

Gene Wilder played a very mischievous character in *Funny About Love*. How did you instruct him?

I told him that here was a guy trying deal with difficult moments by being funny. And Gene Wilder brought a great deal of truth and honesty to it, something he was actually pulling from the very depth of his being, because he had just experienced the tragic loss of his wife.

On the other hand, if a reality-based moment is supposed to be comedy, then the actor has to find a way to play it, even angrily, and to get the comedy out of that anger. For example, Tom Selleck and Steve Guttenberg trying to diaper a baby. Selleck is playing angry—"I should be able to do this"—and it gets very funny.

The crying scene at the reception after the funeral in *Funny About Love*—how did you motivate a comedy actor like Gene Wilder to do it?

Oh, that's an interesting moment. The scene called for Gene Wilder to finally face the reality of the death of his mother. In the character and in the actor, there was a lot of denial going on. The character, Duffy, is trying to joke his way through this scene, trying to be funny about it, denying the emotion. There's a moment where a couple of kids are running and one of them comes running to Gene, bumps into him, and starts to cry. Gene comforts the kid and they sit down. He is holding the kid and saying, "No, no, no, no, no, no." Now the actor has to turn a corner and get into his own emotion.

While the camera was rolling, I said to the kid, "Hug him, hug him hard," and the kid reached up and grabbed hold of Gene Wilder and hugged him real hard, and Gene burst into tears. We did it in one take and it was a great moment of satisfaction for me as a director.

Do you talk to the actors while the camera is rolling?

Not often, but in this particular scene between Gene Wilder and the kid I did, because I saw that Gene was right on the edge and needed something to get him to release emotionally. I got the result I wanted.

Up until that moment Gene Wilder was working at what the script told him to do, which was to comfort this kid, but he wasn't touching his own emotions, he wasn't dealing with them at all. As soon as I said to the kid, "Comfort him, squeeze him hard," Gene cried. I guess it's a matter of instinct based on years of experience being an actor and dealing with actors.

Mary Stuart Masterson was cheerful and crazy and then showed her vulnerable side when she loses the baby. How did you work with her to develop her character? Was it all in the script?

She understood it totally, there was no difficulty. She does this wonderful scene where Gene Wilder comes home, finds her in tears, and puts her in the elevator, saying, "It's going to be all right," comforting her. She had a wonderful sense of what that character was experiencing at that moment, all of the conflicts and all of the anguish. She knew that her character's relationship with Duffy was built on a very shaky framework and that the baby was a connection, because Duffy wanted children so badly, and that if she lost this baby, it was going to be a major, major event in their relationship, having to do with the two of them as much as the life of the child. She understood that and she was able to play a very terrific connection between that moment and the moment later when Duffy comes home and she says, "I'm leaving," because it was pretty clear to her that once the baby was lost, the connection with him was gone.

Do you recall any examples that could illustrate the importance of the director understanding the significance of text and subtext to elicit a great performance from an actor?

I don't see it in those terms, I really don't. I don't come to work on a given day saying to myself, "How am I going to get a great performance out of this actor?"

If we have a script that's working and the actor and I are both in sync about what the script is about, it's a matter of creating an environment in which the actor can do the work that's expected and the work that he or she is being paid for. We are talking about very professional people, people with long years of experience and training. It's not like you pick up somebody off the street and say, "I'm going to make you a brilliant performer or a brilliant star. You come to the studio tomorrow and we're going to do a scene that's going to win you an Academy Award." That's not what it's all about. We are talking about a very, very high degree of professionalism, and collaboration.

This sync element between the actors and the script and the characters they are playing—is this something that you discover in your rehearsals? What do you do in your rehearsals? Do you block or do you focus more on reading the script and discussing it?

Both. It depends on the situation. I have rehearsed scenes on chalk-line sets, where I walk the actors through, which is a way of accomplishing two things: one is technical and the other is emotional. It is a way of helping myself and the cinematographer and the actors prepare for the day when we're going to shoot this scene, because it may have some technical complication and I want everybody to know what the plan is in advance.

Do you have the DP at the rehearsal?

Sure, if possible. The DP and the actors are there so that when we get to the day of the shoot, we don't have to start worrying about "Gee, I didn't know there was going to be a wall here; I didn't know there was going to be a table here."

I think it is a very physical experience for the actors to deal with the connection between the physical and the emotional aspects of the scene. Sometimes there's a very severe physical problem that you have to anticipate. You say, for example, "Look, we cannot do this scene all in one day, because there is a whole set reconstruction that has to be done to shoot the other side of the scene. So we are going to shoot this side of it this day and four days later shoot the other."

When we made *Star Trek IV*, we built three sides of one very, very large set; we didn't build the fourth side, but redressed the end of the set to be the fourth side. The scene was the council chamber sequence. The set was like a United Nations meeting hall. On one side there's a viewing screen, where the president addresses the council. You see the viewing screen and footage of what is being talked about. And on the two long sides, there are people sitting in chairs looking at the screen. At the other end, theoretically, is a large massive door that people make entrances from and walk toward that screen. Well, we never built the other end. What we did, probably saving $50,000, was take away the screen and make a couple of minor changes, and behind it is a door that plays for the other end. So, you say to the actors, "On the day we shoot the screen stuff, you'll be walking toward that screen. On the day we shoot the door stuff, you'll be coming from there. It will be on the same set, but we'll put a door behind you."

That kind of thing certainly has to be talked about with the DP. He has to know where his sources of light are and how his lights should fall.

A good example of a pre-rehearsal of a given, specific physical moment is in *Three Men and a Baby*: I rehearsed with Tom Selleck and Steve Guttenberg the moment that they discover the baby. I had this idea that Tom Selleck comes in from his run around Central Park. He comes up in the elevator and he's got a newspaper. He goes to the door and absent-mindedly, without even thinking about it, still focusing on the newspaper, puts his key in the door, opens it, and walks in right past the baby basket.

It was a dangerous choice in a way. Would the audience believe that he hadn't seen it? Would Selleck be comfortable playing that role? You know, as an actor, I might say, "Well, let me try it and see if I can do that."

It wasn't scripted that way?

No, no. So we rehearsed it on a separate stage—we didn't have the set yet—but I laid it out with chalk on the floor. I laid out the door, I laid out the elevator door, and I said, "Let's see if this works for you guys." And then we watched it happen to see if we believed it.

I did not want to come on the set with that plan in mind and have Tom Selleck say, "Gee, I feel I would stumble on it" or "I can't believe I don't see it."

According to my plan, he has to go inside and then, once inside, realize that he thinks there's something out there, come back out, peek, and realize that the baby's there.

Well, it was kind of scary to do it that way, you know. The other way to do it, of course, would be to have him walk out of the elevator and immediately see this thing sitting there. But I thought it was more fun if we had him go by it as the camera tilts down and reveals it. It was more interesting to me. It had a surprise element to it, and a little fun.

So you place a great deal of importance on rehearsals?

Moments like that, yes, are very important, as are scenes that have some special, specific physical requirement or have a special emotional turn— a corner that the actor has to round emotionally. Other kinds of moments may not be such a big deal. I am very selective.

Can you talk about your editorial process?

For me, the first assembly often is a depressing experience. Everybody goes through this process. You sit down and look at it and say, "Oh, my God, the scenes are flabby, and they're not playing." But the editor is not required to give you a movie on the first assembly. He's required to assemble and show you what you've got. Then you sit down and go to work, reel by reel, scene by scene, with very specific notes: "Let's get off the master here. I'm missing a shot here that I liked a lot, let's use it. Let's get off of him here, and go to her. Let's cut out this line. Let's cut out that entrance, we don't need it; just pop to him and he's already there." What's the best way to get this story told?

What constitutes a great performance from an actor?

I think it's pretty hard to give a great performance unless you've got some worthwhile material to work with. It has to be something that gives the actor the opportunity to rise to the occasion. I think you'd have a tough time putting together the greatest actors and actresses in the world and bring them to a set and say, "Folks, today we are going to shoot great drama, give us a great performance." If it's not there on the paper, it doesn't work.

Great performances have to start with something that inspires, something that touches, something that illuminates something, something that gives you a chance, that gives you a road map at the very least, and at the most, a very detailed pathway for a story to be told in which great and wondrous things—funny or tragic or dramatic—can happen. To get that great moment, you have actors who are in touch with this wonderful opportunity, who have the craft and the skill and the talent to bring their persona to it; they bring an energy to it, an imagination, and they flesh it out and make it become physical in front of your very eyes.

What have been your most thrilling moments as a director?

There are great moments you experience when you are making a movie. Every once in a while, a moment rises above the pain of the physical problems and becomes a greatly satisfying, emotional, or funny moment. You think, "God, that's great stuff that just happened and I think we got it on film," and you're a part of it.

There's also the great moment that comes when you have the opportunity to sit in a screening of your film with a receptive audience and everything is working—they are laughing at the right places and they are surprising you with laughter at stuff you didn't realize was so funny, the pin-drop silences are in the right places, and the audience response at the end is appreciative. That is a great, exhilarating experience. It makes you want to make another movie.

I have spent a number of years as a private pilot, flying single-engine planes. Single-engine piloting has been described as periods of ecstasy punctuated by moments of sheer terror. And I think a similar comment can be made about directing. You have moments of ecstasy and you have moments of terror. You think, "Oh, my God, this is the most horrible day of my life. Why did I take this job? What am I doing here? The weather's wrong, the script is wrong, the camera's wrong, the light is wrong, the actress is wrong, the clothes are wrong. It's just chaos, its terrible and awful, and everybody is angry." You don't want to be there. And then the next day, maybe something wonderful happens and there's a great sense of esprit and suddenly everybody's exclaiming, "Oh, God, making movies is great!"

What do you think are the qualities of the ideal director that you as an actor would want to work with?

He or she should be a great craftsman, a great storyteller, who appreciates what the actor has to offer and can take the actor's offering and integrate it into a great piece of work.

Do you think it's advantageous for a director to study acting?

I don't think you can make a general rule. I'm sure there have been great directors who've never studied acting—great storytellers, people who were great with a camera and great with a story, who had an instinct for it, and didn't have the slightest idea how an actor approaches his work.

On the other hand, it is helpful to the actor if the director understands the actor's process. If you have a simpatico relationship and the actor says, "I'm having trouble here because . . ." and the director can say, "I understand that; we'll see if we can try this and maybe it will work," that's very helpful. But all and all, I think it's terribly important that the director, for everybody's sake, is a great storyteller, which is the essence of the art.

KEVIN HOOKS

Son of veteran television and film actor Robert Hooks, Kevin Hooks began his career following his father's footsteps into television acting. At the age of twelve, he played Cicely Tyson and Paul Winfield's son in the acclaimed feature film *Sounder* (1972), which was nominated for four Academy Awards.

Kevin Hooks earned his action stripes as a big-screen director when he helmed the fast-paced action thriller *Passenger 57* (1992), starring Wesley Snipes and Bruce Payne, and *Fled* (1996), starring Laurence Fishburne, Stephen Baldwin, and Salma Hayek. Before these two films, he directed the comedy feature *Strictly Business* (1991), starring Tommy Davidson and Halle Berry.

In the television arena, Kevin Hooks received a Cable ACE Award nomination for Best Director for his work on TNT's true-life drama *Heat Wave* (1990), which starred Cicely Tyson, Blair Underwood, and James Earl Jones and won an ACE Award for Best Picture. His other long-form credits include the telefilms *Roots: The Gift* (1988), *Murder Without Motive* (1992), *To My Daughter with Love* (1994), and *Boys and Girls* (1995).

He earned two consecutive Emmy nominations for his work on the ABC After School Specials *Teen Father* and *Class Act*. He was honored by his peers with a Directors Guild of America Award for the CBS Schoolbreak Special *Home Sweet Homeless*.

Hooks has also directed episodes of some of television's most successful series, including *Tales from the Crypt*, *I'll Fly Away*, *Equal Justice*, *China Beach*, *The Young Riders*, *Midnight Caller*, *A Year in the Life*, *St. Elsewhere*, and *Doogie Howser, M.D.*

The following interview took place September 30, 1996.

• • • • •

Did the fact that your father, Robert, is an actor have an influence on your decision to become an actor?

He had a tremendous influence on my becoming an actor. I grew up watching him on Broadway, at the Negro Ensemble Company, and of course on television when he did *NYPD*. He never pushed me to act, but there was a passion that came from him. And inevitably, acting was just something that I felt I really wanted to do.

Do you remember how you were cast in *Sounder*?

I started acting when I was nine years old, and the first thing that I did was a bit part with a then-relatively-unknown actor—Al Pacino—on my father's series, *NYPD* in the late sixties. It was a half-hour crime/ detective drama. Hand-held, 16mm, New York City. It was really well done. A pioneer. And from there one thing led to another.

My father had co-founded the Negro Ensemble Company, and one of the creative forces behind it was a writer named Lonne Elder III. Lonne was hired to write the screenplay for *Sounder*, and he called my father and said, "I want Kevin to come out to California to meet with the director and the producer, Martin Ritt and Bob Radnitz. Kevin's perfect for the role. I wrote it with him in mind." And so I came out to

L.A. and met with them, and we hit it off. I guess my acting instincts took over, because I had never studied it, other than watching my dad.

Did they have you read for them?

I was asked to read the material three different times over the course of maybe a week, ultimately ending up at Bob's place in Malibu. I had never seen anything like that—a house right on the ocean. I was from West Philadelphia, so I was really overwhelmed by this whole thing. I remember us walking out on the beach at a certain point, and Bob said to me, "Kiddo, you're going to do this movie. You're the guy." And to this day, I remember that feeling, one of the most perplexing feelings that I'd ever had. I felt great because I knew that this was the reward for the work that I'd put in, but I had no idea what I was getting myself into. I knew that it was a major film, which was a little scary, but the process of making that movie was just incredible, working with Cicely Tyson and Paul Winfield and, of course, Marty Ritt, who was one of the preeminent directors of his time.

How did Martin Ritt work with you? Did he work with you differently than he did with the adults?

I'm sure that it was a much simpler process working with the adults than with a very inexperienced twelve-year-old. But Marty had a great deal of patience, and he was wonderful in that he was able to simplify his needs.

He never was too technical in his presentation of what he asked me to do. He always tried to parallel what he needed from me with stories about other things. And he would always try to pull experiences from my life.

So if he wanted you to cry, he would have you remember something sad that happened to you?

Exactly. Or he would make up scenarios. For example, "What if this were your real father or your real mother? How would you feel about that?" He would put me in a space where, regardless of who the characters in the film were, the emotion was the same.

What did he tell you about the scene where your father comes home after he was in prison, and you run toward him with the dog? That was one of the most emotional moments in the movie.

I remember that the staging of it was probably the most compelling thing about that scene, because we actually had to run almost a quarter of a mile to get to Paul. He was such a small figure when you saw him from the house. He really was a distant figure. And we didn't cheat the space and the distance between us at all. The way Marty shot that scene, the dramatic impact was inherent, it was automatic. He didn't really have to express too much to us, because the scene kind of took over. And I think you see that on the screen.

I remember images of Cicely running down that road, trying to catch her breath and being totally overwhelmed by the thought that her husband had returned. It was a wonderfully shot scene—a case where less was more.

A lot of times the dramatic impact of a scene has as much to do with the staging and the scheduling as anything else. If that scene had been shot toward the beginning of the schedule, it would have meant a lot less to us than it did toward the end of the schedule, because we had become a family by that point. So the thought of him returning had its own dramatic impact on us as a family, something that could be translated to those characters very easily. And Marty understood how to do that, I think, better than anybody I've ever worked with.

Did Martin Ritt have a great influence on the way you work with actors?

Probably more than any director that I ever worked with.

In what ways?

He was able to communicate with actors because he had been an actor early on in his career. He really understood how the mind of an actor works, he understood the psychology.

I think that creative people have a tendency to be very insecure about themselves, because we're very insulated. We don't get an opportunity to take a consensus of what is going to work and what isn't going to work. We have to make those choices for ourselves. And only after we've made those choices are they evaluated for their effectiveness. So I think that actors need to be communicated with in a very delicate manner, and Marty understood that. He understood the simplicity of the communication, especially dealing with me as a twelve-year-old child, which required extraordinary patience. He also understood how to take what the actor has to offer.

It's been said that at least fifty, if not seventy-five, percent of making a film is casting the right people, because ideally you hope to get to a point where you don't have to say much to an actor, because that actor is bringing seventy-five percent of what you need in the first place. Marty understood that. He cast the right people in *Sounder*. And I strive to do the same thing.

I strive to be simple. I strive to use what the actor brings to the table and just act as a guide, to funnel all of our energies into something that the actor trusts, and that we all feel is the right direction to take for this character.

You sound like you have a lot of respect for the actor.

Acting was a great part of my life before I became a director. So I have a tremendous amount of respect for that process, when it is done the right way.

As an actor, can you give me some insight into your character preparation? Are you an actor who does background stories for your characters?

That's very important. I try to create a life for the character, which I think is an actor's responsibility. Good writers, who have spent a lot of time developing their characters, will have done a lot of that work for you, but it's a generalization, I think, of what they see the character being.

The character can only come to life when the actor has been cast. I firmly believe that there is a large part of the actor that moves into the character to really build that person. So I would try to create a life for him, a background of characteristics, people, relatives, and experiences that went into a little mental box I'd carry around with me during the course of a film.

At any given moment during the course of a production, those things become a tremendous influence on the performance level. You will take a character to a level that cannot be understood by anyone other than yourself. I think that's where a great deal of satisfaction and gratification came for me, because I knew that there were levels to a given character that were not on a piece of paper, and that even a director was not always aware of. Directors knew what the end result was, because they saw it, but they were only a small part of that entire process that you had created for yourself. And that's what I think acting is all about. At least it was for me.

Do you think that good directors are open to their actors' ideas about things that may not be in the script?

Absolutely. As long as those ideas don't intrude upon what the director is trying to paint in terms of the relationships. I think that an actor can be responsible for his or her own character, but has to depend on a good director for the relationships. That's something that I can't always see as an actor, but that's clearly what a director's overall responsibility is.

I was very pleased with the majority of directors I worked with, who were very, very open to that process. And again, just because I have this Pandora's box of ideas does not necessarily mean that they all work. There's a lot of discussion. Some of my ideas will be accepted and some will be discarded. It's a collaboration, and I enjoy that process. It's good. It's healthy. But when that openness is not there in a director, it can be very frustrating for an actor.

Some actors don't do much in-depth preparation, some actors like to go with their instincts. What do you expect from your actors?

You have to determine very quickly what an actor's strengths and weaknesses are. I have worked with some actors who have been so prepared you would not believe it, who've created more than one life for their characters, and I'm speaking literally.

I worked with an actor once who had taken a character through two or three lives. At any given time it was, "Well, which character do you want me to play?" But I've also worked with some actors who have brilliant instincts. Laurence Fishburne, for instance, is a guy who really works on instinct better than anybody I've ever seen. And there's an honesty in that, which is truly remarkable. But you have to be a very bright person, a very spiritual person to make that work, because to have good instincts you must have experienced a lot. And I think that your experiences have to have been complex and multi-layered to be really meaningful.

If you look at actors like Laurence Fishburne and Morgan Freeman, the thing that attracts audiences to them is that they are always believable. You are always brought into their world because of their intensity. And when you realize that intensity is instinctual, that's got to be incredibly spiritual. I know it is in Laurence's case.

How does your acting experience help you communicate with actors?

Once you're an actor, you're always an actor. One of the things that I try to do when I prepare a script is think of the characters the way I would if I were an actor. If I can identify with that, then to a large degree, I will have anticipated a lot of the things that the actors will need or want. So when I get to the set, or rehearsal, I've already thought about a number of things, I've anticipated the problems and thought about resolutions. Moreover, I believe there is a trust that actors have for directors who have acted, the same way that basketball players respect coaches who played the game. It's comforting for both the actor and the director to know that there's a trust there.

You've directed TV episodes, MOWs, and features. Does each medium offer a different challenge in working with actors?

To a degree, yes. When you're doing an episodic, the stage that the show is in—meaning whether it's one of the first few episodes of a brand new show or an episode from the fourth season of a hit show—determines where the actors are with their characters.

Early on in my episodic career, I ran into some difficulty in going on established shows and really trying to get some things from actors who had settled into their characters. Obviously, when you do an MOW or a feature, in particular, you're starting from square one with those characters and those actors, and so that collaborative process is probably much more active than it is in episodic television. But again, it just depends on the actors, and whether they're looking to keep their characters fresh and come up with new ways of dealing with things. And that's why you have to be very, very particular and careful in selecting what episodes, if any, you're going to do when you're at a stage in your career like I am, where you go from features to some episodics and cable.

I notice you don't direct yourself.

I have a phobia against it. I put a lot of work and hours into my responsibilities as a director. To add the pressure of learning lines seems overwhelming to me. And I don't know that I would ever feel totally comfortable in a scene that I was shooting, because there's a part of me that would want to be watching it. I've been told by people who do it that you just tape it and then go back and watch it. That sounds reasonable, but at this point, I have a process that I think works pretty well for me, and I would hate to compromise that just for the sake of being in one of my films. I think that if there was a role that I was really passionate about as an actor, and if I was also really passionate about making the film, I would do it.

How did you make the transition from actor to director?

It was a natural progression. I was twenty-four when I started directing, which was the result of being on a television series, *The White Shadow*, for three years.

One day I had a conversation with Bruce Paltrow, who was the executive producer. I told him that I wanted to explore the possibility of directing. And he said to me, "You know, that's a really smart move." I said, "I think so, but what makes you think that?" And he said that there was a distinct advantage to being a director that maybe I didn't realize. He explained to me that as long as I lived I was going to be an actor, maybe a good actor, maybe an excellent actor, but I was always going to be perceived by this town as a black actor. But that as a director I would be evaluated in a very transparent way—my work would determine how successful I would become.

I had never really thought about that before, and he was absolutely right. It was an opportunity to step away from any obvious race discrimination that was written into a script by a writer or added to a script by a director. This was an opportunity to perform on a pretty level playing field, and I was intrigued by that.

So after about a year and a half of observing different directors and editors, I was given the opportunity to direct an episode of *St. Elsewhere*, which Bruce produced. Eventually I did four episodes of that show, and then made my way through every hospital show on the air.

Do you remember the first time you stepped on the set as a director?

I do. It was euphoric. I remember that day, because I felt as though I was extremely prepared to be where I was, so I wasn't really as nervous as I probably would be today if I started all over again.

Why's that?

I was twenty-four years old. I was young and cocky. I felt like I'd worked really hard for this, so I was going to go in and hit a home run. I don't know that I would ever be that secure now, knowing what I know about it. But that was the beauty of it. I was extremely naive about what the job was and what the real responsibility was.

I'll never forget the first time that I was confronted by an actor. It was Ed Flanders, God rest his soul, one of the regulars on *St. Elsewhere*. I had planned out every shot, every angle the night before. I had drawn up diagrams, prepared my shot list. So I explained to Ed what I wanted him to do: He was behind his desk when a rather unsavory character came to his office door, and he was to get up and go to the door to greet this character. We were on the set, doing the rehearsal, and I said, "Okay, Ed, at this point, you get up and go over to the door." And he looked at me with a straight face—he was brilliant at the deadpan—and said, "Why?" And I really didn't have the answer, other than the fact that I had diagrammed this whole scene out that way, and that it was prettier over there than it was at his desk.

That was the first time that I realized that, wow, the actor is going to have some input into this, because what Ed said made sense: There was no way that Ed's character would get up from his desk to go meet this unsavory person. If the President of the United States had come to his door, or if the hospital's Chairman of the Board of Trustees had come to his door, it would've made sense. But this unsavory character did not justify him getting up. Ed was absolutely right!

And that's when I realized what directing was really about—communication. Communication, compromise, and collaboration. The "C" words. That's when I really was turned on by it, because I realized that it was a process that was dependent upon the skills of literally hundreds of people working properly toward the same goal—putting your overall vision on film. And that's where the communication comes in, because I've seen people who have had a tremendous amount of talent and are brilliant visual artists who have not been able or were unwilling to communicate their vision to their cast and crew. And that's tragic.

How do you present your vision?

I work on my communication skills a lot, and I think that I'm very articulate about what it is that I want to do. I'm a very emotional person. I work on emotion. I want the audience to feel what I feel, and if I can do that as a filmmaker, which is a very difficult thing to do, then I think that I've done my job.

The camera should make you feel. And that is something that I work on an awful lot. I think that my camera probably moves a lot, because that, to me, is a way of evoking emotion and feeling, and putting the audience in the midst of a scene, whether it's an emotional dialogue scene with a slow camera move to the characters or the bullet's point of view in *Fled*.

I try to communicate to my cast and crew how I see things and how the shots will be cut together in editing, so they all have a clear understanding of what I'm trying to do, what I'm trying to express. Obviously there are choices about how that can be presented, but what you want to find is the most effective way of presenting that idea. A lot of that has to do with the whole theory of montage. And there has to be a plan of how that's going to go, because each shot is a segment of that montage. Clearly, that gets back to Sergei Eisenstein—*Film Form* and *Film Sense*—and his whole theory of montage, and before that, ancient Japanese culture and the whole idea of their art, how the images are communicated.

I try to communicate all of that to my crew and my actors. It's important that they understand how the final sequence will work. To a degree. Obviously, you don't want to impose all of that upon their work, but at the same time, there are certain things that they may be asked to do that are critical. And for the most part, any information that you can give them about how you are telling the story creates a tremendous sense of trust and security. I think that a problem in relationships with actors is that we, as directors, sometimes have a tendency to be very tunnel-visioned about what it is that we're doing. It's not an intentional thing, it's just that we're so accustomed to developing our ideas alone that, in the rat race of making a picture, we sometimes lose sight of the fact that we haven't communicated an idea clearly. And when that happens, we dissipate the excitement and the enthusiasm of the people around us, because they feel, "Well, if I had known that's what you wanted to do, I could have helped you with it."

It's important to let the actors know what lenses you're shooting with. I may be a hundred yards away, but I've got a telephoto lens shooting a pretty tight close-up. If I don't communicate that to the actors, I may not get the emotion until take seven or eight, when they finally realize, "Oh, you're shoulders and up. I thought this was full-figure."

So it's very crucial to keep everybody in sync?

Absolutely. It develops a tremendous sense of trust. Making a film is like going on a journey. You have to trust your skipper. You have to know that you are safe in his hands, that you are going to get to your destination safely.

Tell me about your casting process.

Let me start with casting directors. Choosing a casting director is every bit as important as choosing a cinematographer or an editor, because from a philosophical standpoint, you have to be on the same page— you have to know what types of actors you want.

What type of film does your cast represent? Do you want to go for slightly off-beat, non-traditional casting, which would see certain actors in roles that you wouldn't ordinarily see them in? Do you want to go traditional, with actors who are truly believable in the roles they're playing? Do you want to go slightly over the top with some and on the nose with others? You have to discuss these questions with your casting director, who has to be confident about his or her ability to cast your movie in a very specific way. And it should be very specific, because your casting determines what type of film you're going to wind up with.

For instance, look at the characters in the Coen brothers movies, which are not necessarily traditionally cast films. All those characters have a distinct look and feel about them, which is unique to Joel and Ethan's vision. And that has to do with collaboration. So I usually try to find a casting director who I see eye-to-eye with, someone who understands what it is that I want to do and is confident that they can bring in those kinds of actors.

I prefer that actors read the material from the script that we're using. Even if it's not the final draft of the script, I like to get an idea of what those words sound like coming from those actors. I generally videotape them, because video is a useful tool to communicate with some of the other people involved in the process, i.e., the studio, the producers, the networks, etc., who are not in the room with you when you are casting or auditioning. But you have to be careful about the over-use of video, because I don't think that it translates emotion very well. Depending on how it's shot, it can come off as very impersonal and cold.

The last thing that you want to do is get excited about an actor because of the energy you got from them in the casting room, and then take a tape of that actor to the studio and have them look at it and find that it does not carry the weight of the performance that you had in the room. That's something that you've got to be very careful of. You want to make sure that if you are videotaping the actors during their audition, you're getting the angles that you would want to capture in the actual film. And that's from a very basic standpoint, i.e., "Let's make sure that we're tight enough on them during this part of the speech."

I do a lot of directing during auditions. I'm very interested in how flexible and quick an actor is in terms of making adjustments. That translates directly to how we're going to work on the set. A lot of actors take a long time to get up to speed with what you're trying to get from them, and obviously, that time turns into money when you're on the set. Not that that should be the primary thought in your mind at that point, but you want to try to put together a cast that is quick to understand what it is that we're all trying to do, a cast that has good instincts. Sometimes that's not always possible. Sometimes an actor may have a quality that is just so incredibly unique that it is worth putting up with some of their other deficiencies.

I try to do a lot of work with actors during the audition process. I'll bring them in more than once, but I try not to bring them in more than three times. It's a really traumatic experience for actors to come back over and over again.

How difficult is your final selection process?

It's difficult for a number of reasons. Ideally, it's difficult because you may have a number of excellent choices you need to narrow down to one. That, based on my own experience, seldom happens. What generally happens is that you wind up with that ideal situation for maybe one or two roles, and then there are always one or two roles for which you just can't find anybody who works. So you're left with a number of choices in one area and no choices in another area.

You want to try to match people physically, which is but one of a number of requirements that go into your choices. And actors know this very well. Quite frequently, an actor will read for something and call his agent afterward, saying, "Wow, I did a great reading. I felt great, they loved me. They laughed, they cried, they were with me the whole way. When do I start?" And the agent will say, "Well, listen, I'm sorry to tell you, it's just not going to work out." And the actor is amazed because he can't believe that he could've done such great work and not gotten the job. But a lot of it has to do with the fact that he wasn't tall enough, or was taller than the star of the movie; he wasn't pretty enough, or was too pretty.

One of the biggest sighs of relief for me in the preproduction process is when I'm cast. You're both totally exhilarated and hoping and praying that it all works out, because you really don't know exactly what you've got. On an individual basis, you know what each person has to offer, but when they all get together, you don't know what's going to happen. Actors tend to feed off one another, which creates a whole different energy that you cannot predict. It can be fascinating to watch, but it also can be excruciating to try to handle.

Any examples?

I don't want to name names. I have been extremely proud of all of the casts that I've worked with. Some of them were more difficult to handle, for lack of a better term, or to read, or to guide, because the energy that was created between them was difficult for me to get my hands around, if you will.

Sometimes I may have a temperamental actor who doesn't agree with my vision, so I try to go back to basics. I try to be as specific as possible about what it is that I'm trying to get. And at the same time, I think that you have to listen to the actors as much as possible, and try to get an understanding of what it is that they're trying to convey. If you can be specific with one another, that will help you find a common ground.

All too often, actors go off in directions that even they can't predict. And you will want to try to find what their goals are, where they are trying to go. But frequently, actors will not have the answer to that. They'll be off on a tangent that somehow feels like the right thing for them to do. It's almost a point at which they can't really see what it is that they're doing. So at that point, it's your job as a director to say, "Okay, let's try to be specific here and figure out what it is that you're going for, because if I can understand that, then I may be able to help you get there." Or you might say, "Wait a minute, hold it, that's an interesting thing to go for here, but it's not necessarily consistent with some of the other things that we've already established. You understand that, don't you?"

I think that the key to a good relationship with actors is that you both have to be good listeners, which is very difficult under the pressures that you have on a film set, where time is money, and if you find yourself in the midst of a conversation that wasn't covered in rehearsals, it's very difficult to have the patience to listen to one another. But it's critical, it must be done, because once you set off on the wrong foot, it can destroy all of the trust that has been built up to that point.

Do you place great importance on rehearsal?

I don't think that I've ever had enough time to rehearse. That is one of the unfortunate things about the films that I've done—they have not, for one reason or another, given me the opportunity to sit down for two weeks and rehearse.

What I try to do in rehearsal is establish a number of things: I try to establish the lines of communication, and with that, a level of trust that will give us a foundation and a springboard from which to work. I try to establish my style as a filmmaker. I try to communicate to the actors what types of things they should expect from me, and hopefully, I get from them a kind of psychoanalysis, if you will, of the people I'm involved with: How am I going to communicate with them? How am I going to deal with them? What things do I have to look out for? How best do I proceed with the dialogue with this actor, as opposed to that actor? I want to establish for myself where the sparks are, which combinations of characters have dynamics that other combinations don't.

The entire process of making a film is a metamorphosis, it's constantly changing. I always make an analogy to an expedition on a ship: You set sail with a crew and you know what your ultimate destination is, but there are so many things that happen along the way that can't be predicted. It's really about damage control and problem solving as much as it is about the creative process.

Do you have any keys to successfully casting a feature film? Any pitfalls to avoid? Any things to look for?

Wow. One of the things that I've learned about casting is that you really have to be aware of the reasons that you are intrigued by a certain actor. And when I say that, I mean that there are a number of different levels of talent that people can bring to the table.

All too often we get caught up in things that are not real—qualities that are presented in the audition process, like a unique ability to audition, which may disguise a lack of real experience or preparation for the actual process.

There are people who can audition really well. But when you bring them back for another audition or you ask them to change things, they'll do the exact same thing again. That's all that's there. So you can't just look at what you see on the surface, you have to dig deeper and find out what is really there. I think that that's something that I am always conscious about when I'm casting.

After days and days of hearing actors read the same material, it becomes less stimulating than when you first started. In a way, the whole process is debilitating, and can become very exhausting. And when you reach that point, you have to be very careful that you're making decisions for the right reasons.

Do you do a shot list before you get on the set for non-action scenes?

In films, as opposed to television, where you have a shot list for everything, the dialogue sequences kind of evolve. But I think you have to have an idea of what things you would like to illuminate, as dictated by the material.

Do you look for what Sydney Pollack calls an "emotional line"?

Yeah, exactly. You look for an emotional line, and you try to follow that. But from a technical standpoint, I think that you have to allow the actors to comfortably express themselves, and sometimes that happens more quickly than at other times.

I think that it is a process that evolves out of the rehearsal. You have to stand the scene up on its feet the way you do in theater, where you sit around a table and discuss a scene for days or weeks, and then finally get up and go to the actual space.

As a director, you clearly want to discover that emotional line, and there will be points during which, technically, you know that you need your camera to be at a certain place. Generally speaking, once I know what the emotional spine of the scene is, because of my television background, my instinct is to get the coverage and then decide in the editing room whether or not I would like to use it. I believe in having options. At other times, a specific camera move would be so dramatically effective that you want to stay with that camera move in lieu of coverage. For example, in *Fled*, the opening shot in front of the crime committee hearing began with the guy delivering the paper. And I knew when we conceived that shot that we didn't want to cut into it until a certain point, so we shot that scene continuously in one long take. We knew that it was elegant, and because the sequence that preceded it had a lot of quick cuts and quick camera moves, we knew that in this sequence we needed a breather, we needed to go into a different kind of mode, and a different speed, if you will.

Once you've you discussed a shot with your DP, do you also discuss it with your actors?

Absolutely. Again that gets back to the communication that we talked about earlier. Sometimes during the course of a film, actors, as well as everybody else, have less of a tendency to forget where they are in the film. All of a sudden they're shooting scene 132, but they've kind of forgotten what scene 129 was about and what scene 136 is going to be. You have to remind them of where we've been and where we're going.

Much of the filmmaking process is making the actor feel comfortable. Some actors don't want to know. They say, "I'm immersed in this person that I'm creating, and that's enough for me. However you want to shoot it is fine. I'd rather not know the details." I respect that, and my tendency and my instinct is to allow them to be as much a part of the process as they want to be. Obviously I don't want to have a cast full of directors, but I do want to let them be a part of it, and feel as though they are participating in the creative thrust of the film. I think that it generates a tremendous amount of positive energy.

When you do your emotional scenes, do you do your close-ups or your wide masters first?

My instinct tells me that there's an inherent danger in shooting close-ups first. I've found that most actors are more comfortable working their way into a certain performance level, which culminates in the close-up. I think that's the very nature of what we have grown accustomed to in films.

There were times when I did my close-ups first, but if memory serves me correctly, I think that we got ourselves into trouble doing that, because once the close-up shot was established and we'd moved back for the wide shot, the actor inevitably saw something in that shot that he or she wanted to incorporate into their close-up.

Now, obviously, there are circumstances where you may have to start with a close-up: You may want to shoot a master at a certain point in the day when the sun is backlighting your master, and you're not going to sit around and wait for that just to start the scene. So you may wind up starting with the closer material, where you see less background.

Again, it's about communicating to your actors about how that sequence is going to work, and what it is you're going to see in that master shot, or that wider shot, so that they can at least evaluate what their choices are and what it is that their character is going to be taking in in that master and what the audience is going to be seeing.

I prefer to start with the wider things and give everyone, not only the actors, but also the crew, an opportunity to see where we're going. It acts like a road map. There are exceptions of course. I'm not a big fan of masters for the sake of shooting masters. I think that television dictates masters more than feature films. The very scope of feature films takes care of the master in and of itself. You can be on a medium or a close shot in a feature film and see an awful lot of background, so you can get away with a little bit more. Films are much more of a sweeping, open kind of picture. You want to make sure that your audience is not confused by a series of what we call "talking heads." People want to know where they are.

Do you like to have actors improvise on the set, or do you limit your improvisations to rehearsal?

That's a tough question to answer yes or no. I think there's always room for improvisation or growth of the material. A film like *Fled*, where you have a relationship with the dynamic that Stephen Baldwin and Laurence Fishburne had, can lend itself to improvisation. It all depends on the situation, the scene, and what it is that you're trying to accomplish within it. Certain situations are more suited toward improvisation than others are. Comedy is an improvisational genre, and so improvisation works quite well in comedy, particularly with people who have comedic instincts. That's what makes Robin Williams brilliant.

So it depends on the situation and the actor?

That's right. It's usually less effective in extremely dramatic moments and scenes. Although I have seen it come out of that, too. When an actor is overcome with emotion, there are some wonderful things that can emerge that just can't be scripted. It really depends on the actor and the situation.

Do you believe that listening and responding is the key to a successful performance?

I think the key to a successful relationship in any walk of life is how well people listen to one another and how well they respond to what they hear. And listening and responding clearly is paramount to an actor's performance.

Do you use a video assist on the set? If so, do you stand by the video assist or the actors?

I do like video assist, but I don't have any set standard in terms of its usage. I can be found in both places, based on where I am needed the most.

In an action picture, I think it is critical for the director to see the monitors for all three cameras that he's got going, to know that he has the cuts that he needs to make that sequence work. Quite frequently, in action sequences, you're cutting all of the angles that you have when the second unit goes to pick up additional angles. It's really important to make sure that you have all of the angles, that you have all the shots. But in a dramatic sequence, my tendency is to be right there with my actors, so that I can look into their eyes. I don't want to depend on the monitor for that.

There are no set rules, really. It depends on the situation. I don't want to be too dependent upon technology. I have to trust my instincts much like the directors in the past who didn't have video assist as a tool and elicited brilliant performances from actors nonetheless.

Tell me about the genesis of *Fled*. Did you initiate it? Was it brought to you? How do you prefer to select your films?

Fled came to me about a year ago. I got a phone call from Preston Whitmore II, who's the writer and executive producer, and he mentioned to me that he had written a script that MGM wanted to make. He had liked my work in the past, and we had had some conversations about doing some things together. He told me that he wanted me to read the script and see if it was something I'd be interested in doing, because he wanted to make sure that I was included in the list of directors considered for the film. I read it and told him that it was a very interesting piece that I felt I could really bring something to. So we set up a meeting between myself and Frank Mancuso, Jr., the producer, and we hit it off right away.

Obviously, it's a lot more competitive to be in that marketplace than it is to develop your own films. You've got more directors who are competing to be involved in a specific project at a studio than in a picture that you and I get together and say, "Hey, I've got an idea. Why don't we write this script together, or hire someone to write. I'll direct, and you'll produce." When you develop something on your own, you don't have to worry about competition, since you're attached to the project already.

At a certain point in this business, when you have developed a number of relationships with writers and actors and talent, you begin quite naturally to develop ideas with those people to be done in a variety of media. All of the films that I have done have been films that were brought to me by either a studio or a producer. It wasn't until two years ago, when I established Hooks Film Works, that I started to develop a number of different ideas, because I haven't really done the picture that I think comes from deep in my heart. And that's what I would love to do.

That's not to say that I haven't been passionate about the films that I've made, but I have not been involved in a film that has germinated from an idea in my own head or in my own heart. And I'm really, really looking forward to that, because I think that the more passionate you are about a project, the better you will be able to express yourself.

Do you feel that you'd have more creative control over films that you would initiate? Films that no one can re-cut?

I've been very fortunate in that I have not had to go through any dreadful experiences in the post-production phase—on editing or otherwise—though I've heard about them. I've done all my pictures with the same editor, and I think that we both put in an awful lot of time to deliver what the studio has requested, whether it's the first director's cut or the final, with all of the notes and cuts, etc. It's a real testament to our collaboration and his talents that we have not had any problems.

Let's say you get notes from ten executives. You agree with eight, but two are totally disruptive to your vision. How do you deal with that?

It's always a difficult thing to maintain your vision at that point, because even if you've been left alone during the production process, everybody tends to want to get the last word in during the editing process. It's very easy to lose sight of your film, as opposed to the film that the studio wants to sell. At the same time, you do have to be cognizant of the fact that it is their money. So it takes a tremendous amount of diplomacy. You have to be extremely careful about how you articulate to them what it is that you're trying to do.

Again, I've been very fortunate in that most of what I have tried to convey in my films have been pretty clear and effective. Now there were some instances, for example, in *Fled*, where we were trying to do certain things with a sequence, and it just never worked for reasons that none of us realized at that time. So you have to be very open-minded, and listen carefully, because sometimes they do have a point.

There are certain situations where you have a note that doesn't necessarily make a lot of sense, and may not be the best thing for the film, but it may be the best thing for the film that is going to be sold on a billboard, sold in a trailer and put into 2,500 theaters. You have to be very careful about how you bridge that gap without stepping on anybody's toes, which is a very tricky, tricky thing to do. You strive to build their trust in you, and that calls for all the communication skills you can muster, because the bottom line is that these are people who you want to maintain a working relationship with.

How long was the shooting schedule on *Fled*?

Sixty days in a number of different locations, with a lot of different people and a lot of stunts and a second unit.

How do you prepare for a film with such complicated logistics?

You pray a lot! [Laughter] I tend to have a lot of meetings with people. I don't like to depend too much on paperwork, because people have a tendency to get the paperwork and not read it or not understand it.

And it's important for me to sit in a room with somebody and explain to them what it is that I'm looking for, and explore various ideas, have them talk to me about some of the things that they've done in the past that are similar or contrast with what it is that I'm looking for. So there's a wonderful kind of give and take, an exploration of ideas that I think culminates in what it is that we finally want to pursue. I have what I call mini-meetings with all the different departments, special effects, stunts, makeup, wardrobe, DP. I talk specifically to all of them, and we go through the script every day for two weeks.

How long was your prep time on *Fled*?

About twelve weeks. Part of the problem with *Fled* was that we were casting in Los Angeles and shooting in Atlanta, so I was constantly going back and forth. Anytime you're shooting on location, you're going to be doing your major casting and staffing out of a major city, like Los Angeles or New York, so there's always a fine line between when you absolutely have to be on the location, scouting and doing those things that they need you to do, and when you are going to be finished up with your casting and staffing in Los Angeles. That was a bit of a juggling act.

After I have my mini-meetings with everybody, I sit down and talk to the group as a whole, and we go through every detail. I try to have at least one meeting a week as I'm progressing and also during the production. I try to get everybody together for lunch, or immediately after work, to look at next week's work as a block and talk about, day-by-day, what it is that we're going to do. Because you have so many people involved in the process, you have to constantly remind people of what it is that you're doing, so that everybody stays on top of it.

A key element here is your first assistant director. You have to have someone who has tremendous organizational skills, because they're a key element in efficiently running your set. It's the difference between staying on schedule and falling behind.

Do you storyboard your big action scenes?

All the action sequences get storyboarded, shot by shot. We may not necessarily use every frame, and we may get some additional frames that are not on the storyboards, but it gives everybody a base from which to work.

There are two main reasons why storyboards are critical. Number one is that it's very difficult to articulate what's in your head to a hundred people. If there's a picture that everybody can look at, it will answer a number of questions, like How much of this are you going to see? We can all look at something that's in front of us and relate to it, which is very important in terms of making sure that everything that needs to be in that frame is included. The other reason, which I think is even more important, is that on *Fled* we had a second unit for about four or five weeks. And the second unit obviously will go out without me.

If you have any kind of visual effects, you need to storyboard. For instance, the sequence with the train, when the guys jump off the bridge and are chased by the train, was visual effects. There was never a time when the two guys were running in front of a train, and the mountain that was behind the train was not there. That was all green-screen work. So we had to storyboard what the first unit was going to shoot live-action and what the visual effects team was going to add in. The only way to make sure that everybody was aware of exactly what they were to do was for us to storyboard.

What are your shooting techniques? Do you shoot run-throughs? Do you shoot rehearsals?

At heart, I'm a perfectionist. I don't like loose ends, so I really try to work my way up to the point where I can feel that everybody's ready to commit it to film.

Obviously in television that's not true. You don't have that luxury. You have to rehearse it, get it up on its feet, get it nailed down, get it lit, and start shooting it as quickly as possible. But in films, I try to work my way into the process so that the momentum is built and the energy has been brought to a level where I feel that we're on the verge of really finding some new things. In other words, I think that there's some value to the theory of spontaneity. And I want the spontaneity to happen on film, so I really try to keep the rehearsals to the mechanics of the scene, and the shot, and the movements. And I want to get an idea of the pacing of it with the actors, where the beats are and where the beats aren't. Then I want to start to film it, because what happens quite naturally is that the stakes are raised and the level of performance is tweaked and things start to happen. And quite frequently, you can over rehearse, and by the time you commit it to film, it's kind of dead. You don't want that to happen. It's a fine line. Success is dictated by your experience and instinct. And it changes every time you do a film, because you're working with a different group of actors.

Every actor has a different way of working. For instance, Stephen Baldwin is the type of actor who likes to go—he likes to talk about it, but he doesn't like to wait around for the technical, mechanical things to happen. We do a take, and he wants to do another take right away. So you try to accommodate that as much as you can, because what he's really saying to you is, "I'm on the verge of something here, I'm feeling good now, so can I take this feeling and make it carry over to the next take?" And I understand that as an actor. There's a window of opportunity for an actor where everything is working and feeling just right, and that's when you know you're going to get the best take. That's what I try to work my way up to.

You need flexibility?

I think so. From an individual standpoint, yeah. But generally speaking, there is a process which works very well for me as a director.

You have to be very observant about when the time is just right, and hopefully, all the other elements are there, too. Quite frequently, you'll have your actors at a point, and suddenly your DP will say, "I'm just going to add something over there. It'll just take me a minute," and it'll spoil that point that you brought your cast to. Everybody's ready to go, and now we've got to take five minutes, which means that the actor goes off and makes a phone call, or gets a cup of tea, and we've got to start all over again.

How do you overcome that?

Again, and I can't say it enough, it is about communicating, about people understanding the process by which you work. I try to be very clear about my priorities. I have no problem telling a DP, in the beginning, when I sit down and talk to them, "Look, I enjoy working with my actors. I want to have as much time to work with them as I can get. As much as I want the pictures to be pretty and want things to work a certain way, I don't want that to intrude upon my time with my actors, because ultimately, we're all here to make sure that we get the best performances from them."

How involved are you in decisions about lenses, lighting, and camera moves?

Very much. When I was a teenager, I used to take a lot of still photographs, so I'm very much involved in the frame and how the camera moves. If you look at most of the films that I've done, particularly the recent films, the camera doesn't sit still for very long. That's my style. I am also very knowledgeable about lenses—what those lenses look like and what effect they have emotionally.

How specific are you in setting up shots with your DP?

My style involves long lenses, compressed images, which is something I adopted while doing television, where you tend to compress your images, and confine the movement within the frame. In features you can go much wider, so I find myself using more of a mixture of long lenses and wide lenses.

Once a DP understands your style, and that's a discussion that you have early on, he knows that there are certain lenses that you like to use, i.e., he knows that you're going to tend to want to go from maybe a 35 or a 50 straight to an 85 or a 100, or a 125, which is slightly more compressed than a 100. Once you've established that in the first few days or so, you don't really have to say what lens to use, because he's going to pull it out of the box anyway. It's, "Do you want to go long-ish here?" And you say, "Yeah," which means he's going to grab that 125.

Tell me about the techniques you use to help actors tap their emotions.

I don't know that I have any set techniques for eliciting emotion from actors. I just try to talk to the actors as much as possible, and remind them of certain things.

In a way, I see myself as the instigator—the guy who kind of tells you what you should be feeling at any given time. Like the corner man in a fight. You come back after each round and the guy tells you exactly emotionally where you should be right now. I just offer little nuggets of information.

In *Fled*, I continually reminded Laurence of the delicate balance of his behavior, meaning that police tend to behave and react to situations in a certain way. There is a certain way of thinking that exists among all police. That's certainly not to say that they all share the same ideology, because we in L.A. know that all too well not to be true. But technique-wise, there were a lot of things that Laurence was doing behaviorally that came from his background of knowing about undercover cops—he had played an undercover cop at least once before in *Deep Cover*, so he had been there before. I was really just reminding him that the audience saw him as a convict, so a certain aspect of his behavior had to reflect that, because that was, on the surface, who his character was. But the underlying character was a much more complex person, so that when he listened to what Stephen Baldwin had to say, or when he came into contact with other people, he used a police technique. He negotiated, rather than immediately responding with violence. Now you only really know that when you look at the movie a second time, and say, "That's why he did it like that, because that's how cops do that."

On the other hand, with Stephen, there was always this naiveté that I would remind him existed with his character. I really just try to be the guide, or the emotional shepherd for the actors.

What did you do to familiarize yourself with the behavior of undercover police?

I have had experiences and relationships, friendships with some people who do that kind of work, all the way from local police to FBI agents. So I have engaged them in conversation about certain attitudes and certain behavioral patterns, and I've been able to relay that to my actors.

I want to be there as a resource for them, somebody they can utilize. When I go to them between takes, I try to come up with one-word clues for them. For example, I did a MOW with Rick Schroder called *To My Daughter with Love*. The story was about a couple in their twenties with a six-year-old daughter, and the wife dies. So Rick's character had to deal with the burden of raising this six-year-old child without a clue about how to do it. I remember that when we started rehearsal, I asked him to do something for me. I said, "Write down all of the things that you think this guy is feeling." They were all one-word things: sad, desperate, vulnerable, overwhelmed—a host of different things. In between takes, I would pull that list out, look at something that maybe he had forgotten about, and say to him, "Devastated." And it would click for him.

I try to simplify things to the point where I don't have to say a lot. I don't want to give the actors a dissertation on what it is that I'm looking for, I want to clue them in with one word or one phrase that zeroes in on something that we've already talked about. So at any given moment, I can say, "Okay, this take is about desperation."

Tell me about the bus explosion in *Fled*. It looked like Fishburne and Baldwin were right there.

You can't make an action movie without that shot—the principals running toward you with the explosion right behind them. We shot that with a long lens, which compresses the images so it looks like your actors are right on top of the background, when in reality, they are a safe distance away.

But I want to talk for a moment about the Air Force base sequence, because that was probably one of the most improvisational sequences that I've ever done. It was something that I really embellished at the moment, because I realized that, in essence, the scene was about a guy who was being prepared to testify to a grand jury, and it was apparent that he was not fully prepared to answer the questions. So I made up a list of questions that weren't scripted, which I gave to the actress who was playing the attorney, and said to her, "Ask him these questions." What I got were totally spontaneous answers, which worked perfectly, because he was nervous, he was unprepared, he wasn't eloquent or articulate. At the same time, we had the steadicam operator do moves that really exaggerated the emotion. I wanted to get the feeling that time was passing, but that we were seeing the passage of this time in the microcosm of a number of minutes. It was the most fun I've ever had doing a sequence, because it was just totally spontaneous.

How did you shoot the bullet's POV as it hit the con in the chest?

I don't know if I should tell you that. [Laughter] I don't want everybody doing it. That was an interesting situation, because it was a shot that I'd seen before in *Robin Hood*, with an arrow, and in another film called *Sniper*.

In my research, I found that it had never been done the same way twice, so we were left to our own invention. We tested a number of different ways and eventually wound up shooting it by cranking the camera down to two frames per second, which is an extremely slow speed, and putting it on a dolly. The combination of the camera move on the dolly and the two frames per second gave us the kind of speed that, while still obviously slower than a bullet, gave that shot the impact that it needed. It's probably the most effective half second that I've ever shot, because you don't expect to see the POV of the bullet.

What about the cable car fight? Was it actually shot on the cable car?

Oh, no, we built a platform, which was about fifty feet in the air, on the side of a mountain, so that we had a 180-degree view. And we put the cable car on something like a lazy-susan, so that wherever the sun was, we could backlight it.

What about the guy falling out?

That was a stunt guy, and that fall was 150 feet into an air bag. We had five cameras on it. That was one of those days where the first unit wished they were with the second unit, because when we went to dailies that night and saw what they had done, we were amazed.

Did you use real actors in the fight scene?

A lot of it, yeah. I always try to keep my actors as involved physically as I can, because I think that people really respond to that.

When working with your dad, do you treat him differently than the other actors on the set?

I've directed my father probably a half dozen times. I find it a real joy to work with him, because he's so professional and so talented. There's a specific, almost unspoken language that we have that makes it very easy to communicate with each other. I don't have that kind of relationship with any other actor. And we have a very good time. We have so much history together. He's like my best friend, and to have your best friend at work with you really gives you an incredible amount of moral support.

The first time we worked together was a very odd experience for me, because I didn't know how to communicate with him at all. It was difficult for me to cross that line—from being a fan to being a director who had to give instructions and directions to another actor. I was not accustomed to looking through the lens and seeing my father's face, so it was difficult to judge just what type of shot—how close or how wide—I wanted on him.

I remember once setting up a basic close-up of him and having difficulty trying to figure out just how to frame his face, only because it was a face I'd been looking at all of my life. Suddenly there were parameters and boundaries in which I had to place that image, his face. Whether I wanted to use a 75, an 85, or a 100mm lens, whether I felt that he was lit properly. With my father at the other end of the camera, it seemed to take on a more important connotation for me. Now, from a technical standpoint, he's no different from any of the other actors that I work with. I'm always pleased to have him there, because he always brings something special to the roles that he does for me.

Do you decide before you get to the set which scenes you're going to spend more time shooting?

The more planning you do prior to getting on the set, the more efficiently your set is going to be run. Generally, on a film, you will have your DP for about two weeks of prep prior to shooting. Now that's not to say that you will not have had any discussions with him earlier, or that you will not have brought him in for a weekend of scouting.

I try to discuss all of my ideas with my DP prior to getting to the set. This way, I not only insure that I set aside the proper amount of time to accomplish my objectives but I also give myself ample time to acquire the proper equipment that I will need to execute the ideas that I want to explore.

In order to make the schedule and to stay on budget, you are forced to prioritize your scenes and decide which sequences are going to be more time-consuming. For me, with my television background, this is not really a problem. I've always been able to do that.

Obviously, on the set, there's a certain amount of spontaneity. You can't be totally prepared for anything. A lot of times you'll see a set one way when you scout it, and then, when you see it lit, you'll say, "Wow, I had no idea it would look like this." And that may inspire you to create something new and refreshing, taking advantage of your environment, which makes filmmaking so wonderful. So you plan in advance to give yourself the time to be spontaneous and experiment a little bit.

How do you choose your DP?

The first thing you look at is totally aesthetic: What do I want my film to look like? And based on that, you come up with a list of people whose work you've been inspired by, whether it's within the genre that you're working in or in some other genre that will benefit you. Secondly, you begin to break that list down by examining their experience within the genre that you're working in.

There are a number of DPs who I would love to work with, who I have not worked with simply by virtue of the fact that action films require someone with experience in a number of areas. They need to be quick and efficient, they need to know how to deal with and coordinate the camera department with the stunt, visual, and special-effects departments. These are things that go beyond a straight dramatic film, and you want to try to find someone who has some experience in these areas. So your list becomes smaller and smaller, based on your criteria.

Eventually you meet with the people who you're interested in, and you start to discuss what their feelings are about the film, based on their reading of the script. How they see it, what their likes and dislikes are, their tastes. And you begin to develop some idea as to how well you will work together, not only from a personality standpoint, but from the standpoint of style and technique. Lastly, I call other directors and/or producers to talk about their experiences with this person. Based on that information, I make a final decision.

The cinematographer is the most crucial of all your key department heads, because the only way to get the imagery that's in your head on film is to have someone who totally understands what you are trying to achieve, and knows how to get it. It's all about collaboration.

Can dealing with composers be difficult?

One of the most difficult things for me to communicate is the musical ideas that I have, the sounds that I hear in my head. Part of the reason for this is that music is a very unique and different language to understand, and certainly to speak. Since I'm not a musician, I don't read music and I don't play, it's very difficult for me to analyze and explain and describe the kinds of things that I hear.

I think that you have to try to be as specific as you can be about what you want your composer to try to achieve, perhaps using musical examples that you've heard or specific types or styles of music that you like and think feel right for the film.

How can you ensure that you're going to get the music you're looking for?

I will have several meetings with the composer prior to their beginning to actually write the music. Once they start, I begin a series of visits to their studio, where I hear just about every cue before it's finalized. I run the music against the picture. And at that point, I can make adjustments. I can say, "Well I like the rhythm here, but I don't like the instrumentation" or "I think this is too melodramatic" or "It's not melodic enough."

Most of the time, composers have studios in their homes, and when they write their music, a lot of it is either computer or synthesizer generated. So it gives you an opportunity to very quickly review a number of ideas.

I ask a lot of questions. When I hear something that sounds odd to me, I'll ask, "What is that instrument?" or "What is that sound?" I like to hear certain things isolated, and with the new equipment, you can isolate a lot more elements within a score than you could before. So I will ask them to kind of peel away certain layers, and in that way I can better understand what instruments I like and what instruments I don't like, and what the music sounds like with or without certain instruments. It's quite a fascinating process, which can be frustrating for me sometimes, because I can't speak that language.

The strip club scene with the music playback: How did you plan and shoot that?

That was a little tricky, playback always is, because if you don't have songs that are already written for those sequences, you have to find songs that you like, use those songs for the playback, and later on, when you hire a composer, or in this case, when we hired a music supervisor who was producing songs for the soundtrack, have him or her write something at that same tempo for the final score.

That's always a very tricky thing, particularly when you have people dancing or have to cut the film to a specific musical beat. Everything is thrown off somewhat when you replace the playback. It's very important to make sure that you have a song that's really in the same tempo as the playback song, so you won't have to change your picture cuts. Also, you must not forget that every time you use playback, it better have sync-pulse on it; otherwise you'll spend hours trying to put it in sync later.

I loved the fact that every time somebody fired at a target in *Fled*, something exploded either in the background of the same POV or on the reverse angle.

It's a style that fascinated me in John Woo's Hong Kong films. He's a master at using the environment to accentuate his action sequences. I thought it was very effective. I wanted to see it used more in American films, so I took it upon myself to incorporate it into my work.

How did you incorporate it into your work?

I screened a copy of *Hard-Boiled* for the cinematographer, production designer, and the effects and stunt departments, making sure that from a production-design standpoint we always had things in those sequences that could explode, and be shot, and accentuate the action.

An action scene that involves pyrotechnics is very time-consuming. Having all of those elements—the guns, the squibs in whatever it is that you're attempting to explode, pottery, glass, people—working together is difficult.

You had many extras in some of your action scenes. Were they choreographed by your first AD? How long does it take to set up something like that?

When you have that many people running through a set like that, you have to very careful about who it is that's getting pushed around, and all that kind of stuff. So you wind up using a combination of extras and stunt people, and you try to place your stunt people in harm's way, if you will, so that those are the people who get pushed aside or fall down the steps.

It's a combination of the AD working with extras and stunt coordinators working with their people. Anytime you're doing that kind of thing with that many people, it takes a long time, because you really have to rehearse and choreograph a number of things.

The most challenging situations that I have had, in terms of staging with extras and stunt people, was on a film that I did for TNT called *Heat Wave*, which was about the Watts riots in 1965. The staging of the riot sequences was one of the most extraordinary experiences that I have ever had, because you are actually photographing hundreds of people totally out of control in a violent situation.

In this particular case, we made twelve stunt captains, and each one of those captains had about twenty people in their group and were responsible for choreographing all of the action and activities of that specific group. You can imagine the number of rehearsals that it took for twelve groups to individually come together, and for us to have all of those groups then meld into one action that was photographed with five cameras going at once.

It was really a remarkable process. We had three cameras on the perimeter, shooting different-size frames, from 150 to 300mm, and we had a couple of hand-held cameras within the action to give you that sense of being right there in the middle of the chaos.

Do you cast your own extras?

Early on, it's very important to me to get a sense of what the extras look like, because obviously I want my film to have a sense of uniformity, and the extras play a great part in that, particularly in large crowd scenes. You want to make sure that you feel as though these people are part of the environment you're creating for the scene.

It's important to me to see some pictures of specific people, particularly stunt players who are going to have special business within the piece. Once everybody has a handle on what it is that we're going for, I let the ADs pick and choose people on their own.

Tell me about shooting the night chase scene in *Fled*, with the Atlanta cop cars pursuing the Mercedes.

That was one of my favorite sequences for one reason: I think that it was the best example of the synergy between the first and the second units, because here was a situation where it wasn't about the second unit cleaning up what we had started.

Basically, I was responsible for all of the material that took place inside the Mercedes, with Laurence and Stephen. All of the shots of the actual chase itself were done by the second unit.

We storyboarded the chase, and went through it with a fine-toothed comb, so I knew exactly what they were going to shoot. Then I made a stylistic as well as a practical choice.

As the first unit, we planned on using a tow rig out on the streets of Atlanta. At this point in Atlanta, it was getting fairly cold, and if you've ever seen a tow rig, it's a very, very cold process, because the tow truck itself, or the insert car, as it's called, is open. The entire crew is sitting on an open truck that is towing the picture vehicle. And it takes quite a bit of time, because every time you change the angle of the camera, you've got to go back to base camp and take the mount off of one side of the car and mount it on the other side.

My second unit director, Mic, had worked on all of the *Lethal Weapon* movies, and he said, "Kevin, I've got an idea for you. Do you remember the scene with the car chase in the opening of *Lethal Weapon II?*" It was the scene that culminated in the car flying through the plate-glass window and turning upside down. Mic told me that all of the shots of Mel inside the car were shot on stage. He said, "We used rear projection, and we were able to move the camera outside of the car in ways that we never could on a tow rig." I realized at that point that, by shooting on stage, we could save a tremendous amount of time just in the convenience, and we could stay a lot warmer. And we could have a lot more flexibility if we did it that way, so we made the decision to do all of the stuff of Laurence and Stephen on stage.

I am exceptionally proud of that sequence, because there's no way that you can look at it and tell me that they're on stage. And I have to give the DP, Matt Leonetti, a lot of credit, because the way he lit the car looked so realistic. Not only did we have rear projection, meaning that if the camera was on the passenger's side of the Mercedes, looking past Stephen Baldwin to Laurence Fishburne, outside of Laurence's window you would see the street projected behind him on what we call a plate, which was shot by the second unit. But to take that one step further, we also reflected in the passenger's side window what would be on the other side of the street. So we had both rear and front projection in most of those shots, which kept the frame alive, kept you from concentrating on any one element of it.

I've never had anyone tell me that it looked phony, because it didn't.

I thought it was executed extremely well. It was a combination of Mic Rodgers' second-unit work with the stunt coordinator and all of the stunt players and Matt Leonetti's ability to create an environment on the stage. And it worked out fabulously with the actors. It kept me much closer to them. I was able to communicate with them like I would in any other sequence. They were warm, they were comfortable. And as it turned out, we were able to accomplish in six hours what we would have needed at least two nights to do. Altogether it took the second unit, I think, four full nights to shoot the plates and car chase.

Tell me about shooting the action scene in the Georgia Dome, which seemed an extremely complicated scene, even for a film like *Fled*, which had many difficult action scenes.

I had virtually no prep time for the Georgia Dome. We had a severe problem finding a location for that sequence. We originally were going to do something in the MARTA (Metropolitan Atlanta Rapid Transit Authority) station, but we could not get a confirmation on that for what seemed like a very long time. Finally we were asked not to use that facility. This happened very late in the schedule, so we had to scramble to find another location and secure it before we could actually rewrite the sequence, which was based on wherever we were going to be.

We looked at a couple of different places, such as Six Flags Over Georgia, which was an amusement park that was shut down for the winter, so it would have been a very controlled environment for us. But we looked at a number of films that had used amusement parks as a backdrop and said, "We've seen this before. Let's try for something a little bit different." We also considered doing it in a very large lumberyard, but it was just too noisy and complicated a proposition, because they wanted to remain in operation while we were there.

Finally, we went to the Georgia Dome. At this point we were about ten days away from beginning that part of the schedule. We secured it on Friday. I went in there for about three hours on Saturday morning and was met by the rest of the technical crew for a tech scout, where I explained to them what areas and things I was going to be shooting. And after just three hours of prep, we started shooting there, I believe, on Monday.

That was probably the largest sequence with the least amount of preparation that I've ever worked on in my career. I wouldn't recommend it to anyone. It was just a matter of circumstance. Sometimes those things happen. And the other challenge at the Georgia Dome was that, even though it was an interior location, because we were working on the concourses, which were exposed to the outside lighting, we really had to work that location like we would work an exterior, because when we lost the light, we could not look toward the windows. We had to be extremely efficient about what we did in that location. We shot that scene in four days.

Do you shoot your action scenes MOS?

All the high speed stuff is MOS, but we try to get all of the ambiance that we can, because action sequences require the most post-production sound. So as much of that as you can pick up live, you do.

How did you cut this film down to ninety-eight minutes?

I usually don't shoot a lot of excess material, because I am very aware of how I am going to cut the film together. I am always cutting in my head, and in that way, I wind up, I think, saving a lot of unnecessary time shooting things that I know I'm not going to use. Particularly in an action film, because you know that these kinds of films are such that people really want to feel like they're constantly on the go.

That I shoot pretty tight and edit very tight has always been a hallmark of mine, a key to my style. I don't linger on things too much. It's getting to the point now where I need longer scripts to ensure that my style is going to be able to deliver. I'm still waiting to do the two-hour movie. I think that *Strictly Business* was around eighty-five minutes. *Passenger 57* was a little more than that.

How do you work with your editor?

My editor and I have done all of my features. I can't imagine working with somebody else. He understands my style. I understand his style. We just work together so well. We communicate with each other. We listen to each other. We experiment. We have a very, very open and honest relationship with each other, which I think has helped the work tremendously.

Can you improve an actor's performance in the editing room?

I think that if you are not improving an actor's performance in the editing room, you're doing something wrong. I think that the whole point of that process is to improve the film, and within that to improve the actor's performance and improve the director's performance throughout.

By the same token, you sometimes have difficulty doing that and achieving what it is that you need to achieve dramatically. There's a fine line there. It's really a measure of degrees that you're trying to experiment with once you get in the editing. What happens in the editing process really infuses the dramatic beats and the ability to really tell the story.

In what sense? Restructuring?

Yeah, to restructure. To decide whether or not you're going to play this line on camera, or whether the reaction to what's being said is more important. The actor gives you all of the beats, then you decide where the beats play best, and in that respect you really do make the performance in the editing room.

Is ADR helpful in restructuring performances?

Sometimes it can be. It really depends on what you're trying to accomplish with ADR, and who's doing it. Some people are better at it than others. I've found that there really is no middle ground with ADR. People are either very good at it, or they're very bad at it.

But yes, it does offer yet another element, and another level of performance that you may not have been able to achieve under the circumstances during shooting. It's another opportunity to close in on something much more personal, much more profitable, because you have had time to step away from the character. And unlike on the set, in ADR, the actors can see what it is that you're trying to tell them. In ADR, they're looking at the finished product. They can see all the cuts and exactly what it is that you're trying to achieve.

How involved do you get in the marketing of your films?

The ultimate marketing decisions are going to be made by the studio, the people who have spent their money and are continuing to spend their money on the marketing and the promotion of the film.

There does seem to be a limit on how much control you have of those particular elements, but I think that it's important that a director's voice continue to be heard throughout that process, up until release.

A filmmaker should be as involved as he can be. From the moment that you, as a filmmaker, decide to make a film, you have made a decision as to what specific audience you are making the film for.

You really need to be aware of, if not involved with, the decision-making process. TV spots. Radio spots. What particular shows are going to be targeted in terms of your television spots. What the look of the poster is, and what that says to your audience. Soundtracks are a huge part of marketing films as well. It's a very, very competitive market out there. I believe that you really have to try to continue to put your mark on your film throughout the entire process.

Do you have any keys to eliciting the best performance from an actor?

The most important thing is to trust, first of all, yourself. Trust your instincts as a director. Trust your emotional instincts, because they're probably the richest attributes that a filmmaker has. Those emotional instincts are full of a wealth of experience, compassion, and passion. And if you trust in yourself, and are able to communicate your passion to your actors, you are well on your way to one of the most enjoyable experiences that you can imagine.

RICHARD BENJAMIN

Raised on Manhattan's west side, Richard Benjamin graduated from New York's High School of Performing Arts and then from Northwestern University, where he majored in drama. His first professional acting job was in Joseph Papp's New York Shakespeare production of *The Taming of the Shrew*. He made his Broadway debut in Neil Simon's *The Odd Couple*.

In 1967, he starred with his wife, Paula Prentiss, in the CBS series *He and She*. In 1969, he made his feature film acting debut opposite Ali McGraw in *Goodbye Columbus*. And he went on to appear in more than twenty feature films, including *Catch-22* (1970), *Diary of a Mad Housewife* (1970), *The Marriage of a Young Stockbroker* (1972), *The Streagle* (1972), *Portnoy's Complaint* (1972), *Westworld* (1973), *The Sunshine Boys* (1975), which earned him a Golden Globe for Best Supporting Actor, *House Calls* (1978), *Love at First Bite* (1979), *Scavenger Hunt* (1979), *The Last Married Couple in America* (1980), *First Family* (1980), and *Saturday the 14th* (1981).

In 1982, he made his feature film directorial debut with the comedy *My Favorite Year*, a film that brought Peter O'Toole an Oscar nomination for Best Actor and established Benjamin as a first-class director. His other directorial credits include *Racing with the Moon* (1984), *City Heat* (1984), *The Money Pit* (1986), *Little Nikita* (1988), *My Stepmother Is an Alien* (1988), *Downtown* (1990), *Mermaids* (1990), *Made in America*

(1993), *Milk Money* (1994), and *Mrs. Winterbourne* (1996).

The following interview took place April 27, 1995.

• • • • •

It would seem a natural progression for an actor to become a director, just as it would seem natural for a dancer to become a choreographer.

It felt very natural for me. I'd always wanted to direct.

Where did you go to school?

I went to the High School of Performing Arts in New York. Then I went to Northwestern and started to direct theater around the Chicago area.

I'd always wanted to direct, but I always wanted to act, too. I like to be involved in everything. When I act in movies, I almost feel like there isn't enough to do.

Having acted both in the theater and in films, which would you say presents the bigger challenge to the actor?

In the theater, once the curtain goes up, you're on your own for two and a half hours, and there's something wonderful and spontaneous about that. Once you're on the stage, you go through the entire performance without the stop and go that you must endure in movies. When you do a play, you rehearse extensively and have previews, which gives you an opportunity to develop and polish a character.

Acting in movies is hard because opening night is at 8:00 in the morning, 2:30 in the afternoon, 5:00 that night. Since most films are shot out of continuity, you never quite know where and when it is. And there's the waiting as the technical crew sets up the shots. And here you are, needing to gear up emotionally for an important scene. It can become pretty chaotic on the set, which makes it a challenge to concentrate. To avoid confusion and maintain character, the best solution is to keep in mind what scene happened previous to the one you're shooting, and what scene follows. You've got to keep all of that together.

How does an actor stay in character when shooting a movie?

You have to put on blinders in some way. Whenever I had some big scene to do, I held it in my head the whole time. So even though people would go, "Oh, sorry, we had a light go down; we're going to be another few minutes," I was still focused and ready once the camera rolled again. I kept my concentration on the thing that I was heading for, which wasn't easy. In the theater you know the curtain's at eight o'clock, and you had better be there.

What inspired you to become an actor?

I saw my uncle Joe Browning, who was a stand-up comedian in vaudeville, perform when I was about five years old. He was talking, and all these people were laughing. I thought they were his friends. I just thought this was the greatest thing in the world. And ever since I can remember, I knew I wanted to do it as well. He was my inspiration.

Did your family approve of your ambition to be an actor?

Yeah. They loved show business. They encouraged me. My father loved comedians. My mother loved the theater.

How did you make the transition from theater to film acting?

I had been doing theater in New York. And then my wife, Paula Prentiss, and I got a television series in California called *He and She*. A few months before that ended and we went back to New York, she said to me, "You ought to read this book. You'd be right for it." It was *Goodbye Columbus*.

Of course, I didn't read it. And the next thing I knew, they were casting this movie. So then I read it and went to see Larry Peerce and Stanley Jaffe and read for them, auditioned, improvised, talked my way into it.

When did you decide you wanted to direct movies?

I always wanted to do it, but I didn't quite know how to get there. I was acting in movies and having a good time, but that wasn't ultimately what I wanted to do. So at a certain point, I went back to my original agent, Phil Gersh, who is basically a director's agent. He knew from conversations we had had years before that I wanted to direct. He said, "Well, what's happened with that? Why aren't you doing that?" "Well, I don't know. How do you get to direct?" He said, "Let me take care of that as long as I know that's what you want to do."

He sent me to see Marvin Worth and Bob Klane, who had written the television pilot for *Where's Poppa*. Marvin said, "If we let you direct this, would you let us know what you're doing?" I said, "What do you mean?" He said, "Well, sometimes we work with people who don't let us know anything." I said, "Of course." And he said, "Okay." So I directed it.

This was your directorial debut?

It was my first thing other than theater. It was done on tape, shot with four cameras, and I actually cut it as I went along. I had a great time, and it turned out very well. The show didn't get put on the air, but the pilot itself was pretty good. And now I had this thing that anybody could see and learn that I could get a performance out of actors.

After that, I was doing something in New York when I got a call from Phil [Gersh] or his son, David. He said there was a movie, *My Favorite Year*, based on the life of Mel Brooks, when he was a young writer with *Your Show of Shows*, and they couldn't find a director for it. They were interested in someone new, and they'd like to meet me. So I read the script and loved it. I knew that whole area because I had grown up there and had worked at NBC. I met with producers Michael Gruskoff and Mel Brooks and we had a great time. We saw eye to eye on the way it should be done, and they said, "Okay, we'll take a chance." It was a big chance for them to take.

When you became a director, did you make a conscious decision not to be an actor anymore?

No, I didn't. I've done some little things here and there and some theater whenever I could. I like acting and I would do it in a second if the timing worked out.

You find so many actors acting in their own films today.

I've been a little reluctant about that because there's so much to do while you're directing. I'm not sure how others do it.

How long did you work with Norm Steinberg on the *My Favorite Year* script?

We worked for something like eight months. We had an office over at MGM where we sat and went over the scenes. We just kept doing it and doing it. And sometimes we'd involve Mel and Michael.

How was your first day on the set of that film? Did you feel butterflies?

Somewhat. I just wanted to make sure that I remembered to say "Action" and "Cut."

What kind of atmosphere or tone do you create for your cast on the set?

I love actors, and I want to make the set a place where they feel safe, and where they will do expansive things—things that are beyond what they think they can do—and not feel that they've been made a fool of.

A fear of failing runs around a movie set, so some actors stay very safe. They do little things, and that way they can't be very bad. But I like it to be big. The bigger it is, the more I like it. Then if I see it's too big or we've gone too far, I can always pull it back.

I like to make the set a place where actors want to be. I like treating actors well. I think they're very special, and I don't like any yelling. I don't like it if the AD yells.

You never yell at an actor?

I would yell at an actor if I see a take that is working wonderfully and the actor cuts it himself, which to me is unforgivable. They may think it isn't going right or they're not happy or comfortable or something, but they should never cut a take because they don't objectively know what it looks like.

When that happens, do you take the actor aside and talk with him?

No. I say, "Roll it now. Don't stop."

I understand that Richard Donner uses a megaphone and often talks to his actors from a distance. What's your technique?

I like to get close. I'm always right by the camera, because I don't use the video monitor.

The thing that drives me crazy on the set is when people are not quiet when we're shooting. When it ruins a good take, that, to me, is like a crime. It's taken over a year to get here and to get that camera pointed in a certain direction on sets that someone has built, with lights that somebody has set, on film that somebody has manufactured in Rochester, or wherever. To get to that moment and say, "My God, that's brilliant" and have somebody who just isn't paying attention ruin it drives me crazy. It's a matter of respect for the actors. Noise distracts and hurts the performance.

How do you deal with your extras?

I like to talk to the extras and tell them what's going on. I talk to them all the time. I want them to understand and be a part of it, not just people crossing in the background, not just part of the scenery. I think that when they know what's happening, they become a part of it.

I think that whoever's on camera is the star of the movie. We may be following Melanie Griffith, but if somebody else happens to be there at that moment, it's their life. And either it's the life of someone who's just walking through a shot or it's the life of somebody who really understands where we are and what's happening.

I imagine you're involved in casting your extras.

That's absolutely important. You can't have a leather-faced outdoors person playing someone who spends his life in an office; they have different body language, skin tones, attitudes. Extras are a big part of the fabric of a movie, so I cannot take chances there.

As a first-time feature film director, did you go in with storyboards?

I storyboard all action sequences so I have something to work from. But I am open to changes. Lots of times something else happens or you find a better shot or it doesn't work out the way you had envisioned, but storyboards are a very good guide, and they're economical too.

When do you do your shot list?

First I rehearse the actors. We work it out together. And when everybody is comfortable with the blocking and business they have to do, I work out a shot list with the director of photography.

When you do your set rehearsal, do you bring in your DP or do it alone?

First I do it alone with the actors, but I keep the script supervisor there. When I get further along, I bring in the operator, DP, and sound person, and we decide how we're going to shoot it.

How many rehearsals do you do?

Until the actors feel comfortable. Then we do some camera rehearsals. Then I send my cast into makeup and we light the set. And during that whole time, I may think of something else I want, which happens even as I'm shooting.

What was the most difficult sequence you ever shot in a movie?

I think the staircase scene in *The Money Pit*, when the staircase starts to collapse and everything starts to fall around Tom Hanks. I had to design the staircase about six months before, because the special effects people had to know how far it had to go before it went to the point where there was no return.

That sequence was the most difficult because the actors are in it— Tom Hanks was in it and so was Shelley Long. And I wanted them to be as safe as possible. So we had all that stuff collapse up until a point and then stop. And then I would get it to another point, and another, until we got to the point of no return. I actually had stunt doubles on the staircase during the part where we had about six cameras running at different speeds, because this was it—there was no coming back.

It's very expensive. You're talking about jokes with a price tag on them. So you say, "Is this funny enough? With this money? Is it still funny even though we're being safe here?" It's all very emotional. Every shot you make in a movie is emotional because it's a decision. And when you make that decision, usually there's no turning back. Once you commit, that's it.

I remember we were shooting something toward the end of one day, and as the staircase started to collapse, Tom grabs a spindle from it. As he looks at the spindle and realizes he's got part of the staircase in his hand, all the spindles all the way down the whole staircase come out, as they're supposed to.

I said, "That was great. We need to do that again." And my crew said, "Well, we can't do it right away." I said, "What do you mean?" They said, "We have to put the spindles back, and they're all different sizes." I said, "You mean to tell me you just can't take those things and simply put them back?" "No, they're all different." It nearly gave me a heart attack, but they were able to put them back overnight and we shot it again first thing in the morning.

What about the elephant scene in *Made in America*?

I didn't have any idea how intelligent those animals are; it was an amazing revelation. At some point, Whoopie's right in front of the she-elephant, and I said to the trainer, "How is the elephant going to stop?" The trainer said, "Trust me, she will never run over anybody." I said, "Are you sure?" I'd heard people say "trust me" before, which are the two worst words you can hear in this business. He said, "If anyone gets right in front of the elephant, she will come to a stop." That elephant was amazing.

But when we had Ted on the elephant going into the water, we didn't know what was going to happen. I said, "Is she going to go in or is she going to stop short of the water?" The trainer said, "She loves water. She's going to go in." I said, "What about Ted?" He said, "It's all fine. But she thinks she's playing. She might want to play with Ted. She might want to roll over on him." So my heart started to pound and I said to myself, "That's all I need now, a giant elephant rolling over on my star."

The trainer must have read my mind because he looked me in the eye and said, "It would be good for Ted to get off as soon as he can." So I told Ted that. But he was so game and so into the moment that he wanted to do it anyway. And he did manage to get off the elephant in time. I sometimes used stunt people on that movie, but many times, on some of the bigger things, it was Ted.

How do you choose your projects, and how involved are you in their development? Do people come to you with projects or do you go out and develop your own ideas?

Mostly people come to me through my agent. Sometimes a script has been developed at a studio, sometimes even with some elements of the cast already attached, and now they're ready to find a director.

How do you feel when you come on a project that already has a cast attached?

It depends on who it is. When I heard that Whoopie was going to do *Made in America*, I jumped on it. Melanie was already involved in *Milk Money*, and that was perfect.

Do most scripts you've worked on require a lot of rewrites?

Some. But if a script is good, I leave it alone. On *Mermaids* I came onto the picture after they'd been shooting four days. I had read the script months before and I loved it. I didn't think it should be changed. And, except for a few very little things, it wasn't.

Made in America was basically the script on the screen. I worked with the writer, Holly Sloan, and we made very few changes. I believe in the original writer. There's something there that is the genesis of the thing. When you start getting further and further away, it gets distorted—the original voice begins to dim, and before you know it, you've got some kind of committee thing. It's homogenized and bland and the idiosyncratic things are gone.

Did you set out to be a comedy director?

Yes. But I'll do a serious film if it touches me in some way that I understand, if I say, "Oh, I know about that" or "I want to express that" or "This means something to me." I like relationships; I like human behavior, and I think trying to explore the human condition is something movies can do in a wonderful way.

Let's talk a little bit about casting. Let's say you have a preproduction schedule and you just have not been able to find the actor you feel one hundred percent sold on. Do you compromise or delay the production?

I don't think you can compromise. Any compromise you make will come back and bite you. Any compromise will be magnified: casting, props—I don't care what it is—you can't let anything slide by.

On the other hand, if I can't cast my first choice, there's not much I can do about it. If the person's not available or doesn't want to do it, I don't chase them unless I believe that they're terribly important. But if that's the case, I don't give up, I just keep pursuing them. And that's happened a few times.

Who has control over the casting of your pictures?

I have mutual approval with the studio. Sometimes there's an impasse, but in my experience, usually we all agree. I go down the list prepared by the casting director and say, "He would be great. He'd be my second choice. He'd be my third." Then I call the studio and they say, "Well, we like him first because . . ."

Have you ever had to compromise your vision to please the studio?

It's pretty collaborative. I haven't run into those kind of things at the studio level. It isn't a game, it's a business. You want them to like the movie so that they're behind it when it's time to release it. And I don't believe in having some kind of confrontational thing, because we're all in this together. Usually there's a way to work it out.

When casting newcomers, will you ever hire an actor without first seeing him on film?

I won't hire an actor without seeing him in person, because I believe, especially in the movies, it's not necessarily their acting ability, it's who they are that's picked up by the camera. If the person is a decent person, I think you see that. If I'm looking for a certain lightness and ease, I trust what happens in the room.

Before you see their reels, do you bring them in for interviews or read them?

No. I will look at their film if I don't know them at all.

What if they don't have any film?

I look at tapes, which may come from all over the country, and I'll say, "I want to see that person" or "I don't want to see that person."

What's your approach on cold readings? Do you tell actors to come in with prepared scenes?

I like the casting director to send actors sides of scenes from the film I'm casting rather than have actors come in with prepared monologues. I like to do readings from the film because, first, I want to see if our material is working. And second, if I think it all works, I want someone who can do it. I don't want to wait until we get out there on the set and then find this person can't get the comedy that's in the scene. Recasting is an expensive proposition. A director must know what an actor can do. That's not to say that mistakes aren't made, but in my case I've been very fortunate. In comedy, I've found that an actor either has that comedy gene or not.

Peter O'Toole was magnificent in *My Favorite Year*. Was he your first choice?

His part was based on the life of Errol Flynn. Peter was one of five actors—Englishmen who you would believe with a sword in their hands—that MGM would make the picture with. I sent him the script and he loved it. I met him and that was that.

How did you find Mark Linn-Baker?

When the casting directors got the script, a number of them said, "Oh, you've got to see Mark." So he was the first actor I saw. And then I went on to see 300 other people before finally going back to cast him.

Tom Hanks and Shelley Long in *The Money Pit*—how did that come about?

Tom I knew about from *Bosom Buddies*. I had rarely seen anyone with that sense of timing. I just thought he was brilliant. I don't know what other pictures of his I had seen. Maybe *Bachelor Party*. He had made a few things.

We all wanted him, but we wanted to meet him first. So myself, Steven Spielberg, Kathy Kennedy, and Frank Marshall had dinner with him. And our eyes were darting around the table because we were saying to each other with our eyes, "Offer it to him now while he's sitting here." After he went out the door, we all turned to one another and said, "Let's hire him. Go get him. We don't want him to even think that we talked about it. We don't even want him to think that we had a discussion." But he had gone. So we said, "Leave a message now so he'll see what time we decided."

To hire a comedienne to play opposite him was very difficult. And Shelley Long, who I wanted, was having a baby. I asked her, "When are you having this baby?" She said, "When does the movie start?" I said, "Well, we can't offer it to you." We went around and around like that. She had the baby, and ten days later she was shooting.

With Whoopie Goldberg already attached to *Made in America*, how did Ted Danson come into the picture?

I wanted somebody who was attractive, and he was on a short list of attractive leading men. Michael Douglas and I had Ted over after he had read the script, and we told him we wanted him. He said, "Why do you want me?" We said, "Because you look good."

You never know if the chemistry between your actors is going to work. In this case, it did. In *Milk Money*, after Melanie Griffith was cast, I asked Ed [Harris] to come in, not to audition, but just to be in the room with Melanie. They just looked great together. I could see that they liked each other and it was going to work. When I saw Ted and Whoopie at the first read-through, I also knew it was going to work.

How many actors do you see on the average before you decide on casting newcomer leads, like the boys in *Milk Money*?

Oh, hundreds. I saw those boys and read them and improvised with them, because there was no experience, no body of work you could rely upon.

You just go with your gut instinct. The bottom line is you don't know until the first day of shooting, so your instinct had better be right. There is always that element of the unknown, which makes the whole process exciting.

Do you check the references of the actors you are going to work with?

Directors talk to directors. It's all very confidential. You need to know what you've got.

What happens if there's an actor who you very badly want to use, who you think would be great for the part, but who you know is going to be a nightmare? What sort of boundaries do you set?

I haven't had that one yet. I refuse to have that one. I legislate on the set that we're not going to have that. I set the boundaries.

I listen to the actors. I pay attention to them. I let them air things out. I try to stay as open and receptive to the actors' ideas as I can, simply because I'm working with people who are very bright and can and sometimes will make great creative contributions—things I may have not thought about, but they, knowing their characters, may have discovered. And if it enhances my vision, why not take advantage of the opportunity?

It is a process of discovery, and sometimes wonderful things happen. But, as a director, you must be definitive about what you're doing. After all, the director has the overall vision of the film. At times, you just have to know when to put your foot down without hurting an actor's feelings. It's a matter of mutual trust, and when that trust exists between an actor and a director, and both are working toward the same goal, magic happens.

Do you have any particular keys to successful casting?

Huh? I don't know. I think one of the things is not to be safe. To be bold. I think it's good to take some risk. If you get exactly what you know you're going to get, it can get to be pretty boring.

What's your philosophy on rehearsals?

I like a week or two of rehearsal. It's a time when you can explore things in depth without the pressure of production. I like to get people moving around and get the discussions out of the way, so we're not wasting time on the set.

Do you like to stick to the script?

Yes. I like to stick mostly to the script, because the dialogue in a script has been worked on for a year, and that dialogue is not speech—it is the essence of speech. Nobody talks like that in real life. They stammer and they "ah, ah, ah" and they interrupt it.

I don't like it when people mess with the script. I don't like it when they put "you know" at the end of everything or add "listen." I like them to pick up their cues and go fast, and if they start throwing things in, they throw the rhythm of the other actors off. Sometimes, I think it's an excuse for not knowing their lines. I believe you can improvise after you know the lines backwards and forwards.

Do you have the writer there during rehearsals and on the set?

To me the script is everything. It's good to have the writer around for rewrites. Also, the writer may see things and say, "Remember, we talked about this a couple of months ago" or "It's better if he says it than if she says it."

How do you determine the look for your films?

On *My Favorite Year*, which was set in the fifties, I got together with the designer, and we both knew the pinks and blacks—the colors of those years. Refrigerators were avocado. But I also wanted that time to be romanticized. I wanted it to be very warm. Sometimes I'll look at other movies with the DP or I'll describe a certain movie and say, "Like that."

How do you decide on your shooting style?

It involves much discussion with my DP. We talk about setups and how long they will take. We agree beforehand on our shooting philosophy, so the DP has the right equipment to give me what I want.

But it all changes once we get on the set: We have to adjust to the circumstances at hand. On the set, the DP may have suggestions, short-cuts, perhaps even more effective visual concepts. I try to stay open to ideas as long as they conform to the emotional keys of the scenes. I don't like the camera to become intrusive. Generally, I like to keep the camera moving.

Studio versus location, which do you prefer?

Locations. But I love soundstages because you can build anything, light anything—you have total control. But there is a certain sense of reality on location that you cannot duplicate on a studio set, and I like to capture that sense of the real.

How involved do you get with your cinematographer in set-ting up shots and selecting lenses and lighting? Do you know each lens and what it accomplishes?

Basically. I know from my own interest in photography that lenses ac-complish different things. A 50mm lens is a more serious, portrait kind of lens, whereas a 35mm lens is more comical to me. So, yes, I'm in-volved in it and involved in the lighting in so much as I have certain things that I need to see that fit into a basic overall pattern in the film. It's all emotional. It's not technical.

How do you feel you convey the emotion through the lens?

In picking the shots. First you have to know, like the actor, what's the emotion in the scene. If it's serious and dramatic, then the lighting needs to reflect that. Sometimes you want to be more intimate with the actor, so you may use a long focal length. If you want to establish the energy and dynamics of a place, you'll go for wider lenses, which may be less intimate but convey a sense of the environment the actors are in, before moving in closer. It all depends on the shot.

It's pretty collaborative. I listen to the DP's suggestions and make a decision. I do like very much to see the actor's eyes. And that dictates the kind of lighting we use.

Do you find that some scenes you shoot require more than one master?

Yes. Sometimes they require the side of that master. And sometimes you have to break it up. In principle, it's good to shoot a master, it keeps you anchored. On the other hand, sometimes it's not required. If I'm going to shoot the scene in a series of close-ups, for example, I like to do it in one long take, because it gives the actors an opportunity to deliver a performance without being cut off. It shows that the scene and the actors have power, because it's holding without a cut. A cut, I think, should only be made when it has to be made. I like to do as much as I can in one long take, because I think it's good for the actors.

Do you think it's good to shoot in continuity if you can?

I want to do the whole movie in continuity if I can.

Are any of your movies shot that way?

They're all done as much like that as possible. If I can, if it doesn't cost too much, I like to say, "We'll come back here." But sometimes you have to stay on a certain set and shoot it out.

Do you use a second unit director for your action scenes and stunts?

I do.

Do you give them a specific shot list?

I say this is what we have to have, but if you find other things, shoot them.

How much do you rely on your script supervisor to remind you of your coverage?

I want them to. A really good script supervisor is invaluable. I like it when somebody says, "You really should get a shot of so and so." Sometimes I'll ask them, "Do I need this?"

What about reshoots?

On *Mermaids* we went back months later and shot two scenes, because when we put the whole picture together, we assumed that the audience had certain information that they didn't have. And they had to have this information. So we went back and reshot.

How difficult was it shooting pickups several months later?

It was a bit of a thing. Winona [Ryder] had cut her hair. We had to put a wig on her, I think. It wasn't easy. It never is simple to get it all back together again.

On _Mermaids_, was it difficult to take on a film after another director departed?

They couldn't shut down the picture. I hit the ground running. I got there on a Sunday and was shooting Monday morning. It sounds challenging and it is. Everybody is looking at you to provide the needed solutions, which can be intimidating since you haven't been through the preproduction process—the casting, the normal directorial prep— but somehow, deep within, you know what to do. It's instinctual, and you do it because you have to. You've accepted the challenge and now you go out there on the set and project the leadership qualities that made you a director to begin with. That's all a part of directing. You never get sick because you can't get sick. You never project insecurities because you are there to provide your cast with strength and support. Those are the rules. And, yes, you'll shoot it because you have to shoot it. It tests you, but it's also fun.

Do you have a preconceived idea about how you're going to orchestrate a scene or do you let the rehearsal flow before deciding how to shoot it?

I have a general idea beforehand, but it changes when the actors are there. The more physical stuff, the more action stuff, is more predetermined because it has to be. But when it's just actors in a room, I give them freedom yet sort of have an idea where it's going.

Jean Renoir said that the director serves as the midwife for the

actor, helping him find himself. How do you structure the performance of actors to find the balance between the emotional needs and the pacing of the scene?

That's what the job is. David Lean said, "Directing is knowing how fast the actor should talk." I think that's true.

As an actor-turned-director, do you have an edge in communicating with actors?

I know what they're thinking and feeling. I can tell when they're really listening and responding to each other, when it all evolves from within, rather than just saying the lines. Having been an actor, I know how to speak with actors, keeping them in the moment. There's a certain language an actor understands. There have been many great actor directors who've never acted in their lives, but for me, my experience as an actor is an asset, and I believe actors feel comfortable with that. They know that I know and it gives them a sense of security: "Well, he knows what he's talking about."

As I mentioned before, the actors have to trust the director. After all, it's their faces up there on the screen, and they want to come off looking good. It is the job of the director to make them look and sound their best.

What tools do you use to explain to the actors what you're looking for? How do you get the best performance from them? For example, do you line-read?

Almost never. Except as a last resort. But some actors actually like it and say, "Well, how would you read this?" And I say, "Like this . . ."

I give the actors a lot of freedom to be spontaneous, but obviously within my own concept of what the scene is all about and what we hope to get from it. Giving the actor freedom opens the door for surprises. Sometimes the surprises work. If they don't, I do another take and tell the actors not to go there or to adjust what they're doing.

Do you speak to the actors while the camera is rolling?

I have done that, knowing I'll loop later. Lots of times I'll just keep rolling when the actors think it's over. Some spontaneous things happen after they think it's all over. And many, many times I'll shoot rehearsals.

Do you ever confidentially tell one actor to do it one way and another actor to do it another way?

Sometimes I have one actor do things to surprise the other actor.

What do such techniques accomplish for you?

Well, spontaneity. I mean, there's nothing like the first time, because they haven't heard it before. I like to shoot that. They're surprised at the way it sounds. They're surprised that when they stop talking somebody else starts. The fastest thing that actors learn is where the jokes are, where the laughs are, even though you don't hear the laughs, because it would ruin the track. But when they're themselves surprised, you can see that in their eyes, and there's something wonderful about it. It's like real life.

Richard Attenborough, an–actor–turned director, talking about

working with actors, once said, "To a degree, you've got to be a psychologist." Is that true?

You're always, continually doing two things at once. While an actor wants to have a discussion with you about a character, you're looking at the sun setting at the same time, aware that you've got only another twenty minutes to get the shot and that you're only going to be in this location for one day. "Yeah, I think we should talk about the character, but let's walk this way while we talk about it." And you guide the actor toward the camera. You're as understanding as possible, and at the same time you get that person in front of the camera.

As an actor, did you create what Martin Ritt has called "the inner life of a character"? As a director, do you expect your actors to do the same?

Well, I don't know if I ever did, but I expect them to.

How can you tell if they've done the work?

Because the camera reads their thoughts. Dialogue is just ten percent of what is there—just the tip of the iceberg. It's what's underneath the dialogue—the inner life—that the camera reads. If actors are just saying lines, the camera will know that, and you'll know that.

You can be up in the stands behind home plate in a baseball stadium and see two people in a conversation way out in center field and know their attitude. You can know if they're angry with each other or not, and I don't mean by the flailing of their arms. How do you know that? By their body language. You don't even need a close-up. You know when someone's turned away from somebody in an upset way or when someone's received really bad news or whatever. You know when someone's just told the funniest joke they've ever heard. You're far away, but you know because it's real. And so the actors have to be real. They have to be like they are in real life. You can't fake it in the movies.

I imagine there's a big difference between acting on stage and in a film.

Yes. What you have to do on stage is create your own long shots and close-ups. In film, you either have that bigness or you fill it in—fill it from the inside.

A close-up can be operatic. That's why I don't believe in this whispery acting. You know, the minimal kind of nothingness. Life is not like that. People have certain points or energies to get across. Sometimes people talk quietly and sometimes they don't. Like we're talking now. And if you get into a close-up and you put your arms way out here somewhere and your hands go out of the frame, but it's full, what's the difference? And you see people, with their faces horribly contorted, receive terribly tragic news in close-ups on the news and that's fine, because that isn't exaggerated. It is the truth.

Do you plan on how you're going to cut a scene before you shoot it or do you cover it from as many angles as possible, so that your editor has as many choices as possible?

I cover things, but not just for the heck of it. I have an idea of what we need to get the story told. That's not to say that I edit in my head. But I have an idea of where the pay-off of this scene is and how it's going to juxtapose with the next scene—what's going to be the last shot of this scene and the first shot of the next one. I think of all those things.

And I think of the pace, because if all the scenes had the same pace, even if it were fast, it wouldn't seem fast because there would be nothing to compare it to. So I try to get different paces and rhythms. Sometimes that's done with cutting and sometimes that's done just with the pace of the actors.

Do you feel some actors require more takes than others?

I find that theater trained actors get more and more powerful as you go along and actors who haven't done much theater do something more spontaneous early on and don't develop increased power.

Who do you prefer to work with then?

Well, it depends. There's something in actors who are so spontaneous and so available emotionally that I like, especially for the movies. But there are times when you've got long scenes to do that theater actors can usually just rattle off. So if the script has long dialogue scenes, like in *My Favorite Year*, I look for theater-trained actors, like Peter O'Toole and Mark Linn-Baker.

Do you believe that editing is the last rewrite?

You make a movie three times: when you work on the script, when you shoot, and lastly, when you edit.

Once you wrap shooting, do you take a break before viewing a cut?

I take a couple of weeks off. When I come back, the editor shows me a rough assembly, which gives me an idea of its length, and how all the scenes are working together. This cut is usually done with minimum input from me, especially if the editor and I are in sync. After we screen this cut, we start working together, reel by reel. First, the broader strokes. Then we get into more and more detail. And sometimes I look at a scene and say, "Don't touch this."

Do you stay involved with the film beyond delivery of the director's cut?

Oh, yeah. I stay involved until it's released. Through sound effects and music. Everything. It's all important to me.

I think sound and music are giant factors. And, again, it's all emotional. You can't have someone else do it for you. You've got in your head what you think this whole thing is, including the music. And I've been there where I've had to say, "Well, you know, I think you have to do that again. The violins are not strong enough there."

Are you involved in marketing your films?

Yes, I am. For example, I knew from the first second that Warner Bros. showed it to me that the poster for *Made In America* was wonderful, that I didn't have to meddle because it was so definitive. I said, "This is perfect. You don't have to do anything anymore." And we all knew it, because we knew what movie we had made and that that poster defined it. What I'm always looking for is a definition of the movie. If I don't like a poster, I'll say so, I'll say what I feel. But at the same time, I'll also say, "I'm not selling the movie." I don't want to interfere with them to the point where they come back to me with, "Well, we had a poster, we had advertising, but you didn't like it. And you see, the picture didn't open."

It's both political and sensitive; it's like walking between the rain-drops without getting wet. You have to know when and how to fight without getting your head chopped off. I must say, I've been very fortunate in the last bunch of movies at Paramount. They have a terrific bunch there. I love what they did for the trailer of *Milk Money*. And also the one sheet. Warner Bros. is the same way. But there have been times when I've said, "This isn't the movie, and I don't think it's appealing." And then you finally get to the point where you say, "Okay, you're going to sell it."

As a filmmaker, which phase of the overall process do you like the best?

I like them all. But I especially like to get out there on the set and start shooting. It is your moment of truth as a filmmaker, stepping out on that set and saying, "Action." It's when all the dreams and all the efforts that went into seeing the film get made become a reality. That's what keeps my adrenaline pumping and my spirit inspired.

MEL GIBSON

Mel Gibson first caught the world's attention as the star of George Miller's *Mad Max* (1979), and within in a relatively short time, established himself as one of the most popular international superstars.

Born in upstate New York in 1956, Gibson and his family moved to Australia when he was twelve. After high school, he enrolled in Sydney's National Institute of Dramatic Art, and while still a student, made his screen acting debut in a film called *Summer City* (1977). In 1979, he starred in *Tim*, for which he won an Australian Film Institute Best Actor Award. His role in Peter Weir's *Gallipoli* (1981) won Gibson a second Australian Film Institute Best Actor Award, and soon he worked again with Weir in *The Year of Living Dangerously* (1983).

Gibson's other films include *The Road Warrior* (1981), *The Bounty* (1984), *The River* (1984), *Mrs. Soffel* (1984), *Mad Max Beyond the Thunderdome* (1985), the enormously popular *Lethal Weapon* trilogy (1987, 1990, 1991), *Tequila Sunrise* (1988), *Bird on a Wire* (1990), *Air America* (1990), *Hamlet* (1990) *Young Forever* (1992), and *Maverick* (1994)

Mel Gibson made his directorial debut with the critically acclaimed *A Man Without a Face* (1993), in which he also starred. He won a Golden Globe and an Academy Award as Best Director for his stirring historical epic *Braveheart* (1995), in which, again, he also starred.

The following interview took place November 15, 1995.

· · · · ·

What kind of training helps make an actor a great screen performer?

By going to acting classes, you achieve some sort of economy of channeling whatever it is that you've got inside of you. But ultimately, a lot of acting is instinct—you've got it or you don't. You can learn technique, but if the instinct is not already in you, it's not going to get planted in you by taking classes.

You've worked with many great actors. Did you learn a lot from, let's say, Anthony Hopkins, Patrick McGoohan, Paul Scofield, or Glenn Close?

You can't help but take from these people because they are so giving. They put it all out there. You can't see exactly how they do it, but there are certain indications that tip you off about their methods. Their methods may not work for you at all, but they're always so interesting to watch.

I find a great deal of diversity in the types of roles that you've played: a sensitive, slightly retarded boy in *Tim*, an innocent at war in *Gallipoli*, a mythical warrior in the *Mad Max* series, a novice political journalist in *The Year of Living Dangerously*, a farmer in *The River*, a rogue cop and drug dealer trying to go straight in *Tequila Sunrise*, a Danish prince in *Hamlet*, an innocently imprisoned man in *Mrs. Soffel*, a gambler in *Maverick*, a crazy cop in the *Lethal Weapon* series, an adventurer-pilot in *Air America* and a freedom fighter in *Braveheart*. Is there some connecting thread that drew you to playing these characters?

Yeah, of course. I try to satisfy both art and commerciality, if possible. But it's not always possible. I think it's easier to reconcile those two things as a director, working on something like a *Braveheart*.

What sort of research and preparation goes into the creation of a character? Do you create backstories? How did you prepare for your role in *The Year of Living Dangerously*, for example?

It depends on what I'm playing. That particular story came from a novel that was loosely based on true events, so there was a very good backstory provided—a political correspondent in troubled Indonesia in 1965. For *Gallipoli*, I had an opportunity to meet some of the veterans of that battle. For *Hamlet*, there was an abundance of material apart from Shakespeare's play, and there was an abundance of previous performances to study. For *Lethal Weapon* and *Tequila Sunrise*, I went on "ride alongs" in squad cars.

I was fortunate on the *Lethal* films to actually find a cop who had the same kind of profile—he had served in the war in Vietnam, been a Navy Seal. He had some terrible experiences over there. The effect on him was extraordinary. He wasn't a normal guy. He came out of the service and couldn't settle down, so he joined the police force and killed a couple of guys in the line of duty. The police said, "You're killing too many guys," and fired him. He was very much on the edge and often contemplated knocking himself off.

What about Wallace in *Braveheart*? Did you find a wealth of material on him that helped you to create his character?

There wasn't much material, really. Mainly, what exist are a lot of poems and legends. Wallace was worshipped as a hero, and it was difficult to separate fiction from fantasy. Even today, many questions about the nature and the character of the man remain shrouded in mystery. There was a very good book, *William Wallace*, by a man named Andrew Fisher, who is probably the most unbiased and honest of all the Wallace historians. I talked with Fisher, and I reviewed the legends and the poems, which helped me get into the character.

You read things, and if you find something of interest, you seize it and make it your own. Your research provides you with a firm foundation from which to jump off. So I do create backstories; they help me anchor the character.

What do you look for in a script?

I look to be intrigued, entertained. It has to affect me emotionally somehow.

How do you go about developing your projects?

I get a copious amount of scripts submitted to me.

Script writing must be one of the most difficult things to do. I think it is a very peculiar art. I'm not a script writer. It's much easier for me to look at someone else's work and fiddle around with it than to start from scratch and try to knock something together. I haven't got that kind of talent.

When a script comes to you, do you look at a reader's coverage before you read the script?

Not always. I do have readers cover the material, but if it's from someone I know, whose taste I trust, I'll read it myself.

What about *A Man Without a Face* and *Braveheart*?

I had a woman working for me in development who found *A Man Without a Face* under a rock somewhere up in Nova Scotia. She said that it had possibilities and that I should read it. For *Braveheart*, I met the writer, Randall Wallace, and the producer, Alan Ladd, Jr., who had a great deal of passion for the story, so I read it.

Did you make it a point to observe the directors that you worked with? What key principles, in terms of eliciting excellent performances from your actors and telling your story, did you absorb?

The first thing I learned was to have an overview of what I want to achieve with the performances—how those performances help tell my story. And if possible, to give it as many layers as I can without getting muddy and obscured. A key thing I learned was to look for clarity in a performance.

How do you develop a scene?

First of all, as a director, I have to provide the actors with an environment on the set where they feel secure and relaxed, so they can concentrate without any distractions on their performances. When you hire actors, you're not hiring robots; you hire living, breathing, thinking people with their own opinions and ideas, which are all valid, unless you decide together that they are not.

We're not talking ego here; no one knows their characters like the actors, so I have a tendency to be open to ideas I may not have seen myself. There's a lot of discussion, and if I feel they've got good stuff,

I'm going to go along with it. I know that if I can make an actor feel supported, that I'm there to listen and take his suggestions into consideration, I'm going to develop a trust, and then he'll give me the best he's got. I'm an actor. I've been there. I know.

In most cases, on the films I've worked on as an actor, the good director provides you with a safe environment and calls you in and says, "What do you got for me?" If you feel free and relaxed and secure enough, you offer him a smorgasbord of things. Then he can pick and choose or tell you that you are right up the pole and why don't you try something else, hoping that you understand exactly what he's talking about.

In most cases, when I would get in front of the camera, I just kind of followed my nose, followed my instincts, and talked about it afterward. Usually I'm on the right track or close enough. But not always. Sometimes I have failed miserably, because a scene isn't right.

We are all capable of not doing our best work, from the props guy to the camera guy to the director to the actor. Sometimes, no matter how hard you work at it, it doesn't work, which can be very frustrating. That's one of the reasons I try to resolve the script before we get on the set.

If the script is not right, nothing is going to work. It all begins with the script; it's the foundation of any great movie. I learned that as an actor; I know it as a director.

You go back a long way with director Peter Weir. In a *Playboy* interview, you said that there's something mystical about the way Weir achieves a mood, an ambiance, an atmosphere. How much influence has he had on you as a director?

Certainly, he is one of the directors I've worked with who is more in tune with the acting process. Some have not been in tune at all. Peter is very astute as far as performing is concerned. He was born like that. I'm sure I have, to a degree, subconsciously taken some things from him. Some of the things he would do technically to achieve an ambiance or a mood I would find so curious. For example, he would shoot a sequence and edit it together in the wrong order, or in an order that defied logic, which produces a curious kind of knowledge of something that was going to happen before it happens. It enhances performance, because it keeps you on your toes, not knowing what to expect.

You've worked with some very good directors: Mark Rydell, Richard Donner, Steve Miner, Franco Zeffirelli, Gillian Armstrong, Roger Spottiswoode, George Miller, and Peter Weir. I imagine they all work differently. Which ones profoundly inspired you both as an actor and as a director?

Yes, they all work differently. I suppose there are many ways to approach screen acting and storytelling. Mark Rydell is a method actor. He talks about motivation, and then gives you enough rope to go out and hang yourself. Richard Donner understands the value of performance. He has a tendency to talk right in the middle of the take, yell over the top of it. He's very boisterous and a lot of fun—he's the perfect example of a director who creates an environment where his actors can just feel free as birds to experiment with anything. You say, "Hey, what if I do this?" And he says, "Try it." Nothing's too crazy for him. Gillian Armstrong also gives you the opportunity to expand and experiment. When I worked with her, there were some days when she was fighting the clock and the budget, yet allowed Matthew Modine and I to horse around for an hour. And when we came up with something that was different, she filmed it.

To have that kind of trust from your director, it's very important for the actors to trust their director. It's the first rule in establishing the actor-director relationship. There's no room for petty grievances. They block your creativity, your performance. The director has to give the actors the feeling that they have the overall picture of what needs to be achieved, and that he is not going to let them go astray, go somewhere that has no connection with the overall direction of the film. It's something that I always look for in a director, and definitely practice as a director.

Tell me about working with George Miller, the doctor-turned-director.

Fantastic. Here is the mathematician, the Einstein of filmmaking. I always think how fortunate I am that I got to work with him and Peter Weir, two really great directors, early in my career. George works like he's in a laboratory, I guess it's that doctor thing, experimenting, dabbling with the elements in the film. He's extremely technical—understanding the camera and the lenses and the film speed. He has a very practical approach, which is unorthodox but brilliant.

I'd say I pulled the best out of three people I worked for: Peter Weir, George Miller, and Richard Donner, excellent people to learn from. From a writer-turned-director, Bob Towne, I learned the economy of words. I think it's advantageous for a director to also be a writer, or at least have a firm understanding of the mechanics of screenwriting.

Why did you decide to become a director? Was it a natural progression for you as an actor?

Yes. Look at what we were just talking about: writer Bob Towne, doctor George Miller, Peter Weir. They come from different places and use different tools and means, but they all share the desire and the need to tell a story. And that's what I've been doing as an actor, telling stories.

How did you go about doing your first feature film? Did you do any shorts first, or you did just decide, "Hell, I'm going to plunge in and do it"?

I decided to just step up to the plate and take a swing at it. I fooled around with video cameras and stuff, and it's amazing how much you learn from screwing around with video and trying to make sequences, but I decided to just step into it. It's scary, but it's fun.

Did you seek advice from some of the directors you had worked with? Did any of them become your mentor?

I would say things like, "Hey, I'm going to direct this film, and I'm scared," and hope for some words of wisdom. And occasionally they'd come. I actually talked to Clint Eastwood on the phone. I said, "Man, I'm kind of nervous here." He said, "You've probably got a lot more subliminal stuff in your head than you realize." And he was right. Besides you're not alone in this thing; there's a wealth of experienced people all around you who are experts in their particular fields, and they are there to support you. Whenever I didn't know something, I would look to their experience to bail me out. I didn't have one specific godfather, but the advice of many.

Why did you choose *Man Without a Face* as your first feature rather than an action film or a more visual kind of film?

I thought the story was strong and I liked the characters. And it was a small film. Going out there for the first time, I didn't want to do anything too extravagant. I wanted to see what I could achieve with a minimal amount of fuss.

On the surface it probably seemed like a simple film to do, but I imagine once you got in to it, it wasn't that simple. You not only directed it but also starred in it.

I must admit I was terrified, and it proved to be quite trying at times, but you just get through it.

Was it very stressful for you to both act and direct?

Man Without a Face was far more stressful than *Braveheart* because it was the first time I had to face that struggle.

How did you overcome it?

I overcame it by relaxing, by realizing what's there, by learning from my mistakes, and by simply going into it the next time with a lot more confidence.

Was it difficult to cast the role of the boy, Chuck, and the role of the girl, Megan?

Looking was a long process, but it wasn't difficult once I saw them. The boy, Nick Stahl, was extraordinary for his age, and displayed something I'd never really seen before in a child actor. Nick was unusual because his dialogue would come out in response to an obvious thought process he was going through, whereas most of the other kids who came in and read tried to lay a veneer of emotion over it, which is wrong. They had been taught bad habits. This kid would think and experience. It took him twice as long to do the reading, but he was slowly going through the process. I watched this in amazement—I'd never seen this in anyone so young.

Why did you choose to play McLeod? Did you first consider other actors?

Yeah, I did. They either couldn't make it or didn't want to do it. Let's face it, it wasn't the greatest part in the world, but I thought it was interesting. I figured, "Hey, I've got to be there anyway, I might as well slap on the pizza and take a crack at it."

You could have cast a star to play Catherine, the boy's mother. Why did you chose a relatively unknown actress?

I saw her in a Michael J. Fox film, *The Secret of My Success*. She played the lascivious aunt, and she was really funny. Her comic timing was great. I looked at her work and thought, "My God, she's terrific." And once you know, you know. It's very simple.

Do you believe that rehearsals are necessary? What do you focus on in rehearsals, if you have them?

Rehearsals are really nice to have. What I think you achieve is a chance to analyze the scenes and break them down and talk about what you think they're about, and what you think the characters are about. And you try and find some kind of unity of purpose with your cast in those meetings where you just sit around the table and talk. I don't actually start blocking scenes; I think that is not usually important in the rehearsal stage. I find it limiting.

Some of the scenes you know approximately how you're going to shoot, and what things you must do to save time and money yet do as truthfully as possible. The battle scenes in *Braveheart* were very, very carefully planned as to the strategies and the terrain that we needed and all the things that I specifically wanted to see. We planned them out thoroughly with shot lists and storyboards, because they were going to be so chaotic that we had to know beforehand exactly what we were going to do. You can't just go into something like that with no preparation. You've got to be very specific. But I've got to tell you, as much as we preplanned, and in great detail, once we got to the set, we deviated from those plans to a good degree.

We were able to respond so well to conditions on the field because we were so organized. In some situations, the more organized you are, the more latitude you have to respond to the moment and improvise without creating too much havoc.

How much rehearsal time did you have on *Braveheart*?

Braveheart went like lightening. We started preproduction in March and we were shooting by June. That in itself is an incredible feat, considering the size of the picture and the elements that we needed to gather. Everyone worked very hard.

We didn't have rehearsals because there were so many cast members—sixty-eight speaking parts—and these people were scattered all over Europe. We literally couldn't get them there at the same time. When I met all these thousands of actors and actresses during the casting period, we would sit down and talk about the script and the part for about fifteen or twenty minutes, and in a way, that's kind of a rehearsal. It was very, very sketchy; we didn't actually have a formal rehearsal time.

Do you think not having a rehearsal hurts an actor's performance in any way?

Obviously it would have made things a bit easier for them if they'd been given an opportunity to rehearse, but I don't think anyone was hurt by the lack of it. I mean, you can see it on the screen. The cast did a magnificent job.

How was your first day on the set as a first-time director on *Man Without a Face*? **Did you feel the need to do something spectacular to prove to yourself and the cast and the crew that you knew what you were doing?**

I was very nervous but, at the same time, exhilarated. I didn't sleep much the night before: I kept thinking about how I would have to step out there with everyone looking at me, expecting me to provide leadership.

It's different from being an actor, where you're just a piece of the entire puzzle. As a director, the responsibility for the entire vision, for running the entire operation, rests completely on your shoulders. That can be very intimidating, and I'm not easily intimidated. By my second film, *Braveheart*, they looked at me like I knew what I was doing, which was nice.

What kind of scene did you shoot on the first day of *Man Without a Face*? **Did you select something that you knew you could handle easily?**

Not necessarily. It was the scene in the graveyard, with the girl singing a song and the kid who comes along on his bike and watches her by the fence. I thought that was fairly ambitious for the first day of shooting.

How much help did Nick Stahl need to create and maintain his high level of performance?

I made him feel really comfortable. Once you give Nick the ball to run with, he's courageous enough to grab hold of it with both hands and give it his best. As the film progressed, day by day, I saw him gain more and more confidence. We improvised things that right off the bat were so wonderful that I just marveled at this kid. As he progressed, he needed less and less messing with. He started to do the right thing naturally, so I figured why mess with it? He's a very talented kid.

Do you like rehearsing emotional scenes both as an actor and as a director?

I don't, actually. I do rehearse them. I mark them; we block them through. But you don't give it anything until you start rolling. Usually, the first couple of takes go astray, like stray bullets, and then you settle into something, usually around take three or four. I don't do a lot of takes.

It's spontaneous?

Yeah, I think so. Often in rehearsal, if you haven't learned your lines, you'll start off, then get a response that will elicit another response, which may not be the one that is scripted, but it may be a better response because it's the next logical thought. I'm not saying you shouldn't learn your lines. And some writers may resent me, but sometimes the actor has to make the lines live, make them real, and for the most part, they enhance what's there.

Do you find that child actors have to be directed differently than adults?

I was fortunate in that both my young actors were very cerebral and instinctive, and had the maturity to listen and respond to one another.

Listening and responding, not just anticipating your cues from the other actors, is the key to good acting. The more loving and giving you are to your counterpart actor, the more truthful your performance will be. That, to me, is the essence of it all. And that also applies to the director, who must have the capacity to recognize when actors are listening and responding to each other.

How does a director cultivate that kind of ability?

Instinct is something that you're born with, and experience sharpens it, which is why I think in terms of working with actors and pulling a better performance out of them. A director who has acting experience, or at least an in-depth understanding of the process an actor goes through, has an edge in seeing subtleties that an untrained eye or ear may not pick up. So even if a director is not an actor, he should immerse himself in the mechanics and the language of acting. It's all a matter of preparation—doing your homework before you ever set foot on the set—and it all begins with observation and communication.

How did you cast James Robinson, who played young Wallace in *Braveheart*?

It was the biggest piece of luck. He was Scottish. He could do an accent. He used a very cerebral approach to things that you could read in his face. He was a minimalist, which was fantastic. All I had to do was talk to the boy and he'd go and do it. It was all thought-processes; it was very poetic. And he had these magnificent, very expressive eyes. He was a real find.

How did you get him to cry during the funeral scene?

I helped him a bit. [Laughter] I didn't want the kid to cry until the girl hands him the flower, and then he permits himself to show his grief. It was very technical, I asked him not to do anything except look at her and I just sprayed some menthol crystals in his eyes. It saved a lot of time.

When you do emotional scenes, do you shoot your close-ups first?

Doing a wide master gives an actor the opportunity to warm up and to get hold of the emotional key of a scene; though sometimes, when I need to save time, I go into the close-ups immediately and maybe don't even shoot a master. But, to do that, you've got to really have thought it out, so you don't get stuck in the editing room. Which brings into mind cutaways. They're crucial. If you're doing a long scene, and it drags out, you have something to cut away to.

Doing close-ups is always important. In *Braveheart* I shot my close-ups but didn't linger on them. It was a little puzzle for me to get inside people and stay true to the scope of the film at the same time. I had to maintain a certain balance. You can create that balance during the shooting, but sometimes you need to find that balance in the editing room, so you had better cover yourself.

In *Man Without a Face*, how did you pull off the back-to-back scenes that grew in emotional intensity? When Chuck finds his sister in bed with her boyfriend and when he cries in McLeod's arms and the explosive scene with his mom?

You start with some kind of blueprint in your head, and you build from that. You get to the set, you watch the camera blocking, you start to see possibilities of how you're going to shoot it, and you talk to the actors, making sure they understand what the purpose of the scene is, where the emotions lie. You do a take or two and you start to shape it, develop a rhythm. You turn it up or slow it down a bit, and you get to a point where something happens that starts sparks inside the actors. And then something wonderful happens, something you didn't even anticipate—a change in delivery, an attitude, a line change.

I found the end scene where the adult Chuck looks at McLeod at his military academy graduation very moving. Was that difficult to direct, since this kid was a day player coming in for just one scene in which he had to have emotional intensity?

It wasn't. Somebody spotted this kid in an elevator in Cincinnati. He had an extraordinary face that expressed innocence. He wasn't an actor; he was just a guy. I was very by-the-numbers with him about the exact kind of beat I wanted to see. I told him to be very still and not even move his eyes, just stare for five seconds. I explained the whole backstory to him and he was quite relaxed about it.

Did you do many rewrites on the *Braveheart* script?

We never did what you might call a formal rewrite, because Randy

Wallace put his heart and soul into the script. I read it and it got inside me. During preproduction, Randy came over to London and we just tweaked all the scenes, moving them around. It was just a process of adapting it here and there, and then being spontaneous when we had to on the set. Randy was the one and only writer. Some of the best scenes in the film were in the first draft.

Occasionally, I'd fiddle a bit with this or that. A director has to make it work for his own sensibility. But some writers are too close to their scripts, they get upset when you make changes. Luckily, Randy was cool. I understood his vision, it affected me on a very fundamental, visceral level, and he knew it. I only tried to enhance the power of what was already there.

Did you visualize yourself playing Wallace when you read the script, or did you consider other actors?

I didn't visualize myself playing Wallace at all. I visualized a kind of fearsome-looking, primal character—dirty and funky, just out of the cave. Yet I wanted him to express a certain level of intelligence and education—he did speak French and Latin. So while at first I didn't think I was right for the part, images just kept hitting me—the script was such that it got inside my head, and for about a year, I created little scenes before I nodded off to sleep. I was making this movie in my head, but I still had no intention of doing it. Now that's funny, isn't it?

So what made you finally decide to do it?

I was in my trailer with my assistant, and he said, "What are you going to do next?" I said, "Hell, I don't know. I haven't read anything that I like." And then I said, "Well, I read one thing that I really can't get out of my system." So I told him the story, blow by blow, image by image, and he said, "Wow, I've got to read this, it sounds great." And I said, "It does sound pretty good, doesn't it?" So he read it and said, "You've got to do this." I went back to Allan Ladd, Jr., the producer, and said, "Look, I want to do it, but I'd like to direct it. Is that cool?" and he said, "I have no problem with it." So, bingo.

Tell me about casting *Braveheart*.

We had England's, Ireland's, and Scotland's best actors available to us. There was such a wealth of talent that sometimes it was almost difficult to make a choice.

I don't like reading actors. I don't think you really find out very much by getting anyone to read. I go through a different process. I like meeting the actors and talking with them, getting a sense of who they are. We talk about anything, and eventually I get some vision about who the person is, what they are about.

Did you videotape any of these conversations?

No, not the ones I was involved in. Patsy Pollock, the casting director, did some work on her own where she'd put people on tape and bring it to me.

Was Patrick McGoohan your first choice for Longshanks, King Edward I?

Longshanks was the most difficult part to cast. I couldn't find anyone I thought could do it. I had looked at everybody Patsy provided me with, and then the first AD asked, "What about Pat McGoohan?" I said, "Pat McGoohan? Is he still alive?"

Patrick and I met, and I thought he was just great. I said, "Here's a guy with presence. He's got to be the king." He stands about 6'2" or 6'3", so he's tall enough. He has this intense concentration; and his eyes kind of just stare at you, cold and penetrating. He has a very austere presence and an aura about him that demands respect. He is classically trained, which in this particular case was very important, and he has all the authority and age and weight. There was just one problem—his nose. The only thing that didn't look like a king was his small Irish nose. So I said, "Put a nose on him, and he'll be perfect." We brought him in and sculpted a fake nose—a stronger, bigger nose, sort of a Roman beak. And he looked perfect, as I had imagined him.

And his beard was great.

He grew it himself, and the hair and makeup people trimmed it up. With the nose and beard, he personified my vision of Longshanks, King Edward I, so I just let him go. He portrayed the character of the king as cold and calculating, right on the edge of being a psychopath, which I was pleased with.

Why did you cast Sophie Marceau as Princess Isabelle?

I interviewed many actresses from all over Europe, and they were all beautiful, but when Sophie came in she reminded me of a Vermeer painting. The character was French, which she is, and she had regal bearing and practically perfect features. I thought, "My God, if I was in the royal line many years ago, I would have procured people in my court who looked like her." You may say I was living my fantasies.

Not only did she fulfill all my expectations about what a French queen should look like, she could turn on the performance, too. There were some scenes where she and Peter Hanly, who played Prince Edward, were fantastic that I ended up taking out of the final cut.

He was good. He was a nasty villain.

Unfortunately, the scenes that I had to remove made you understand him better: He was a villain, a murderer, but I made him understandable to the audience. It really killed me to take those scenes out, but I had to in the interest of time and the film as a whole.

Tell me something about casting Catherine McCormack. I fell in love with her.

Everybody says that. Murron was killed fairly early in the story. To create a big impact on the audience, we determined that we must find someone who you'd immediately love and emotionally connect with to play the character. Catherine McCormack had done practically nothing before. She is very attractive, but not in a way that would stand out in a village, and that's the quality I was looking for. She and I talked, and I just knew she was right. Sometimes that's all it takes.

Another standout was Angus McFadyen. I thought he had tremendous passion. I really sensed the inner conflict that he was experiencing. I really believed him. How did you find him?

I had cast someone else in the part, but that person got another job. Then Angus wandered in. He seemed to be unsure of who he was because he had this kind of demon struggling inside of him. He just was right for the character he was to portray.

Is there an element of luck in casting?

I suppose you can call it that. You have to be flexible with your vision. You can easily get stuck thinking you need this or that particular actor, then that actor is unavailable and you suddenly have to recast. A certain panic sets in because you're hard-pressed for time. Then another actor walks in and turns out to be better than you had anticipated. That's one of the gratifying things that makes casting the exciting process it is. So I try to stay open-minded.

James Cosmo, Brendan Gleeson, David O'Hara, Peter Hanly—they were all marvelous. You have an incredible eye. So how did you find those actors?

We cast in both England and Ireland, and it was the same old process—drag actors into a room and talk to them. I had a very specific picture in my mind for the Hamish character—a big dude with red hair, who had to be fierce and tough, yet have the innocence of a boy. I asked my casting people if they could find him for me, and was told that there was a good actor in Ireland I should see named Brendon Gleeson. He walked into the room, and I said, "That's the guy, right there." Instant decision. It was a good experience.

And David O'Hara?

Here was the only person who ever got fired from The Royal Shakespeare Company. He is the sweetest guy in the world, but he's got this streak of the devil in him, kind of a lawlessness, which the character required. I offered him the part straight away. Fifteen minutes was all it took to figure that out.

Weren't you concerned with his reputation?

You have to be willing to take a risk. I knew he was wild, but I said to myself, "If some of his wildness plays on the screen, it'll be great." I took the risk, and it paid off magnificently.

Did you personally supervise the casting of your extras or did you leave it to your ADs?

The extras were the Irish Army. We told them not to shave and not to get haircuts for a while. We told them the story and they really got into the whole spirit of it.

Do you have any keys to successful casting?

I trust my instincts, and I'm willing to take risks. That's what I operate on, I won't have it any other way. I've done it in both my films, and it's paid off. Though along the way, I made a couple of goofs, too. Luckily they were only in small parts.

Tell me about selecting your key creative team. John Toll's photography was stupendous, as were the production design and the costumes.

John Toll was relatively new, or he was at that time. Now he's got an Oscar. He's a hardworking, inventive, and gifted cinematographer. I was looking at cinematographers, and the list is long because there are so many good ones, when I heard that this guy used to be the operator for Conrad Hall. I said, "Well, that's not a bad school." I heard that he had shot a film that wasn't finished yet, *Legends of the Fall*, so I called up

Ed Zwick. Ed's a very nice guy, so he said, "Hey, come to the editing room. I'll show you two or three reels."

I went, and I looked at a workprint that was filthy and had scratches and tape marks all over it, but it was undeniably beautiful. I said, "This guy's great." And I went after him. Incidentally, I met my editor Steve Rosenblum in the same room. He had done *Glory*.

I loved the costumes.

Charles Knode's the best. This is a case in point of a guy who came in at the end of the list, but once we sat down, within five minutes, I gave him the job just from listening to him talk. He did the research, and he impressed me with his intelligence and knowledge of history.

What sort of directorial homework did you do while planning this production? Why did you chose Ireland over Scotland?

It all came down to efficiency, in cost and artistically. You haven't really got the highlands in Ireland, but what you do have is a more gentle, undulating country. In Scotland it was just going to be too difficult to pull all the elements together.

Were the opening shots of *Braveheart* shot in Scotland or Ireland?

Oh, that was Scotland.

You sent a second unit there?

No, I went up myself. We shot the first six weeks in Scotland. All the

Scottish village stuff and the magistrate. The big battles were filmed in Ireland because we couldn't find the proper terrain in Scotland, where it's rocky and not horse-friendly. In fact, Scotland doesn't have many horses, whereas in Ireland, they export them. And we couldn't get the cooperation of the army in Scotland, but the Irish government said, "Here, use our reserves."

Did you have to pay them by the hour?

We paid them daily rates. It turned out to be economical for us to do it that way. We had the cooperation of the Minster of the Arts, who influenced the Minister of the Defense, who allowed us to utilize the army not only as extras, but also to use the barracks to house them and to use their firing ranges as the battlefield. The barracks were over a hill, half a mile away from the set, so these guys could walk to work. There also was a racetrack two miles away where all the horses were stabled and fed and taken care of in a proper way. And Dublin was forty-five minutes away, so everyone in the crew and cast could live in civilized conditions.

How long did it take to film the Sterling battle?

Six weeks.

When I watched the Sterling battle scenes, I thought of *Spartacus*. Did you look at any films that involved major battle scenes?

I watched many of those, because I wanted to understand what makes something like that work on the screen. I wanted to see a battle that I had not seen before. I wanted to get into the sheer ferocity and chaos of it. I didn't want to see anything that looked like a stunt. Oddly, you know, in almost all those old films you can see the strings. But I'm not trying to belittle them, we've got more tools now and know more about this sort of stuff than we did in the fifties. And they had to sanitize those kinds of things in the fifties. We didn't have those restrictions, and we had more sophisticated equipment to work with.

When do you set your shots? Before or after rehearsals?

You go in with certain visions, always prepared to change them, and you do change them in ninety percent of the cases. It all depends on the nature of the scene. For example, the battle scenes in *Braveheart* were very specifically planned with a storyboard, because we needed a bible to at least fall back on if we didn't know what to do next. Everything else we got was gravy, because I had something like seven or eight cameras on all the time.

Sometimes we knock off a shot list the night before. Sometimes the nature of the scene is more dependent upon performance than the mechanics of things, so you let the rehearsal and the blocking sort of dictate what the shot list will be.

How much latitude do you give your actors to explore and experiment on the set and in rehearsals? Can you, as a director, help actors make the right choices if they are unable to come up with them themselves?

Absolutely. It's your job to be an objective pair of eyes, to be supportive, to guide the actors. You have the overall vision, and if the actors are deviating from your overall vision, you bring them back. You remind them of the objectives of the characters if they're going too far over the top or if they're not going far enough. You're there as almost a parent. You keep the performance level consistent.

Do you work with video assist?

I find video assist helpful because you can be truly objective and watch the whole shot—the composition, the mood, the performance. It's not the best view, but it gives you a pretty good indication that you haven't completely destroyed your reputation, so you can feel pretty comfortable and move on.

How involved do you get with your cinematographer in setting angles and selecting lenses? Do you discuss each scene individually or do you just discuss a basic concept and let the DP go with it?

On *Braveheart*, in particular, I had very specific things that I wanted to see, specific speeds that I wanted to explore, specific lens sizes to get certain emotional effects. For example, when Wallace rides into the village in slo-mo, I knew specifically what I wanted to see. It was one of those scenes you stay up at night and think about how to best attack. I wanted to see the fear in the horse's eyes and build suspense with the slo-mo, until finally, Wallace whacks the English soldier in the head with his sword. You probably didn't even notice it, but he gets hit in the head three times with center cutting. A slow one, and then you cut immediately from 96 frames to 20 frames a second. It created a powerful impact. I described it to the DP and let him work out the technical details which made the shot possible.

What about the lighting? Do you leave that pretty much to the DP? There was a lot of great lighting in *Braveheart*. For example, the two-shot in the prison cell of Wallace and Princess Isabelle enmeshed in a blue-tinted beam of light.

I wouldn't presume to tell John Toll how to light something. We talked about that scene beforehand, the mood I wanted to establish, and then I left it up to him. Also, when it came to lenses, setups, and angles, I'd discuss them with him, and where I didn't have a real specific idea, he would come to the rescue with good, creative suggestions, which made this movie a really lovely collaborative experience.

Did you choreograph the battle scene with your stunt people?

There was myself, a camera guy, the first assistant, my line producer, and the stunt guy, all sitting around a table with little plastic soldiers, talking and laughing and horsing around and creating these battles. From that came ideas, a shot list, everything.

I did feel like I choreographed it, because I wanted it to make sense as a battle. I wanted it to be understandable, make you feel that you were actually there, participating, feeling your adrenaline pumping with excitement and fear. I wanted you right in the middle of the chaos and the hell of it, the ferocity of it. But I also wanted to make it clear, like a sporting event where you know who's who, so there would be a personal emotional connection, not just a bunch of strangers slamming each other.

In *Spartacus*, for example, you could see the strategies, and you knew who was who. But that movie missed the real visceral battle stuff. I wanted *Braveheart* to go beyond what was done there. We also enhanced the Sterling battle scene digitally, giving the audience the illusion that we had a much greater number of troops than we actually had.

I loved the touch of the priest praying with the soldiers before the battle. Was that in the script or was that something that you came up with?

I wrote that in because I figured that those guys would have been around—battlefield absolutions were pretty common in those days. I had it improvised right there on the set.

How many feet of film did you shoot on *Braveheart*? How many days of shooting did you have?

It was scheduled for eighty-five but we actually shot 105 days, and we still never broke the budget. We shot almost a million feet of film.

Did you have a lot of reshoots and pickups?

Not a lot. I reshot one thing—the horses hitting the stakes—in Arizona. I reshot the point of view of the Scot soldiers, with the horses coming to take the impact of the impalement. I had to get a wide-angle lens at a low angle, line up the ten horses and the guys in costumes, and get the horses to ride up to the camera and rear like they had just been stuck by something.

How different was it to step out on the set as the director of an epic the size of *Braveheart* after doing a small, personal film such as *A Man Without a Face*? Did you feel overwhelmed by the challenges that you were up against?

I think it was easier, because I'd got a lot of my insecurities out of the way on the first film. I'd been through it and I knew that I could do it. I was confident that I'd overcome the challenges with a solid team of professionals behind me. I knew that, to survive, I had to conserve energy and strength and always be physically fit, because making any movie is definitely a test of endurance, and especially a film like *Braveheart*, where I faced an epic struggle.

Like everything in life, it's a matter of attitude. I went in looking to make it a fun experience, and no matter what we had to deal with, I always reminded myself not to lose sight of that goal. Essentially, you can only do one day's work at a time. And when I focused on that, I knew it was no more difficult than my first film, because I did one day's work at a time there, too, except that we shot *A Man Without a Face* in forty-eight days and we had 105 days to do this one. It was like the same workload, just longer. Logistically it was a lot more difficult, but then I had a larger crew to handle it.

Do you look for an inner world beyond the script as you direct the actors?

Oh, absolutely. Sometimes if what is written is too obvious, I will change the lines. The old line is subtext. Maybe you lay something over the top to hide it a little bit.

How did you help the actors create their characters? For example, what kind of direction did you give Patrick McGoohan?

It was interesting. I gave him the script to read and he said, "This man is diabolically evil." So he had that one down himself. He knew what he had to do when he came in, and he did it with great charm.

In fact, I remember sort of venting at one point. I said, "Why don't you say the trouble with Scotland is it is full of Scots," and everyone chuckled. It's sinister and kind of amusing at the same time. It's a scary "ethnic cleansing" kind of moment, which is what he was doing— thirteenth-century ethnic cleansing. It's always been like that. People have always tried to knock people off because they are different.

What sort of direction did you give Sophie and Catherine?

We would talk endlessly about the rhythms and the tone of the scene, what I'd want from them, and whether I thought they should cry.

And Robert the Bruce's emotional outbursts with his father, how did you handle those?

That was probably one of the most interesting experiences I've had as a director, because it wasn't happening. He was blocked that day, and we kept doing it and doing it. He was trying to find the right access point for it, and I didn't want to jump in there and do it for him. It was killing me; we did twenty takes, just exploring and exploring, and I didn't know how to make it believable.

We were both exhausted but we just kept working with it. Suddenly I thought of Arthur Miller's *Death of a Salesman*, and I said, "Do you remember the scene in *Death of a Salesman* where he gives that speech about the pen and what the hell am I running down the stairs for? That's the kind of feeling I need." And something clicked for him. He came into the room and did it. I was watching the monitor and started crying. I thought it was beautiful. I said, "Cut, that's it. We only need one."

Here's a guy who had all the right instincts and everything; he just needed to feel comfortable enough to let it go. It turned out to be one of the best moments in the film.

Do you do several run-throughs first, or do you shoot the rehearsals?

We do a little run-through, a couple of times, so it feels loose and everybody knows what they are doing and the guys have got their marks and moves down.

How do you deal with a temperamental actor who disagrees with your vision?

I've worked with many actors, and some of them have been, at times, inclined toward temperament. And I can understand it because I've gotten to the point where I get pretty cranky. But yelling is counterproductive on the set. The crew doesn't like it either; they get upset. We're all a part of the process. And I believe that it should be fun. You shouldn't have unnecessary pressures that make people uncomfortable.

Everybody must have some kind of inner peace in order to perform their best. So patience is a key ingredient in being a successful director. You have to set an example on the set. What you put out is essentially what you get back. If you present hostility, that's what you are going to get back.

What happens if you have one actor who needs a lot of takes and another actor in the same scene who doesn't?

I keep doing it until I get it right on both sides, but I never let it get out of control. As a general rule, I don't allow myself more than three or four takes.

Is it very difficult to be behind the camera, setting up the scene, and then suddenly have got to jump in front and be the character?

Not at all. Basically, it's easy, because it gives you a whole other kind of security—you know exactly what you are dealing with in a technical way.

Let's say you got the best performance an actor thinks he's capable of giving you, but you still need more. What do you do? How do you inspire him to give you more?

It's very hard to be specific. It's experimentation, playing around, exploring another way of doing it, and saying, "Okay, we've got some good stuff. Let's try another one. And this time get wild, go somewhere else." Sometimes that works and sometimes it doesn't. You keep adjusting it until it feels right.

Has having actors from different schools and with different techniques ever been a problem? Maybe one intellectualizes while the other works from the gut. Do they clash? How do you balance them?

I'm still trying to figure out your question. It has never been a problem. The actors always seem to fall right in and help each other. The process of good acting requires interaction, and that means giving, showing consideration for the other performer.

It's my own experience that the best way to help yourself become better in performance is to do all that you can to make the person opposite you look as good as possible. Give them everything, and they will do the same for you. That's the secret of good performance.

Do you feel that a happy actor will give you a better perfor-mance? How do you keep the actors happy?

Absolutely. How do you keep them happy? You just keep things light on the set. You can be working your buns off trying to accomplish something and have fun, too. That's happiness in a way—kind of a tortured happiness—overcoming the challenges and enjoying the process. It gives you a sense of triumph. There have been a few times when I've gotten a real buzz trying certain things, not knowing whether they would work, but having an idea that this is the right way to go.

When you shoot a scene, what's your attention most focused on: the performance or the visual choreography or what?

You have to look at the whole picture. And every scene is different. Some scenes are more dependent on action and others on performance by the actors. You just take it scene by scene.

Do you shoot by the book—master and coverage?

Each case is different. I go by what the moment dictates. Sometimes you have a very strong sense of image and exactly what you want to see. I'm not concerned with doing it by the numbers. But some scenes require the old-school method of wide masters going into close-ups.

Do you think you can improve performances in the editing?

It's really just a question of quantity and quality, isn't it? You have choices, and sometimes the take that you thought was the best doesn't turn out to be the best, so you go with another one. I always keep three or four takes, so I can pull little bits from them.

How do you work with your editor?

You shoot the material, you give it to him, and he knocks out the first assembly. From there, you've got to guide the editor, look over his shoulder while he's doing it, and just talk.

We had a wonderful time on *Braveheart*; it was a good process creatively. There's so much that the editor contributes. At one point, he said to me, "Essentially, what we are doing here is the final rewrite," which is true. You can restructure things by moving the sequence of scenes, you can rewrite lines by cutting some out or adding some in ADR. It's a long process, but never long enough. At some point, you've got to say, "Okay, I've got to stop."

I thought you did a brilliant job in editing it *Braveheart*. You didn't lose any of its essence.

We had versions where we did cut the essence right out, and then we went back and reinvented it somehow. Editing is like a puzzle—you pull things from here and there, and sometimes just a few frames make a big difference in the emotional impact of a scene. It's one of the most enjoyable filmmaking processes.

How did you work with your composer, James Horner? Did you give him specific musical ideas, or did you more or less give him the freedom to experiment?

Even before we started shooting, I talked to James on the phone, asking, "What did they have back then?"

The music in Scotland at that time was terrible. They had Gregorian chants and stuff that you really can't listen to. I thought we should have more melodic music, but still something primitive, something with old instruments and lots of drums and primitive beats and stuff somewhere between Celtic and Native American—lots of rhythms. At the same time, there were places where you had to have the overlay of a big score.

I had very specific notions about the kinds of things I wanted to hear, and I shared them with James. He took them away and came back with what I thought was fantastic.

What sort of music did you use on your temp tracks?

We had quite a large temp mix. I bought lots and lots of recordings of pipes and fiddles and other film soundtracks that seemed to fit.

Sometimes you kind of get married to the temp music, and when you hear the score, it doesn't fit with what you had in mind anymore.

Yeah, but this score was so good that it didn't take much getting used to at all.

Braveheart **was an epic, with battles and political intrigue, yet also an intimate story of people and their personal tragedies and triumphs. It resonated with me long after I saw it.**

Characters always come first. And that's what I care about.

PAUL MAZURSKY

P aul Mazursky's films are often personal, intimate observations of the human condition.

Born in Brooklyn, he started his acting career in the off-Broadway production of *He Who Gets Slapped*. In 1953, he appeared in Stanley Kubrick's first film, *Fear and Desire*, and in 1955, in Richard Brooks' *The Blackboard Jungle*. He also landed roles in such live television shows as *The Kraft Theater* and *Robert Montgomery Presents*. Moving to Los Angeles in 1959, he teamed up with humorist Larry Tucker to write for *The Danny Kaye Show* and other television programs.

Mazursky made his feature film debut as a director with *Bob & Carol & Ted & Alice* (1969), which he also co-wrote. The screenplay for this film received an Academy Award nomination along with best screenplay citations from the Writers Guild of America and the National Society of Film Critics. Subsequently, Mazursky would write or co-write and produce or co-produce most of the films he directs. *Alex in Wonderland* (1970) dealt with his personal reaction to success and *Blume in Love* (1973) is an exploration of marriage and love. *Harry and Tonto* (1974), dealing with aging parents, won its star, Art Carney, an Academy Award, and its Mazursky-Greenfeld screenplay received an Oscar nomination. *Next Stop, Greenwich Village* (1976) was based on his experiences as a young actor and featured future stars Jeff Goldblum and Christopher Walken. Mazursky's depiction of a woman's struggle for self-identity and love, *An Unmarried Woman* (1978), won Jill Clayburgh best actress honors at the Cannes Film Festival and an Oscar nomination, and its screenplay received an Academy Award. Mazursky's exploration of the human condition continued with *Willie and Phil* (1980) and *Tempest* (1982), culminating with the poignant comedy/drama *Moscow on the Hudson* (1984). Two years later, Mazursky's comedy *Down and Out in Beverly Hills* (1986) became a blockbuster hit. Since then, Mazursky has directed *Moon Over Parador* (1988); a powerful drama based on the novel by Isaac Bashevis Singer, *Enemies: A Love Story* (1989), which earned three Oscar nominations and won Mazursky the New York Film Critics Award as best director; *The Pickle* (1993); and *Faithful* (1996), which was written by Chazz Palminteri.

Mazursky's numerous film appearances include most of the films listed above as well as *Punchline*, *Carlito's Way*, and *Miami Rhapsody*.

The following interview took place January 15, 1996.

• • • • •

Did you start out with the goal of becoming a writer or an actor?

I was an actor, in the theater, and that was all I thought about. I studied acting with Lee Strasberg.

I got a part in Stan Kubrick's first feature film, *Fear and Desire.* Then I was cast in *Blackboard Jungle* and went to California to do the part. I started to get a little work as a television actor, but I was only getting serious dramatic parts, and I thought I was very funny. So back in New York, I started to work on a nightclub act. I was also acting in some theater and live TV at that time. I had some pretty good parts, but never made much money.

Somewhere around this point, I directed an off-Broadway revue and started to think more about directing. I did some work in San Francisco and Los Angeles, and one thing led to another. I started to write for Danny Kaye's television series, together with my writing partner Larry Tucker. We lasted four full years, and I suddenly said, "I don't think I'm going to do this forever," and I started thinking about my career as an actor and my directing in the theater, and I started to write screenplays. I wrote a couple with somebody else, Larry and I wrote one that never got made, and then we wrote *I Love You, Alice B. Toklas!*, which we also produced. I was going to be the director, but it didn't work out. We were on the movie for the full run, and I learned a lot. Then we wrote *Bob & Carol & Ted & Alice*, which I directed. And since then, I've been directing and writing movies.

Can you tell me a little bit about your family background, growing up in Brooklyn? How much influence did your family have on you?

Their influence is my memories of them, which I've used in my writing. My family was not in show business. My father was a laborer with a printing company. He helped wrap the papers and put them on the trucks. My mother was a very good stenographer and played piano part-time in a ballet school. In terms of show business, she was a real influence on me. She took me to the opera—the dollar seats; she took me to see foreign movies; and she took me to the Apollo Theater in Harlem. My mother was a wild, gypsy lady, lower-middle-class Jewish, born in the United States, who loved art and life.

Another person who had an influence on me was my grandfather. He played the violin and told me stories about Russia. He had deserted the Russian Army in 1905, jumped off a train, because of anti-

Semitism. He met my grandmother on the boat going from Hamburg, Germany, to the United States. He taught me about reading Pushkin and Dostoyevsky. So my mother and grandfather created some intellectual atmosphere, which motivated me to read and to play violin and piano. But I was the only one in my neighborhood that I know who ended up moving to Greenwich Village.

Can you tell me about the agony and ecstasy of your acting career?

Mostly I found it difficult to get enough work. I looked eighteen years old until I was thirty. When I was in *Blackboard Jungle*, I was twenty-four and looked sixteen. I played a high school kid. The ecstasy was working, the agony was being out of work most of the time, which is the life of an actor. There's a certain glamour to it, when you're young, but it soon disappears when you've got to pay the rent, even though it's only $50 a month.

Being out of work, never knowing if I'd get a job, was a constant anxiety. So it's easy for me to understand how anxious actors really are. Even if the actors are stars, they're naked, they're exposed. They're the ones who have to do it. Understanding that alone is already a step toward being a better director. But like many things in this life, there are no rules. Federico Fellini didn't know anything about the art of acting, he just knew what he wanted and knew how to get it.

Looking at your films, I get the sense that you like to investigate and satirize the absurd side of our quest for love and meaning and happiness and our overcoming of the obstacles we create. What do you think draws you to stories and characters in transition?

You never know a hundred percent what draws you. I saw my movie *The Tempest* again for the first time in a decade, and finally, after all these years, I really understood the movie. It was about forgiveness. It was about having a huge anger, a huge rage, and a lot of confusion, and finally doing the thing that a human is capable of, which is to forgive, thereby freeing yourself. I don't always know why I'm making a picture.

I made *Down and Out in Beverly Hills* because I was walking down the street one day and saw this homeless guy, with a little dog, pushing a wagon. And I suddenly remembered an old French movie that I'd seen where a bum jumps in the Seine and tries to kill himself. I suddenly saw this guy doing that in a Beverly Hills swimming pool, and the idea just came to me on how to make that movie. *Next Stop, Greenwich Village* was about my own life. *Unmarried Woman*: A woman, a friend of ours, one day very proudly told my wife and myself she'd just bought a new house. She showed us the deed, and on the deed it had her name, and next to her name it said, "an unmarried woman." I said, "Unmarried, what a peculiar way to label somebody." So I started to talk to women who were divorced, and that led to a movie about an unmarried woman getting her life together after her husband leaves her for another woman.

My mind is constantly fertile with ideas, no matter what is going on around me. Josh Greenfeld, with whom I wrote *Blume in Love*, was assigned to write a piece about me for *Look* magazine. While he was writing the piece, we started talking about what it would be like when we're seventy; we were about forty at the time, and this dreaming led us to come up with the idea for the movie *Harry and Tonto*. It was a wonderful script, but nobody wanted to do it, saying, "It's too depressing." So I sat down and started to write. I just wrote: "This guy is sitting in a café in Venice, looking at all the lovers." And I wrote it all almost not knowing where the next thing was coming from. It became *Blume in Love*. It came out of living in Italy. I had just lived with my family in Rome for four months, and I had been to Venice. It came out of some trouble in my own marriage.

Bob & Carol & Ted & Alice came out of a *Time* magazine article I read that had a photo of Fritz Perls, the Gestalt psychologist, sitting in a hot tub with five or six naked people. It was a new kind of therapy. My wife and I did it for a long weekend, which resulted in that movie.

Every movie has it's own place and experience. I don't sit down and say, "I want to make a movie about . . ." Ideas are strange things, they have to possess you before you can write them, and there's no explaining the manner in which it happens. It's art. The writing is in many ways the hardest thing.

When you collaborate, do you and the other writer actually sit in a room together and write?

Larry and I sat in a room together almost all the time. I would type. Sometimes we'd improvise. We went to Palm Springs for *Bob & Carol* and improvised about eighty pages, just talking out the dialogue. We'd do it on a tape. He'd be Bob, I'd be Carol. And vice versa. Then we'd write out whole scenes sometimes, in the normal way, then rewrite, polish, change, whatever.

Do you do use a step outline to start with, or you sort of jump into it?

I usually have an outline. I put down notes that give me an idea of where it's going, but not always. I didn't do that with *Blume in Love*. I didn't know where I was going when I started it, I just did it, one piece at a time. I wrote a scene where the guy's sitting in a café talking about how great it is to be in love. He's in love, too. Unfortunately, he's in love with his ex-wife.

For *Bob & Carol*, we wrote treatments first, because we were going to try to get money for it. We had done *Toklas* on spec, and we wanted to get paid to write *Bob & Carol*. We wrote this very clear treatment and everyone thought it was too dirty. So we said the hell with it, and we wrote the whole script. The minute we'd written it, we made a deal with Mike Frankovich. And he said to me, "Who do you want to direct it?" I said, "If I don't direct it, we're not selling it." And he said, "What have you done?" I said I'd directed a little theater, but I'd been an actor for a while. "Alright, I'll let you know tomorrow." The next day he called back and said, "It's a deal." That was it. He was a great man, a great guy.

Do you recall what your first day on the set was like?

Panic. I'd done a lot of preparation, a lot of rehearsal. I felt I could do it, but the day I arrived for the first shot, I suddenly realized the enormity of the scene. The crew, the stars, Natalie Wood, everyone staring at me: "Where would you like to start?"

What did you do?

I said to the DP, "Well, what do you think?" He said, "Why don't we seat them how you think they'd be seated, do a little rehearsal, and then pick out the first shot." He helped me, and I started to get a feel of how to do it. He said to me, "Anytime you're in trouble, anytime you're not sure what to do, let's do a crane shot." I said, "Why?" And he looked at me with this grin and said, "We'll go up on the crane and figure out what to do; while we're up on the crane, nobody will hear us."

By the second day, I was cocky, thought I knew it already, but I really didn't. You can't learn about directing a movie without directing one. I learned a lot making that movie. I didn't go to film school. I did study editing at USC at night, but I didn't know anything about cameras and lenses.

Do you think it's necessary for a director to know these things?

I think it's very helpful. I really do. Most writers who start directing don't know these things. I learned through doing, and I'm still learning even now. I learn something on every picture I do.

Do you have a specific approach to shooting a scene?

I like to do long takes, where I'm on a single of you talking to me, and you get up to go get a piece of fruit in the outer office and still hear me talking, and I see the secretary doing the phone, and you come back in—it's still the same shot and I'm still here. You sit next to me, and now it's a two-shot. I like to do that kind of thing a lot. I like to do three pages in one shot. But there's no scene in any movie that fifty different directors couldn't have done fifty different ways.

What were some of the lessons you learned in *Bob & Carol* that helped you get good performances from actors?

Since I'd never made a movie before, I did what I felt I had to do, which was have a lot of rehearsal. In that movie, I had two full weeks of rehearsal. Now I try to get three. You never really have a full rehearsal every day since you also are trying on clothes and costumes and seeing locations. You end up getting about three days a week.

Again I say to you, no rules, because there are directors, and good ones, who don't want to spoil the pristine moment, don't want rehearsal. They don't want the actor to know everything. I don't believe in that—unless you're not supposed to know the person at all, then I don't rehearse. But if you're supposed to have a relationship like the one in *An Unmarried Woman*, where these people have been married for fifteen, sixteen years, I want to rehearse. And I do all kinds of tricks.

Like what?

I'll read the scenes through a few times, and while we're still rehearsing, I'll say, "Look, I got to go do something for an hour, why don't you guys just talk among yourselves, do whatever you want." I do that to get the actors to be with each other, hang out together.

I'll ask them sometimes to go to dinner, go to the movies. I'll take them all ice skating. I want them to experience some things with me, some things without me, so by the time we shoot, they're not a real married couple, but they're a lot more like a married couple. They're not meeting on the set and saying, "How do you do, I'm going to play your husband."

I also do a certain amount of rehearsing, especially in difficult scenes, where I let the actors be bad, let them experiment, let them do whatever they want. Go crazy. Then we can talk about it a little bit.

If there's any rule, and I've said there's none, it's don't say anything unless you have to. Don't direct if there's nothing to say. If they're doing it great, let 'em. That's it. You don't have to constantly push them, but if you get an idea, you shouldn't be afraid of expressing it.

One of the problems that I've never had but seems to be around now is the actor getting ten million dollars and the director getting a million. How is the director going to tell the actor what to do?

I was at a director's meeting recently, and a very well-known director said that now that there's video on the set, everyone connected with the movie thinks they can do it better—everybody looks at the tape and says, "Pretty good, but here's how I would've done it." Including the grips and the craft-service people.

Do you block scenes?

I block, I rehearse, and sometimes I have a performance in front of as much of a crew as has been hired. I also rehearse on the set, if the set is available. It's enormously helpful because, believe me, most people who read the script don't have a very strong idea of what this thing is really going to be until they see it. Each department reads the script for what they need: What clothing are they going to wear? What kind of set does he want?

I usually spend an extra month working with the production designer. The normal thing is ten weeks of prep; I try to take fourteen, because I want to allow time to talk to the production designer, and to dream, to imagine myself playing the parts, to imagine how the stage is. I explore ideas with the DP.

Preparation's the name of the game. You prep the entire script, try to think of how it's going to look, and then start from the beginning and do it again. And then do it again. Clearly, you have to see the locations in order to do that, and I don't need the actors at this stage. I do it without the actors. I do it in my mind. I do sketches, and sometimes videos, using whoever's around to stand in key shots. I did a lot of *Moscow on the Hudson* on video, enough to make clear certain ideas. It's inspiring. You do anything you can to help free yourself of your conventional mind. You play music. Music inspires you.

When you did *Unmarried Woman*, did you have that musical theme in mind already?

I worked with Bill Conti. We had a temp track and then Bill wrote the theme.

In *Tempest*, I played some of the same music you hear in the movie while I was rehearsing, and dreaming about it. Remember, it's free while you're dreaming. If you change your mind, throw it out. It can inspire you, give the actors an emotional connection.

We want to be, as much as possible, unafraid to really risk, which is to really get into yourself if you're acting or directing, or whatever it is you're doing, to free yourself of the safety net that most of us create for ourselves.

I spend a lot of time thinking about the movies I do. On the surface, things may look simple, but a great deal of thought goes into a movie. What's important is that there are no rules on how to make a movie. It's an individual thing that's organic to the director and how he visualizes a movie. It's a collaboration with other creative minds, but ultimately, it's the director's vision, especially if the director is also the writer.

Do you ever have conflicts between actors who like to prepare a great deal and actors who work more by instinct?

Every actor works differently. I understand that. I find a way to reach each of them on their own level.

How did you help Nick Nolte create his character in *Down and Out in Beverly Hills*?

I wanted Nick to hang out with the homeless down at this mission, and he did. He started growing his beard and looking dirty and wearing the clothes a couple weeks before rehearsal. And when we got to the rehearsal, he didn't take a shower for probably two weeks. Bette Midler said, "Jesus, he stinks. Can't you get him to take a shower?" She thought his method kind of thing went too far. And I said, "I've got no control over Nick." We were playing a little game with her, and it worked, it was helpful.

Do you believe an actor should do that kind of thing, start from the outside?

There are no set conventions on how an actor prepares. It really depends on the role. I would think that if you were going to play a homeless person, it'd be helpful to you to really experience it, go down and talk to some of them, because the clichés are too easy to do, they're a dime a dozen. For example, I said to Raul Julia in *Tempest*, "If I were you, I'd go to Greece, spend a week with people who herd goats, be around goats, get a feeling of the animals, and be comfortable." And he did that.

Tell me about casting Lena Olin in *Enemies: A Love Story*?

I'd seen Lena in *The Unbearable Lightness of Being* and thought she was overwhelming. When it came time to cast Marcia, I think I showed it to a couple of actresses who were afraid of it, or something, or were stupid, and then I remembered Lena. I arranged to meet her in London. We had a two-hour breakfast and my heart was pounding—she's overwhelmingly beautiful and very smart. And I said, "Do you think you can do this accent?" She said, "Yes, I guarantee you I can do it." I said, "Fine. You got the part."

All actors work differently in rehearsal; some go very slowly, they barely can be heard in the early rehearsals. Lena gives you the full performance right away. And it can be a shock at first—it's so rich, it's so emotional and complicated. She can do it and you can't tell her not to.

Do you communicate differently with American actors than you do with foreign actors?

In my experience, the foreign actors never give you a hard time. I remember the great, great Fernando Rey, who played the servant to the dictator in *Moon Over Parador*. After one day of rehearsal, I treated him like a king. I would say, "Fernando, could you possibly move from here to there, and sit when you say that?" On the second day, he said to me, "Paul, do me a favor, I know you like me very much and you respect me, but please treat me like the cur dog of an actor that I am." He's one of the greatest actors of our time; he was delightful, unpretentious.

Lena Olin didn't want a stand-in. She said, "Why should she stand in for me?" I said, "You're going to get tired." But she insisted, "I don't need a stand-in," and she was available every time we needed her on set for lighting or what have you. It's delightful to work with actors who have great attitudes. So to answer your question, I don't have a different way of communicating with foreign actors.

It's obvious to me that you enjoy acting in your own films. How stressful is it to act and direct?

Usually it's not. Don't forget, I'm not playing the main part, like Woody Allen does.

You had an intense part in *Enemies: A Love Story*.

Yes, but it only took one day. It was very tough and I felt very pressured. I had to do a lot of physical stuff. Go down with a tray, get food, pay for the food, do this huge, long scene. At first I was nervous, but finally I got the rhythm and used the pressure of the moment in the performance.

In the movie I just did, *Faithful*, I play a psychiatrist. I have a big, big part, but in all my scenes, I'm by myself, so it was much easier. I'm getting the hang of it and it suits me just fine.

Do you use video assist when you direct yourself?

I use it. When you have long, complicated tracking shots, video is very useful. The trick with video is to not watch it when you're directing the scene. Look at it afterwards. As much as I can, I stand by the camera and watch the actors. I look at their eyes. You can't tell shit from the video. Video never tells you which is the best take. It tells you what the composition is.

Why do you write or co-write all your films? Is it more difficult to internalize or visualize other people's material?

I was a writer before I made movies, so it's not a problem of internalizing or conceptualizing other people's material. I love writing, and if I have the opportunity to collaborate in the writing, why not? Why should I do somebody else's vision? So far it's worked well for me, although I didn't write my last film, *Faithful*. It was written by a very talented actor/writer, Chazz Palminteri.

Is it advantageous for writers to direct their own scripts?

I don't think there are any rules. I don't think you should direct unless you have a mad passion to do it. It's too hard. You're living with something for a minimum of a year, and sometimes longer. Look at Oliver Stone's *Platoon* and Richard Attenborough's *Gandhi.*

I know many writers who feel passionately about the scripts they write, and I can understand their pain in seeing their work mutilated by another person who may not understand the writer's vision or who has a totally different interpretation in mind. Writing is such an individualist art. You sit in a room and create the visions you have. You see these visions so clearly in your mind's eye that you get connected to them emotionally, and you write it with great love, especially if it's a spec script. You invest so much of yourself, and then the baby is taken away and given a new mother.

Some writers are fortunate and their scripts are enhanced by a talented, genius director. We've seen it happen many times. But for each success story there are many disappointments. To writers, it's a matter of protecting the integrity of their work; it's a matter of preserving their sanity; it's a matter of survival.

Not all writers can direct; some are born with the talent and ability, but others, who think they can direct, end up wishing another director had done their film. They may be too close emotionally and therefore too rigid.

If there is a terrific collaboration between a writer and a director, there's nothing healthier than a fresh point of view. But if a writer has done some previous directing on stage or TV, or shorts, and feels compelled to direct his own script, then he should direct it. It's an individual thing. I write scripts for myself to direct. It's my vision as a writer, and it's my vision as a director. I feel very comfortable with that. But if someone else has written material I can get passionate about, I'm open.

Do you shoot close-ups first in highly emotional scenes?

No. I almost always do the masters. I generally don't do too many close-ups. I want to save them for the absolute right moment. I want to see what it's about; I don't look at just the face. If I have a specific emotional reason to draw attention to what the character is thinking or feeling inside, I save close-ups for that. But everyone works their own way. I am sure that many directors do it totally opposite from me. Look at *Dead Man Walking*—so much of it was in tight close-ups.

When Shelley Winters played the character based on your mom in *Next Stop, Greenwich Village*, did you have her meet your mother?

My mom was dead. Shelley asked me questions, and some of them were uncanny. She asked, "Did your mother know how to type?" How would she know that? I told her as much as I could about my mother. And that was it.

Was it logistically difficult to shoot a period film in New York?

It wasn't that bad. It was very tough for the actors in certain sequences, because it was supposed to be winter and I shot them in the summer. It gets real hot and muggy in New York in the summer, and here they were, wearing long, heavy overcoats, running in the streets. Almost the whole movie was shot on location. Some of our locations were on fifth-floor walkups. That was brutal.

How did you do the storm in *Tempest*?

It was all made up. It was a combination of all the arts of movie making. We prepared it shot by shot. The storyboard had great detail, and we then figured out what we would do with the camera, what we would do to make thunder. Some of it was shot in a real location, some of it was shot on Stage 22 in a Rome studio, where I reproduced the outside porch of the house.

For the choppy water, we had a miracle happen during the location part of the shoot. The water had been calm for two months, but when we went down to shoot that scene where the boat turns over, the water got rough. Vittorio Gassman, Susan Sarandon, John Cassavetes, and Gena Rowlands all went into the water. They went out and had to swim back. It was unbelievable.

You said that *Tempest* was about forgiveness. I saw that too, especially when Cassavetes and Rowlands were doing the tango. Was there a metaphor that you wanted to express with the tango?

Well, yeah. I don't like to use too many words to describe what you might feel. Dancing is the closest we come to holding and touching, getting closer without making love. We can embrace somebody in a dance, we can be close. And there was something I just loved about the tango as the dance of passion.

To go back to *An Unmarried Woman*, how did you cast Alan Bates? Was he written as English?

No. He was written as a New York Jew. Alan said, "I can't do an American." I said, "I'll make him British." And I did some research.

Why couldn't you find an American actor for it?

I just didn't find one I felt was right. I knew Alan Bates from other films. I flew over to England, met him, and thought he was perfect for the part. I made the character a British Jew. That was the end of that. And I justified it: There are a lot of British painters living in New York; I had him study painting. And you've got to remember that had I made the movie in the forties or fifties, half the stars in Hollywood were British or Irish playing Americans.

Was the therapist an actress?

No, she was a therapist, the real thing. That scene was written, but improvised. I told her to start with my lines, but if at any point she felt she wanted to do something from her experience, not to worry about me, and she put in some of her own stuff, which Jill Clayburgh responded to. I told Jill, "She's probably going to stay with the script, but if she goes off it, since she's never acted, go with it." And it worked.

When Jill Clayburgh's character runs away after her husband tells her he's having an affair, she throws up. It looked so real, did you plan it?

It was in the script. I wanted her pain to be visceral, not intellectual. You can only imagine intellectually what it's like if the guy you've been living with for sixteen years breaks down in the street, starts to cry, and says to you, "I want a divorce. I fell in love with another woman. I met her in Bloomingdale's." There were a lot of ways to react, but I wanted her to be sick. She's filled with rage and disbelief and has no idea what's going to happen. She ends up throwing up, and it helped. Then I had her walk away.

How did you direct Alan Bates as Saul Kaplan?

I didn't tell Alan much. I just rehearsed. He was right there.

What about that fight scene with Charlie. Was that done with a stunt person?

I rehearsed it with a stunt person to make sure they didn't kill each other.

But you let them do it on their own?

Yeah, and I made it rough—bizarre rough, more like a wrestling thing, like what really happens at a party. People don't throw clean punches. They only do that in Westerns.

Cliff Gorman was very good; he's a great actor. I'd seen him do *Lenny* and *Boys in the Band*. When he's up in the loft with her, it's the first time she's going to have sex with a guy since her husband. She's got her things off, and he takes her by each nipple with his fingers and pulls her toward him. I never told him to do that; he did that on his own. And she let him do it. I thought it was a great beat.

That wild laughter when Charlie was kissing her legs: Was that scripted, or something that just came out of the actress?

It was not scripted. Jill played it as any woman would feel it, having sex with a man after being married for a long period of time. It's like a new thing; it's bizarre. I'm not a woman, I can only imagine the first time she experiences another person. I talked to some women, and it's as scary an experience for them as it is for a man. Jill and I talked about it, and being a woman, she understood what a woman would feel going through that kind of an experience, and she gave the performance an edge, a raw edge. I wanted the audience to share viscerally what her character was feeling, and she was able to execute it, which is the result of a director being specific about communicating his needs to an actor and an actor using her intelligence and imagination to create a special moment. It was very moving for me. Jill is an exceptional actress.

You moved the skating scene in *An Unmarried Woman* from where it originally appeared in the script. And where you placed it seemed to work so much better. Did that happen in the editing?

In the script, she goes skating before she has met Saul. But after I saw the cut, I said to the editor, "We need to feel her sense of triumph in having found a man she loves, so seeing her at the skating rink earlier in the film doesn't make sense. But if we place the scene much later in the movie, after she has fallen in love, then we get to share her joy." It made a profound difference.

That's the wonder of editing. On paper, a scene and its placement may look fine, but once you shoot the film, the structure, the story, the characters take on new life and new dimensions. And in editing, you get the opportunity to improve on your original concepts, which is wonderful.

What attracted you to the theme of forgiveness in *Tempest*?

I had to be half-crazy to make that movie, because it was very difficult to do. At that time, I didn't even think about the theme so much as I thought it was a wonderful entertainment. I loved the play, and I tried to figure out how to adapt it and get everything in it.

I thought it was about a combination of things. It's about an architect, and I consider architects artists, it's about an artist having a midlife crisis, a nervous breakdown. And everything that happens in this movie could be a total figment of his imagination. If you want, he makes magic, he makes the storm. I was asked, "Did the storm really happen, or did he make it up?" And I said, "Whatever you think. I don't have the answers to everything."

Directing comedy versus drama: Which is more challenging?

They're so different. What's great about comedy is if it doesn't make you laugh, it's no good and you know it. So it's a little easier, you have more latitude than you do with drama.

In *Down and Out in Beverly Hills*, when I told Nick Nolte to eat dog food with the dog, I knew it was going to be funny, but I didn't know it would be *that* funny until I saw Nick do it. Nick really put his face into that food. I knew it would be funny when the dog psychiatrist says to the dog, "Now I want you to eat, here's some food," and the dog takes the dish and flings it. I thought it'd be funny when Nick does yoga and the boy and Bette imitate him, but I wasn't sure.

Some things you don't know. Take, for example, when Nick has sex with Bette. It's one of the most hilarious scenes I've ever seen. She's rolling around on the bed, saying, "Take me." And the dog is rolling on his back. And then, when she says, "Oh!" I cut outside and you see Little Richard going, "My God"; the maid going, "Wow"; and the fountains popping up. I wrote it in the script, but I didn't know if it was going to work until I saw it, when we cut it all together.

Do you find it difficult to direct nude scenes?

It depends on the actors. I close off the set. I try to pretend it's ordinary. I tell the actors that if there's anything bothering them, "You tell me, and I'll do it." Some people are more comfortable than others. I think there's an unfairness toward women in almost every movie. They're constantly showing women's breasts and this and that. They rarely show a guy's penis. So women often are a little resentful that you're asking them to expose themselves.

Do you have any keys to successful casting?

I think you've got to be wide open. Trust your taste and judgment, and the casting director.

I needed a cab driver in *Harry and Tonto*, and I was having trouble casting the part. One day I was in a taxi on my way to the casting director's office, and this lady cab driver started to talk to me—endless talking, hilarious talking. So when we got to my destination, I said, "How would you like to be in a movie?" She said, "What do you mean?" I said, "Keep the meter running, I'll pay for it." She came in and read for me and I gave her the part. And it was a big part. For reasons I can never tell you, she never blew a line, she did take after take, perfectly, brilliantly, for two days. Who knows why? She never acted again.

There are no rules. You go with the moment. You cast by the numbers or you cast by a moment's inspiration, and sometimes you strike gold. The key here is being open to those opportunities.

Do you read actors?

Oh yeah, I read them. I read with them. Very often, I'll read the other part because I'm good at it. I can shift and change and do things. I can get a sense of where they're at. The whole thing about casting is having a concept in your head about who can play what. I cast people by reading them, by seeing their work, and sometimes just by getting a sense of who they are if they're new.

I don't set any rules and regulations. The new ones are tougher to cast because there's no body of work you can look at. I've started a lot of people, or have done their second film: Kris Kristofferson, *Blume in Love*. Dyan Cannon, in *Bob & Carol*, never had been in a movie. She came in and read. She was great. I screen-tested her. I don't screen-test everybody. I don't worry about the camera; I want the right person for the part.

Obviously, if I want someone who's got to look unbelievably beautiful or if I have any fear, I'll do a camera test. But usually, when I see someone like Lena Olin, whom I'd seen in *The Unbearable Lightness of Being*, I don't need my cameraman to tell me that she can look beautiful. But if they don't have footage, I read them and get a sense of who they are. I put them on video so I can remember them and look them over again, and I bring them back a second and third time.

Casting is an art you can't teach. You can learn, but you have to go through the experience of casting. It's scary. I cast a part in one of my movies, I'm not going to tell you which, where a girl read great. Great. Twice. Then, when we shot the scene, she couldn't do it. I tried every trick I knew to free her up, to relax her. But I couldn't get her relaxed. It could have been the fault of the scene, it could have been my fault, it could have been that the girl was just plain unable to do it. I never used that scene in the movie. I had to just eliminate it. And this happened after carefully reading her, because she didn't have much experience. I misjudged. Today, I would've recast the part and done it again with another actress, just to see if it would really work.

I've misjudged a couple of other things in some of my casting. Usually you can't fix it, so you do the best you can.

Casting correctly is crucial to the success of any movie. That's why you see a lot of people playing the same kind of character over and over again. Whoever's casting knows that that guy can play a gangster and be tough. That woman can play sexy or whatever. That's why a lot of actors are dissatisfied; they don't want to always play the same character—they want to be challenged. But it's the directors' fears that keep them where they are.

There's nothing worse than bad casting, just as it's the greatest thrill for a director when an actor is right on. For the writer it's an even greater ecstasy to see an actor bring to life what the writer had in his or her imagination, it's something visceral, it fills you with admiration, respect, and love for the actor. It's one of the payoffs as a director and as a writer. All the hard work seems worthwhile when the actor reaches and fulfills your expectations, and every one of us wants to achieve that new plateau of excellence. So I try not to rush casting. If I have to call an actor back again and again, I do it until I am convinced that my decision is right. Then I go with it, hoping I was right. There are no rules.

When you're casting newcomers, how do they convince you that they can do the job?

I'll cast the actor I believe the most, the actor I think is closest to the part.

I loved that panning shot of the immigrants before the swearing-in ceremony in *Moscow on the Hudson*.

I cast all the extras with the help of an extra casting person and the first AD. We got pictures, and I went to the open casting with my AD, my production designer Pato Guzman, and the cameraman and just picked out faces. I'll cast all the parts like that if they're really going to be seen. You just have to.

The shots of the bus with the Russian guard, the circus people traveling through New York—all these little bits you had—were they done by the second unit?

No, I did them. I love using a second unit, but in this scene I wanted to really see every image that they would see and feel their experience of seeing New York for the first time. My grandfather and grandmother came to New York in 1907, and here we were, shooting almost eighty years later, and experiencing freedom was still exciting.

When you work with the second unit director, do you give him specific shots?

They get a shot list. On *Tempest*, Don Cameron, the editor, did a wonderful job of second unit. He shot many things that worked for the storm—shots of burrows and chickens with wind blowing, pieces of the coast, water lapping. We never could've gotten that storm without the work he did. He made a great contribution as an editor, too. I've had great luck with the editors I've worked with.

Do you think it's best to do an extensive shot list before you report to the set or after the set rehearsal?

I do a shot list the night before. In the morning, I give it to the script girl. I probably give one to the AD, too. And I discuss what we're going to do with the cameraman: "We'll get a master here. We'll cover this one this way."

So you already visualize it in your head.

Yeah, I've blocked it long before, in rehearsals. The first shot of the day usually takes the longest to light, set up, rehearse. But from there it goes quicker. You've got to be patient, in my opinion. And everything I'm saying to you is merely my opinion. I want to make it clear that I don't write rules. I don't know any rules. In my opinion, have a little patience with the cameraman on the first shot, and you'll be better off. So he takes a half hour longer than you thought, so what? Once the first shot—the master—is out of the way, coverage is easier.

Do you talk to your actors while the camera is rolling? Do you give them line readings?

I don't give my actors line readings. I'm not there to tell the actors how to do it. I give them the freedom to create. Once in a while, I'll give them direction as the camera rolls. Generally I try not to. But sometimes the actors say, "Do me a favor. Do it for me. Don't keep telling me X, Y, Z, just do it." It's a dangerous thing for me to do, because I'm a good actor. I'll probably give a good line reading, but not exactly what they should be doing. I don't want them to do *my* version; I want them to do *their* version. So I very rarely give line readings. I just say, "a little more surprise," or something of that nature.

What happens when you have one actor who needs a lot of takes to get going and another one who doesn't?

You do the best you can. There's no secret. I don't have a simple answer. Sometimes there's just nothing you can do except do it. Sometimes fatigue helps an actor. Sometimes you trick them a little—you say, "We got it. I'm satisfied. But just for fun, let's do one more." The one more you do is usually better. But sometimes the first take is the best, you never get it any better.

Enemies was full of subtexts and memories. Did you do a lot of rehearsals?

That was a hard film. We did two weeks of rehearsing. And the actors did two weeks of homework that I gave them—movies to see, documentaries about the period and the concentration camps; dinners with survivors; meals in Jewish restaurants—work to make them really understand how the trauma had effected the people who lived through that horrendous experience. I hoped to enable the actors to personalize the experience so they could draw upon it in their performances.

What was the hardest scene emotionally to direct in that film?

The two most difficult scenes were when Anjelica Huston discusses the children with Ron Silver, the dreams that she has of the children, memories that will not go away. Very emotional. And the scene at the end when Lena Olin tells him to go, and he puts his arms around her, not knowing that she's contemplating killing herself. It was an overwhelming scene to shoot, and it was overwhelming on the screen. I think Lena Olin is one of the greatest actresses in the universe. Remember her suicide scene, when she looks in the mirror and she smiles that odd, strange smile?

Was it something she created on her own?

No, I talked to her about it. I told her what I thought was happening.

That when she finally takes the pills, she's free at last from her pain. The thought of her freedom gave her a strange release. She agreed and executed it wonderfully. If they don't get it, you talk it over until they do. That's why you are the director. You have the whole vision in your head, and it's your job to communicate that vision to the actor.

I know you tried to stay faithful to the book by Isaac Bashevis Singer. Did you have the actors read the book?

That was up to them. I didn't tell them to read the book. Ron Silver read it; he used to carry it around with him, and he would tell me, "Look, the scene is great, but in the book he also says . . ." That was one of the reasons I didn't tell the actors to read the book. You stay as close as possible, but sometimes not everything translates well to the screen. I stayed as close as I could to Singer's book.

Do you look for an emotional spine in each scene?

I don't say, "This is the spine, this is the thing." I'm just trying to understand it as I go along.

How did you accomplish the change of seasons in that movie?

With great difficulty, but also with great preparation. I did three seasons—snow, summer in the morning, fall in the early afternoon, and snow for another season—in one scene in one day on Coney Island. All in one day.

Parador must have been a great challenge. You had huge crowds in almost every scene. How did you plan something like that?

It was tough, but we prepared well. Pato Guzman and I went to the locations in Brazil with a video camera and started to imagine what they would look like filled with marching crowds. And we kept polishing and polishing. But when we finally got to shooting it, if ever I was scared, it was with that picture. I had seven or eight thousand people in the piazza when Richard Dreyfuss made his speeches for the big night-time carnival. The lighting was planned well in advance. I had four cameras, and we shot for two nights.

How did Richard Dreyfuss prepare for this kind of a role?

Playing the American actor was easy for him, he's a great actor. He started speaking with a high voice and it didn't work. Then he found it. He likes to work spontaneously; he's not big on doing a lot of research

I found it very unusual that you played the mother. How did that off-the-wall casting come about?

Actually it came up by accident and turned out to be great fun for me. A mistake was made in booking the actress who was supposed to play the mother. She was booked for the wrong month. I couldn't find a replacement, so I went to Richard Dreyfuss and said, "Let me read this part with you." I read it and he said, "Do it." So I went to the costume guy and said, "Can you make me a dress for tomorrow?" When I screened the movie for Maurice Jarre, he said, "It's a great movie. I really love it, but I particularly love that woman who played the mother. Who is she?" I said, "That's Carlotta Gerson. She's a great Argentinean actress, but she's a pain in the ass." And he said, with his face right up to mine, "Why is she a pain in the ass?" I said, "Maurice, don't I look familiar to you?" He said, "What are you talking about?" And I said, "I played her." He cried, "Oh my god!" He almost fainted.

Do you care to share any choice bits of wisdom about the actor/director relationship?

Go with your instincts. Prepare as much as you can. Be a friend to the actor, but if he's off, don't be afraid to tell him the truth.

I want to know about the challenges you faced directing *Faithful*, a movie you didn't write.

The script was brought to me by my agents. I read it and I liked it; I thought it was very amusing. It's a black comedy written by Chazz Palminteri, whom I liked very much in *A Bronx Tale*. I met with Chazz and we talked about ways of opening up the script a little. He was in agreement with me, and to make a long story short, I said I'd do it. I made the movie, and it was a very nice experience.

What is it about?

It's a movie about a woman in her mid-forties, played by Cher, who lives in a beautiful house in Westchester. We find out that she's kind of suicidal. Then we meet her husband, played by Ryan O'Neal, the owner of a big trucking company who's hired a hit man to kill her, coincidentally, on the day that she's decided to kill herself, which is a wonderful piece of irony.

The hit man gets to the house, ties her up in a chair and says he's not going to kill her until he gets a phone call from the husband. And she gets really crazed and angry about her husband, but she's not afraid to die. Her lack of fear, and the fact that the husband doesn't call right away, gets the hit man very crazy and nervous. He begins to doubt himself a little bit—he's never killed a woman. He's a guy who kills other wiseguys. He gets so nervous that he calls his therapist. He's a hit man in therapy, which is funny. I play the therapist.

And it all reaches a point where the woman begins to want to live and so she starts to work on him. She offers him sexual favors, all kinds of things, and you're not quite sure about the outcome of that evening. Then the husband comes home, assuming she's dead. Well, she's alive. And now you have this fabulous encounter between her and her husband, where she pretends that she knows nothing, and she's all dressed up and looking great.

Then the thing unravels in a way that I don't want to tell you. I really like the picture, I think it's a good movie. It's sort of Hitchcockian in the sense that you're not totally sure what the truth is.

Was Cher already attached to it when you came on board?

Nobody was attached to it. I cast the movie, with the agreement of the producer, Bob De Niro.

From a performance point of view, what was the most challenging scene in the film?

The whole movie was challenging, because a lot of it takes place in one house. And she's tied up.

I found all kinds of realistic reasons why he'd move her from room to room: He's hungry. He's thirsty. She wants to go to the bathroom. He wants to check out this room, that door, this door, to make sure nothing's going on. The phone rings—he's constantly going to the phones and he always drags her with him. And as he goes from room to room, it gets interesting. It's fun to see it.

How important is it for a director to have final cut?

I didn't have final cut on *Faithful*. I've never had final cut. Listen, any-body who can get final cut should get it. But I don't think there are more than five or ten people who can get it.

It's absurd. The film is supposed to be the director's vision, right? So you put your heart and soul and creative impulse into a piece of work that you know is correct and you're never really sure if the integ-rity of your expression will be violated. That's one good reason to do your own material, because they don't second-guess you as much.

Obviously, if someone produces and finances your movie, or if you get hired as a director, you've got to pay attention to what they say. But when there is a creative difference, sometimes you've just got to stand up and fight for what you believe is your right as an artist. And if the conflict is not resolved to your satisfaction, you always have the option to remove your name from the film, which rarely happens. It's not something I'd like to do. You've got to choose your battles. It can get very political, and sometimes the DGA has to intervene on behalf of the director. But you don't want to create enemies, so it's a fine balancing act for the director.

MELANIE MAYRON

A native of Philadelphia and a graduate of the American Academy of Dramatic Arts in New York City, Melanie Mayron was one of the last six actors to be admitted to the Actors Studio by Lee Strasberg before he died.

She spent a year in the national touring company of *Godspell*, and starred in many films, including *Harry and Tonto* (1974), *Car Wash* (1976), *You Light Up My Life* (1977), *Girl Friends* (1978), the CBS Special *Playing For Time* (1980), *Missing* (1982), *The Last of the Cowboys* (1982), *The Boss' Wife* (1986), *Checking Out* (1989), *My Blue Heaven* (1990), and *Drop Zone* (1994).

A regular cast member on the acclaimed TV series *thirtysomething*, she made her directing debut on an episode of that series. She also wrote, directed, and starred in an episode of *Tribeca*, "Stepping Back." She has directed an episode of ABC's *Sirens*, several episodes of *New York Undercover*, and a remake of *Freaky Friday* for Disney.

She made her feature film directorial debut in 1995 with *The Baby-Sitters Club*.

The following interview took place February 13, 1996.

· · · · ·

What challenges faced you as a first-time episodic television director?

I was given the show that was the hardest out of *thirtysomething*'s eighty-eight episodes. The show boarded out to ten ten-hour days, when, normally, *thirtysomething* was shot in eight ten-hour days. And the show wasn't in Michael and Hope's house. It was about the shooting of a commercial, so we had more locations than usual, and had to shoot the commercial itself, which took two additional days to do.

On my first day of shooting, I did the second day of the commercial, and on my second day, I did the first day of the commercial. So I had to do eighteen pages on my first two days of directing.

The first day, we were in San Pedro, Fisherman's Wharf, and the second day, we were in a big warehouse in downtown L.A. And I had to get everything, because we were only going to be at these locations once.

The first day, I had two cameras and had to do a fifteen-setup montage. You know if you've got fifteen setups in a day on *thirtysomething*, you're going for the brass ring. What I had to do was enormous. It wasn't, What's the first time you direct going to be like? It was, How's anybody going to get this show done in this amount of time?

The first day, we did fifty-four setups with two cameras in a ten-hour day. I did a lot of hand-held, because I figured the only way I would make this work, and save time, was to get the camera off the dolly. I did all the action in "oners," blocking in a way that not only saved time but also got the necessary coverage. The second day, down at the warehouse, I had one camera and we did thirty-nine setups.

Can you explain the term "oners"?

It means shooting the whole scene in one take, with different sizes and movements and people moving in and out of the frame. You go from a three-shot to a single close-up, and back to a two-shot. Or you may have a long steadicam shot of people, walking and talking, who'll go from a hall into a room while the camera stays right with them, covering them in different angles.

Does it take much longer to light a scene like that?

There's a trick that I picked up on *thirtysomething*, because the whole deal with an episodic is that you don't want to take too much time lighting. If you come in one end of the room and walk all the way across to the other end of the room with the camera following you, every direction in the room has to be lit, and that's going to take a lot of time. But if you just light a limited area and shoot everything in one direction, you save time. So when time is limited, I always work toward getting away from costly and time-consuming relighting on turnarounds, unless they're coverage that's absolutely crucial for the story, because they will kill you.

In the *New York Undercover* episodes that you've done, I notice that you have a talent for evoking emotion with your camera placement and lenses. Did you make it your business to learn specifically what you can accomplish with the your camera placement and the use of various lenses?

I love photography. For years I took actors' headshots, many shot with a 105mm portrait lens. And on sets I've worked on as an actress, I've always sat close to the camera, watching what they were doing and asking a lot of questions.

On *thirtysomething*, they were always doing close-ups with an 85 or a 150 or a 100, because those lenses are going to give intimacy. You could work with a DP, if you didn't know about lenses, who might do a close-up in a 50, so everything's in focus, including the face. But there's no intimacy, there's no softness around it. You're not drawn right into the eyes or the face; you're just seeing the whole picture, which looks kind of flat.

A director should definitely be aware of what lenses can accomplish, just as a camera placed in an extremely low angle, looking at an actor's face, would convey a different emotion from a camera placed high above the actor. And a moving camera behind an actor going up a semi-lit staircase would evoke fear, suspense.

Do you think that what you learned as an actress has served you well as a director?

Without a doubt. It's like what Kevin Costner said to me on the set of *Baby-Sitters*: "Nobody knows what your job is unless they've done it."

You're the only one out there having to make someone's reality work in front of the camera. While they're pulling at your face, pulling at your hair, pinning your pants, or taping your bra with a wireless mike, you've got to pretend, for example, you're drunk and be emotional, create all these realities within you so that when they yell, "Action!" you're there, giving the best performance of your life.

No one knows what that's like until they've done it. And just being a good actor and knowing what I have to do—just knowing my craft—helps me when I'm directing other actors, because I can see when they're working and when they're not. And I can help.

How can you detect when actors are working and when they're not?

You see that they're general—just basically playing the lines—not playing the reality that isn't the lines. Nine times out of ten, it's not what lines you're playing, it's what you're really thinking, what you're doing.

"Acting is behavior," is what Lee Strasberg always said. You go to the theater or see a movie, and nine times out of ten, the biggest laughs are in response to some physical business somebody did, not some line. Someone is trying to make a good impression and they trip. It's happened to all of us at one time or another in our lives, so we identify with what the actor is doing and laugh. Action comes from recreating an experience.

In the "Toy Soldiers" episode of *New York Undercover* that I did, Lauren Valdez, the actress, whose character's ex-husband died, has a scene with a priest. He said to her, "Were you in love with him?" And she said, "Yeah." Then he said, "You're sure everything's fine?" And she said, "Sure." But she wasn't thinking, she was just saying it.

I thought it could be more interesting. So I said to her, "Have you made a substitution for Louis?" I didn't think she had; I thought she was just playing the line. Lauren's a wonderful actress, but I think in an episodic, because of the time constraints, actors get into just playing the lines a lot of the time. I said, "Who was your husband to you? Maybe he was the love of your life, and even though you knew it could never work out with him, he still captured your heart. So when you say, 'Yeah,' it's not so easy. You have an emotional reference. And then, when you see his murderer and freak out, there's a reason—you really cared about him."

Had we not made that choice, that scene wouldn't have worked on that level of emotional intensity. Just being specific about that choice, and reaching beyond what was on paper and giving it a life—giving the character a humanity, a personal experience—made that entire storyline more effective.

Another thing Lee Strasberg always said was, "You're as good as your choices." A director can help an actor reach those decisions, but for a director to be able to do that, there has to be a perception of what's required in the development of a character. Sometimes it's something that happens intuitively on the set as you're blocking for the camera. You may not have even seen it in rehearsal. And on episodics there are no rehearsals. A knowledgeable director will see and grasp the opportunity to enrich a scene with a couple of well-placed words to the actor.

On a police series like *Undercover*, cops have an attitude, a body language. Did you consult a technical advisor or just depended on the actors, because they'd already been doing it for a while?

On episodics, where actors do a role week after week, they know who their characters are more than I could presume to, so I just listen to them. They've been around cops, they've done a lot of homework, and they have experience. They informed me on a lot of the cop business, the gun things. For example, I said, "You come and hold your gun here." And the actor said, "I'm right in a direct line of fire with her. I would never do that." So I said, "Oh, well, where would you be?" "I'd be over here." "Okay, that's cool. We'll shoot you over there. That shot will work."

How is acting in a TV series different from acting in a movie? Are there different sets of rules for character development and performance?

Character development is the same and performance is the same, except that you really never have rehearsal in TV, at least not in one-camera television. In multi-camera sitcoms, they rehearse a week. In episodics, you don't have the time to give an actor the opportunity to help in the blocking by experimenting—doing what they think the character will do in the given circumstance.

Blocking in episodics is dictated by the director: "Okay, you take this salad bowl and walk over here and get the plate and put everything on the plate." The actor has to learn all the business, then go to hair and makeup, then come back and have one more time to practice it. Then it's shot.

While I think you get some terrific performances from actors on TV, feature-film performances are superior because the actors have had an opportunity to rehearse, try things out, polish the script to perfection, etc.

You studied method acting. How did that help you in your acting career? Take the good-bye crying scene in *Harry and Tonto*, for example.

I did that movie before I actually studied with Lee Strasberg. I spent the whole shooting day walking down the side of the road trying to cry: "My dog died, my this died." I was making up everything, because I thought, "Oh no, they're going to say 'action' and I've got to cry, and I don't know if I can do that." I never wanted to live through a day like that again. So I said, "I've got to learn the craft."

They've got a great deal of money invested in a crew and all the equipment and locations, so when it comes right down to it, when they say "action," you've got to deliver the goods. That's your job as an actor, and if you can't do it when it's demanded of you, sixty people will be standing around waiting for you to get it together. And if you don't get it right, you're going to have to do it over and over again, and that's not the mark of the professional.

Did you finally get yourself to cry?

I had thought about everything under the sun, and on the first take, I was just about to cry. The director, Paul Mazursky, yelled "Action!" and then looked around and cried, "Somebody forgot the cat!" I was supposed to say good-bye to Harry and Tonto, the cat, but the cat trainer forgot to put the cat in Harry's arms. "Cut, cut. Where's the cat?"

I started to get angry. Here I was, really emotional, vulnerable, about to cry, and then: "What the hell happened to that cat trainer? How dare she? Here I am all ready to go, and she doesn't have the cat."

At that point, I was not ready to cry, I was too angry. How was I going to cry if I was angry? They rolled the camera for the next take, and of course, I didn't cry. Paul Mazursky said, "Melanie, you want to take a minute?" I took a few minutes and then said, "Okay, I'm ready." They rolled the camera, and just as the scene started, an airplane went overhead, so they had to cut the take. It was a close-up and couldn't be used with the airplane noise. Again, Paul said, "Melanie, take a few minutes." I did, and then nodded "I'm ready." Paul yelled, "Action!" and the camera battery went out. So this was "welcome to your first emotional scene in a major motion picture." And now I was frozen, because I was angry and frustrated.

In a situation like that, Lee Strasberg would say, "use it," use all the emotions and cry because of them. But I didn't know how to do that. So we did another take, and of course I was frozen, nothing came out. So Paul Mazursky took me aside, put his arm around me, and said, "Melanie, look at him," meaning Art Carney, who I'd had so much fun with, "he's old, isn't he?" And I nodded. "You never know when you're going to see him again, do you?" And with that realization, I just broke down and cried, and Paul put his arm around me, tight, and said, "Okay, let's roll."

Paul spoke about the reality of the moment, which pulled me right into it, and basically, that's how the method works. If you're specific about a moment in your real life, no matter what the lines are or what the situation is, and it works in the reality of the moment that you are experiencing, then as you've embodied that moment it becomes your truth, and it will work.

Once you went to Lee Strasberg, did you find the stuff that you learned during the shooting of this scene was affirmed?

Absolutely. He was wonderful. He always started very constructively: "What did you work on?" He'd start with the positive, and then he'd say where he thought you could be more specific, or do things differently.

I was among the last six actors who got accepted at The Actors Studio before Lee died. I was really lucky to have gone to the Studio when he was there. I had opened *Godspell* on Broadway, but I was more nervous doing a scene in class for Lee Strasberg than I was opening on Broadway.

What does an actor gain from acting school?

Well, I think you either have a gift or you don't. When I directed *The Baby-Sitters Club*, there was a little six-year-old girl playing a small part, and we cut to her all through the film, because she always had something going on. You just looked at her face and she was there, thinking. She was into it.

If you aren't exactly born with the gift, classes are very helpful, because you learn technique that will help you harness whatever is inside you. If you are born with the gift, it's a matter of taking control of your talent, giving it shape and discipline. I'm all for acting school.

Do you think directors should study acting?

As an actor, I very rarely had a director who would tell the actors anything that helped. What Paul Mazursky said to me in *Harry and Tonto*
was rare.

Costa-Gavras is another director who understands the process that
actors go through in creating characters, in projecting their inner-emo-
tions on the screen. I had an extraordinary moment with him, which
is a good example of what I'm talking about, in *Missing*.

There was a scene where Sissy Spacek's husband, Charlie, played
by John Shea, goes to get a newspaper and leaves me—I played Terry, a
photographer friend who came from New York to visit them—at a
newsstand, where guards come and arrest me.

Costa was shooting across this big square in Mexico City, with a
300mm lens tight on my face. Because the camera was so far away, and
I didn't know what lens they were using, I didn't really know what to
do. So Costa ran up to me and said, in his accent, "Now Melanie, you
know the camera, very long lens; so we're very tight on your face now."
I said, "Oh, okay, thanks." And he said, "So the guards, they come.
They're leading you away. You look at Charlie, and you go, 'Help! Help
me! Look at me! Look at me! Do something! Do something!'" I'm
thinking, I don't have any lines in this scene; oh my god, he's giving
me all these lines. I'm trying to remember everything he said: "Help,
help! Look at me! Do something!" Then he said, "But of course it's all
with your eyes." And he patted my arm and said, "Okay, we shoot."
And I thought, oh, okay. Because the camera sees your thoughts.

If you're thinking the right thing, it's going to be right. Sure, just
as there are actors who have the gift, there must be directors who have
that genius within them, who know and understand the acting process
without ever having studied it. But for those who don't have that gift,

acting classes are a good idea, which is why I think an actor-turned-director has more insight into working with actors. They've been there. They understand. They know.

Do you think that a classically trained actor with extensive theater experience, somebody coming out of New York, let's say, has an edge over an instinctive film actor?

Yeah, I think they have an edge, because they have more craft. Anyone can be brilliant, can do something intuitively spectacular. But can they do it for the next take? Can they do it for the next setup? All the takes for the next setup? Will they pull off that level of work all day long? Will they be consistent, so it all cuts together?

Actors who are in the theater train and know how to take advantage of their body language and play bigger than life. They have to do a show eight times a week. And they can't be brilliant one night, and not so another. They have to maintain a level of professional excellence. That's being able to repeat. And that's craft.

In film acting, someone who has schooling, who can repeat what they do, over and over, will have a leg up on the actor who doesn't have that schooling. I've seen it time and again with actors who do film: If you're someone who's been around and studied, when it's your turn to do your emotional work, you're right there every take, every setup. Someone else might not be, or might need a lot of work.

How do you do your emotional preparation just before the camera rolls?

That depends on whatever the specific of the moment needs. I do certain exercises—effective memory, specific prop. For example, if I had to do the good-bye scene from *Harry and Tonto* again, having now gained the craft, I would substite who Harry is, or who Art Carney is, for somebody specific in my life. And I would substitute one of the three Tonto prop cats for a specific pet in my life. And I would maybe do an effective memory of a comparable moment when I was saying good-bye to someone I cared a lot about and might never see again. I would personalize the moment and the experience so that it was true to me—so that me, Melanie, could have a reaction. The camera's right there in your face. What you do has to be right.

You only have seven twelve-hour days to do forty-five minutes worth of film in episodic TV. How do you plan your shooting to accommodate such a tight schedule and yet deliver quality?

One of the things I do is pick which scenes are more important than others, because I want to cover and take more time on the more important scenes.

Did you plan on becoming an actress?

Yes. When I was fifteen, I saw Cyril Richard in *A Midsummer Night's Dream* at the American Shakespeare Festival in Stratford, Connecticut, and I was knocked out. It was the first play I'd ever seen, and I said, "That's it, I'm going to be an actor." My first desire and goal in life was to be a veterinarian. I guess my goals shifted. And when my family visited Israel, we went to the Wailing Wall in Jerusalem, where I wrote a note to God. At the Wailing Wall, you write a note to God, stick it in a crack between the rocks, and know that God's going to fulfill your prayer request. I wrote, "Listen, God, I want to be an actress. I want to make people laugh, I want to make people cry. You wouldn't have given me this desire if you weren't going to make good on it. So you'd better. Otherwise I'm going to have a miserable life. Signed, Melanie, Philadelphia, Pennsylvania, USA."

What inspired you to direct?

Some kids take to football or basketball or whatever, but my dad put a camera in my hands when I was eight, and I took to photography. I've been taking pictures ever since then. Later I bought a 35mm camera with 200mm and 50mm lenses and shot stills with those two lenses until I was able to buy myself a 24mm lens, which expanded my range and taught me more about what can be accomplished. Shooting stills, I learned a lot about the emotionality lenses can achieve, and about lighting and composition.

I was twenty-one when I did *Harry and Tonto* and was introduced to the Panavision camera and lenses. I was very curious, so I constantly talked with the DP and the camera operator. Ever since then, I've been paying attention to the camera and its movement and the lenses they use.

On *Missing*, there was a scene where Jack Lemon and Sissy Spacek were in a makeshift morgue, and there was a shot of all these bodies. The camera panned up to the ceiling, which was glass, and you saw all these bodies up there, too. Pretty horrifying. Costa had shot his master. And I had taken a shot of the room with my Polaroid from a little further over to the left than he was, let's say eight to ten feet. He looked at my Polaroid and liked my angle better than the angle he had shot. He said to me that he wished he had shot from that angle rather than where he did, but he was rushed that day and had to move on to the coverage. The next day he said to me, "Melanie, you make a good director. You have a good eye. You know where to put the camera." I guess, subconsciously, that stuck with me.

You've worked with many fine directors, but the two directors you seem to refer to most often are Costa-Gavras and Paul Mazursky. Were they the two who most influenced you?

Yes. And also Danny Mann, who directed *Playing for Time*. I thought he was amazing with the actors and knew what he was doing with the camera.

I've also learned a lot from other actors I've worked with. In *Playing for Time*, I had the opportunity to work with Venessa Redgrave. It was a dream working with her. It was magic working with her. She is just consummate about everything she does. When you work with someone wonderful, like her, they elevate everything you do, they inspire you to greatness. She took me under her wing and was very supportive and loving to me.

Paul Mazursky told me that acting is all about giving—the more giving you are to the other actors, the better the results.

That very much describes Vanessa. She was that way from the moment I met her. She's passionate about her acting and she's passionate about her politics. She radiates excellence. She's so brilliant because she cares so much. I was very inspired by her example.

Another person I learned a lot from was my writing/producing partner, Catlin Adams, who was an AFI graduate. She had been an actor and became a director.

We did a short, *Little Shiny Shoes*, and then we wrote an *Afterschool Special* that she shot. Then we raised three and a half million dollars and made *Sticky Fingers*, starring Helen Slater, which Catlin and I wrote and produced and Catlin directed.

When you have a creative writing/producing partner like her, you learn a lot because, doing projects together, you see what she's doing. Catlin always made a shot list, and she always passed it around to all the department heads. She prepped really well. I absorbed everything I could from her.

You were a cast regular on *thirtysomething*. Tell me about your breakthrough as a director on that show.

I went to the producers of the show and just said, "Look, I just produced this movie right before I got on the show. And I produced this short. And I've been writing since I was twenty-one. Will you guys give me a chance to direct an episode?" It took a while, but during the third season they did. And they were very pleased with it, so they let me do another one during the fourth season.

How do you select a lens for emotion?

I do a lot of hand-held stuff for TV, and with hand-held, you can't really go on a long lens, because everything's going to shake too much. So we shoot on 35mm and maybe 29mm lenses. The movement itself—just the jitteryness—gave us the emotion for a big argument scene. I said to the operator, "Don't be so good. Don't hold the camera so still. Move it around. Look like a bad operator, it'll help."

You can get away with that more on a small screen than you can on the big screen. When you do hand-held on a movie, you have to be sure no one throws up.

You directed television episodes of *Tribeca*, *New York Undercover*, *Sirens*, and *thirtysomething*, and then you did the feature film *The Baby-Sitters Club*. How did you approach each of these challenges emotionally and technically?

A lot depends on the story and the parameters dictated by the production. The producers on *Baby-Sitters Club* specifically said they didn't want me to shoot the style that I usually do in TV. They didn't want a lot of oners; they didn't want a lot of hand-held. They wanted it to be a more classically shot film. I had one great steadicam sequence in the house—a movement in and out of all these rooms—that was cut. It made me sick to cut it, but I had to live with it.

For the last *New York Undercover* I did, "Toy Soldiers," I redesigned a dolly that had been made up for *Sirens*—a little platform on wheels that they would put an apple box in so the operator could scoot himself all around with a hand-held camera. So for this scene in a church, which if you shot eye-level was just marble and boring, I wanted to shoot very low, so I could get the stained-glass windows and the arches—a very impressive shot. I wanted the operator to be able to be down so that he could shoot up, but I also needed him to be able to move around. So they built this dolly for me, which I modified and we used for most of the shots. I wouldn't have been able to get that sequence without that makeshift dolly.

These decisions are made after I read the script, scout locations, and start to visualize what I'm going to do. Each situation is different, and I adjust to it emotionally and technically. There are no set rules. Some wonderful things happen by pure coincidence—you start out with a plan and then things change, ideas that you didn't think about suddenly pop. I try to stay open and flexible, because the surprises can give you a new level of excitement.

The big difference between doing TV and doing a feature is time. Doing a feature gives you more time to think. Doing episodic TV, time is so much of the essence that you're always scrambling to find the most innovative ways to save time, which forces you to be more ingenious, more creative in overcoming the challenges. But you don't always get the optimal results you can get when you have the time to think and rethink your shots.

I'm curious about your directorial debut on *thirtysomething*. How cooperative were your co-cast members? Did everybody feel comfortable with you, or did they adopt a look-see attitude?

When you work on a series you develop a sense of family. We were such a tight group; everybody was so loving and supportive and had such an open heart. It was really a wonderful, wonderful time.

Did you have to overcome fears or doubts? Did you sleep the night before?

I actually did. [Laughter] We don't lose too much sleep in my family. The shoot started on Thursday, and Thursday and Friday were the bad days. So I thought, "If I can live till Saturday, the rest of the show will be a breeze." And it actually worked out that way. Once I survived the first two days, the rest of the shoot was a breeze.

How were you chosen to direct your first feature film, *The Baby-Sitters Club*?

Jane Startz, the producer, co-founder, and executive vice president of Scholastic Productions Inc., saw my *Tribeca* episode entitled "Stepping Back," which I wrote, directed, and starred in. I was given a lot of freedom with that episode, and it became like a forty-five minute independent film—a showcase of what I could do.

How long were you involved in rewrites for *The Baby-Sitters Club*?

For about three months. We did about twelve drafts, because there were three companies involved and we had a lot of notes. And then there were a lot of changes during production.

When I met with the producers, they never asked me what I thought of the script. Instead they asked, "How soon can you start?" and "What are your dates?" I remember I went home, called my agent, and said, "You know, they never asked me what I thought of the script. I have some problems with it, and I'd like to make a few changes. But nobody's asked."

Tell me about casting the leads in *The Baby-Sitters Club*. I understand that you looked at 6,000 girls nationwide.

First of all, I didn't interview that many. There was a talent search in six cities—the production company hired casting directors in Chicago, New York, and all these places to take a look at people, and those local casting directors sent the best of their city to the Los Angeles casting directors, Mary Artz and Barbara Cohen, who went through all the tapes and only showed me those they thought were the best. But I did see a lot of candidates in New York and in L.A.

For three months we were in negotiations with Natalie Portman. During the rewrites and preproduction we thought Natalie was going to play Kristy. Natalie was a huge fan of the book and really wanted to do the movie. We cast everybody around her, and then maybe three, three-and-a-half weeks before we started shooting, we found out that the deal fell through.

So suddenly they got me on a plane to New York, where I saw the girl who starred in *Secret Garden* on Broadway and the girl who starred in the film *Secret Garden*. I saw any girl who could possibly play the part. The thing is, thirteen, or twelve and a half, is a funny age for boys and girls, because everybody's developing at different rates. And the Kristy character still had to be tomboyish; she couldn't be womanly. So I might find a really good actress who's maybe fifteen, who looks fifteen, and is a little too womanly.

I was racking my brain, and I was in an acting class that Catlin had. Sissy Spacek had sent her two nephews to study in Catlin's class, and Sissy's nephew Steve was in class with me. He said, "You know, Schuyler's acting now in school plays." Sky (Schuyler's nickname) is Sissy and Jack Fisk's daughter. I'd seen her the day after she was born, but then they all moved to Virginia and I never managed to see Sky again.

So I called Jack and Sissy and said, "I'm faxing you a couple of scenes. Put Sky on tape, because she's twelve and a half and Steven says she's acting now. She could be right."

They taped her, and I couldn't believe it—she was it. She was just fabulous and looked right. She was real spunky and energetic, and Kristy had to be a leader, a troublemaker, and vulnerable. Sky had everything. I started to weep. I shouted, "I've got her. I've found her. I can't believe it."

So when you see that gift, that actor who personifies the character, you just know?

Paul Mazursky said to me when I did *Harry and Tonto*, "Melanie, casting is ninety-nine percent of the success of any picture. You can have the best script, the best director, the best producer, but if you don't care about who's playing what part, it's all over.

Do you cast by reading actors or just talking with them and getting a sense of who they are?

If it's an actor I know, I don't really have to read them. With the kids, I talked to them a lot, just to see what they were like, what their personalities were, because it's a little hit-or-miss as to what their craft will be like. We'd talk and then we'd read.

In the case of this *New York Undercover* episode that involved Rwandan boys, we needed actors who could do a Rwandan accent. I saw a lot of wonderful actors, but they were just talking American hip talk—they were unable to do the accent. And then a few did a sort of pseudo-African kind of foreign thing that sounded convincing, so I said, "Look, I don't know whether it sounds like Rwandan, but it sounds good enough."

Do you tape your readings?

In *The Baby-Sitters Club* we did, because the producers had to see it—Columbia had to see it, the producers in New York, Scholastic, had to see it. But normally I don't always tape the actors.

Do you have any keys to successful casting?

If the actors move you in some way or elevate the material in some way or open your heart and touch you in some way, they're the right people.

Tell me about working with the young cast of *The Baby-Sitters Club*. How much rehearsal did you have? And what did you try to accomplish during rehearsal periods?

We didn't have a solid rehearsal on *The Baby-Sitters Club*. A lot of it consisted of the girls getting their hair done. But we had a few hours every day in which mainly the core group, seven friends, got to know each other.

That was important, because they had to pretend in the movie that they were a group of friends. It was a week of bonding more than rehearsing. We read through the script, and we did improvisations with them as the characters in different situations. At the beginning of the film, we had seven little strangers, and by the end of the film, they were The Baby-Sitters Club.

Once I got on the set, I blocked it and shot it. Obviously, I would have loved more rehearsal with the young actors. But I was allocated only one week, so I chose to do what I thought was best for the actors—the bonding thing took precedence. With the adults, I knew they would do a great job for me in no time, and they did.

Some directors don't like rehearsals. Do you prefer to have rehearsals?

I do, so there's less to discuss on the set, where time is money. But sometimes something can be too rehearsed, which kills it. There has to be a balance. And as a director, you have to be intuitive enough to know this. Being an actor helps.

What techniques did you use to stimulate *The Baby-Sitters Club*'s young actors in tapping their emotions and giving you their best performance?

I talked the young actors through the emotional scenes because they were young and not very experienced. I felt they needed guidance.

For example, I would say, "Okay, in this scene, you're feeling this because . . ."

On *The Baby-Sitters Club*, did you plan shots after your set rehearsals or before you had an opportunity to see the actors use the set?

I had a lot of things planned. I had the first couple of weeks planned, but we ran into rain. So we had about six days during which we wound up going to places that we weren't prepared to go, places we had never tech-scouted.

We were literally making it up: "Who's ready?" "So-and-so and so-and-so." "What scene are they in?" "They're in scene 70." "Oh, you mean the scene at the arts and crafts area?" "Yeah." "Well, what's sunny?" "That path." "Okay, let's do Scene 70, and then we'll be walking down the path." The production designer says, "What are they doing? How about a puppet parade?" "Great, let's have it."

We had a week of this. I felt like I was directing the Civil War. But you know what? The stuff we did there came out wonderfully, and nobody would ever know we were at the Disney Ranch when we should've been at the house.

How collaborative was your relationship with your DP on this film?

I told my DP, Willy Kurant, where I wanted the camera and if it was a dolly shot or whatever, and then he'd give me his input. He was phenomenal. He had some wonderful ideas. It really was a good give-and-take. When we had the luxury of being able to scout some places together, it was nice, because we could talk about stuff.

Did you sit down before the start of the film and go over the script to get an idea of how you were going to shoot it and how you were going to express certain emotions?

I showed him some movies I liked—movies I generally liked the lighting of. And then things kept changing: We had clouds, and we couldn't light the whole field. He said, "If you want to do the big field shot, we need a million lights, and we don't have them." So we had to do it on a long lens, and just do the girls in the bushes. It was supposed to be Connecticut—we couldn't have Peter Horton walk all the way across the road, because we see a palm tree. Exit the shot; start another shot.

A lot of things came up where I had something designed in my head that we actually couldn't do. There were a lot of compromises.

But compromise is also the mother of invention, as they say. You find innovative ways to overcome challenges; they sharpen your creative impulses. I moved fast, really fast. And I knew Willy would be fast, because he was just so gifted and so experienced. He could move things around and be ready for the next shot in six minutes. And it would look spectacular.

How were you hired as a director on *New York Undercover*?

I did my first *New York Undercover* right after *Baby-Sitters Club* came out. Don Kurt, who was a producer, was also a co-producer on *Tribeca*. And he was in a situation where he needed a show done in six days and without a second unit, instead of seven days and a couple second-unit days. He knew my *Tribeca* episode, "Stepping Back," which I directed and acted in every scene and shot in seven twelve-hour days. He said, "I need somebody who can do it fast, and I know you can."

So I did it, but it wasn't a show with any action. I thought it would be. I thought, "This could really help me, because people might think I only direct people stuff or kid stuff. This could show another side of what I do."

They were happy because I brought it in $57,000 under budget. I brought *Freaky Friday* in $267,000 under budget, and I'm proud of that.

You wrote, directed, and starred in "Stepping Back." How challenging is it to wear so many hats on a production, especially on a short schedule?

We had a few fourteen- and fifteen-hour days. Monday, the first day, we were in New York, Seventeenth Street and Third Avenue. We were all around the square there, and used that block for a lot of locations. Then that night we had a scene with Richard Lewis, Carol Kane, Adam Arkin, and Roberta Wallach in the kitchen. That was a long day. We knew it was going to be a long day, so we did a oner in the kitchen. You just have to be creative with time.

Having Carol and Richard and Adam, we knew it was going to be professional and wonderful. Carol is a genius and Richard is such a character and Adam is so sincere. They just have to say their lines and it's spectacular. If you cast right, you will save time, especially when you're wearing more than one hat and shooting on a short schedule.

Was it difficult for you to be both an actor and the director?

It was hard. I had directed, and I'd been around a lot of episodic timing, so I knew you had to work fast. Usually in features, when an actor stars in something they're directing, they have video playback and can watch each take and see themselves.

I bought a video camera and blocked with a stand-in, so I could set up the camera shot. And then, right before we started rolling film, I did a rehearsal with me in it. Taping the rehearsal helped me a lot, because I'd watch myself in the shot and adjust my body movement. But I couldn't play back each take, because if I shot a take and then took the time to watch it, I'd use up the time of shooting two takes. And I didn't have time to spare. So if it felt good, looked good, I'd print and move on.

How many pages did you shoot per day?

We did nine pages a day with one camera. I did a lot of oners. When my editor, who cut Brian de Palma's last couple of films, saw the dailies, she said, "Boy, this director must've had a bad experience with an editor because all I had to do was cut the heads and tails together."

Some industry insiders say directing episodics is like directing traffic—there's no creativity. But I saw plenty of creativity in your selection of shots, which created an ambiance of danger and tension and a sense of humanity all at the same time. Not at all your typical TV coverage. When you were hired, did the producers ask you to look at previous episodes or tell you how to go about doing the show?

I asked to look at some episodes. I watched them and I didn't really see much of New York. I said, "Here they are, shooting in New York. They've got their setup at Sixteenth and Tenth Avenue, and I hardly see New York. They could be in Valencia, shooting a lot of close-ups in a warehouse. I want to open it up. I want to shoot as much wide-angle as I can. I want to see the city." Only a few of their directors show the city, so my episodes didn't really look like what their shows usually look like.

Was the shot on the internal affairs investigator organic to this show?

No. There were eight scenes in the interrogation room. I started the first scene of questioning at eye level, and then in each subsequent scene I lowered the camera a little. I thought that as they progressively attacked each cop, it should become a little eerier, a little weirder, more like a pressure cooker.

It did create that feeling. You certainly did create emotion with the lenses and the camera.

These are things that come to you on the set at times, not things you plan on. You're on the set with the actors, and you say to yourself, "How am I going to convey such and such emotion, make my audience a participant rather than just an observer?" And these ideas begin to emerge as you exchange ideas with your DP. As a director, you have to keep your mind open to spontaneous sparks of creativity.

How much latitude do you give your actors to explore and experiment? For example, the soldier's speech in "Toy Soldiers," which was highly emotional and evoked a heightened sense of who this guy is—dangerous, crazy.

When you have a great actor, you just let him go, knowing and trusting that he's going to do nothing less than interesting and great. We ran it, he had his rehearsal, he knew what he was doing. I loved it. I might have said one thing or another, but not too much, because he was just right on. Sometimes, casting the right actor is just luck. He's available when at another time he may not have been, and he needs this role as an opportunity to expand his talent to the next level.

I believe in giving my actors as much latitude as they need, and if they go over the top a bit too far, it's my job to catch that and perhaps bring them down, change their delivery somewhat. But if they're right on and steaming along, I let them go, let them express themselves, because most actors' instincts are good. Sometimes, especially in a scene as emotionally explosive as the scene you mentioned, there's something deep within the actor that needs to be projected. And when it erupts, it's magic. Having been an actor for so long, I sense it, I feel it, I share that experience. And all I can do is acknowledge that they did something wonderful.

These are the moments that make the job of directing so gratifying—when you know you're communicating on an almost spiritual level with an actor, even if you haven't said a word. I am there to encourage and empower the actors, never to limit or criticize. And once actors know and feel they are supported, they will give you their best performance. Trust is the important factor in the actor-director relationship. It's something I consciously work on achieving.

Tell me about planning and shooting the action scenes in the *Undercover* shows. How do you conceptualize a scene that balances and integrates violent action and human emotional elements, which you did so nicely in the "Toy Soldiers" episode?

For the murder scene in the church, for example, I sat down with my little Apple PowerBook and started visualizing it, writing down every shot that I needed.

For that sequence I did everything on the dolly until the shot where we go down to the gun, which started a hand-held sequence to produce tension. Certain shots went from hand-held to hand-held on the dolly.

I'd envision her POV when she comes in, a shot of him, his face, the machine gun. There's a shot of him standing up. There's a shot of her coming down the aisle and sitting down. The kid getting confession, the priest giving confession, the people getting confession, the killer's POV of him getting confession, the killer's face, his walk down the aisle. It's a process of fitting together all the pieces of the puzzle, because there's no dialogue.

Did you shoot them chronologically?

No. The order was determined by the direction we were looking. We grouped shots to accommodate the lighting.

I had only one day to shoot in the church, and I had this action/ murder scene, which would have taken several days on a feature, and then I had three other acting scenes in the church. We shot forty-one setups in a fourteen hour day. I have never had a day like that in my life.

One camera. We flew. One take: "Okay, print. Change the lens. Now we're here. Action! Cut! Okay, check the gate. Now we're here." I take chances because I have no other alternative, and fortunately, I've been very lucky so far.

For the garage scene, where they're coming in and firing at each other, I didn't have a stunt coordinator, because there really wasn't a stunt. I had two cameras, and we blocked out the action and then figured out how to get all the pieces. I love that, though, because I'm good at thinking of the pieces. I'm a detail person.

Did shooting in New York's freezing cold present any technical or logistical challenges?

We were there the week of the blizzard. The actors get to sit in their little mobile homes and be warm. I'm out there with ten layers of clothes on. I'm uncomfortable. My toes are cold, but I have a job to do, so I take my mind off of the physical hardships and focus on what I need to accomplish. This is the job that I've chosen to do, so I live with it. Next time I may be in Tahiti for three months, right?

Do you ever have to deal with a temperamental actor who disagrees with your concepts and interpretations of the character and story?

You have to not get angry. If you do get angry, you have to rise above your anger, try to be really loving, and see the actor's side of it. And then just explain why you want it done in a particular way. I even go so far as to explain my vision—why I'm shooting the way I am and how I plan to cut the scene.

What do you do when one actor in a scene needs more takes than another? Or when one actor is cerebral and intellectual and another works by gut instinct?

It's hard. I had that situation on *Freaky Friday* with Shelley Long and Alan Rosenberg. They both worked very differently. Shelley needed more takes to get warmed up, while Alan was best right off the bat. So I rehearsed a lot without rolling the camera. But I told Alan not to try to get into it that much, just rehearse it for the lines, for the business. I didn't want him to blow it all before we rolled the camera, so I said,

"Just be kind of technical about it." And when Shelley felt she was starting to cook, I said, "Let's shoot."

You just let everybody do what they need to do. Because I'm an actor, I'm respectful of the process, whatever anybody's process is. If someone needs a lot of time for an emotional scene, I'll just say, "Let me know when you're ready."

Do you speak to your actors while the camera's rolling?

Yes. I started doing that on *Baby-Sitters Club*. I talked through everything, except probably the scenes with the grownups. And I did that on some of the *Undercover* close-ups too. So even if I have to do more ADR, if it helps to get a better performance from the actor, it becomes a priority.

Do you ever play games, like telling one actor to do a scene one way and confidentially telling another actor to do it differently?

Not very often, but in *Baby-Sitters Club*, Larisa Oleynik, who played Dawn, had to be squirted with a little flower that squirts water. On the very first take, her reaction was great, but we needed to do it again, because there was a camera problem. This time she was anticipating getting squirted before the water actually hit her, so I pulled the actor Asher Metchik aside and said to him, "Squirt her, but this time I'm going to tell her that you're not going to squirt her." I said to her, "Larisa, he's not going to squirt you this time, okay?" And this time it worked.

Do you have any specific techniques for getting the actors to listen and respond to each other?

It's all in the casting. It's so much about the level of who you get. If you cast well and you've got good actors, they're going to listen and they're going to respond.

If you're casting relatively new actors, do you find several you like, then bring them together to let them improv a little bit?

In *Baby-Sitters Club* we did, especially with Bre Blair, who played Stacey, and the boyfriend. We did it to see how they would react. Sometimes it doesn't work. It's like love. If the chemistry is right, it's right.

Do you ever let a scene run if you're aware of a technical problem?

That would be a waste of time. I don't want to get to the end of an emotional scene and have the sound man say, "It was bad, because the battery went out in the middle of the take." He should have cut the take because the actors just acted their guts out and now it's no good, which is unfair to the actors.

That's happened to me way too many times as an actor. So I say to the camera operator, "If there's a technical problem, just cut." To the sound man, I'll say, "I want you always in my line of vision." If there's a plane, sometimes they can mix it out, so I'll ask, "Is that going to ruin the take?" And he might respond, "It's okay." But if it's bad, he'll put his thumb down, and we'll cut. I'd rather do that and keep the momentum going: "Okay, look, there's a problem. Sorry. Let's go right away." You start right over again and keep the energy up. If there's another problem: "Cut. Sorry. Okay, let's go again right away."

Everybody's an expert on your crew, and I don't pretend to be a sound expert, I don't pretend to be an expert about what's being seen through the lens of a camera. I want to preserve the energy of my actors. I'm always thinking of the actors first.

What constitutes an excellent film performance?

Truth and honesty. Vulnerability. That's what you see when you go to the movies and identify with the characters—the soul of the actors coming out on the screen, because that's what the camera sees. That's why you can't fake it. That's why I really wanted to get my acting craft together. I wanted to be able to do the best of comedy, and the best of comedy is being able to do the best of drama, which then you throw comic timing on top of.

You have to have craft in this business, as an actor and as a director. I've been on sets where directors don't know what they're doing. They might not have a shot list; they might just want to work it out on the set. Well, a lot of time's wasted working it out there. Craft is really the key, because craft will also give you flexibility when you run into a situation where you have to improvise.

If you want to be a director and you've had some acting classes, you've had to get up there as an actor to do some scenes—you know what an actor needs to go through and you're going to be more sensitive to the actors that you're directing. If you're a director, you should know about cameras and know what the lenses do. You'll be a better director if you can pick lens sizes based on the emotionality of the moment, which will help you visually convey what you want to convey.

Herbert Ross, John Badham, Paul Mazursky, Costa-Gavras—they all know what they're doing. There's never a moment wasted. They do their homework; they're prepared. Today it seems that so many of the best directors are actors—have the actor's sensibility—and possess a wonderful camera vision. And it's just inherent that in all the years you spend learning to be a good actor, you also develop a strong sense of storytelling.

Can you improve a performance in the editing?

Yeah. A lot of times, editors don't know what you were doing: "How come you were talking through that close-up?" "Because I wanted this moment, and I wanted to double-cut that moment."

You must make sure the editor is in sync with your vision, your interpretation of the key story, the emotional points, and whose point of view a scene is shot from. And that applies to action scenes as well.

You have to stay on top of the editing so that your vision is not deluded. Editing gives you an opportunity to fix your mistakes, any performance problems, and sometimes script problems in terms of structure and dialogue. Editing is great because the pressure of the clock running on the set is off your shoulders, you're rested. It gives your mind an opportunity to think and get creative. You can add moments where there were none; you can alter the pace of a scene and improve on the rhythm of a performance. Editing is another area where a director needs to be proficient. It's a matter of protecting your vision.

RONALD F. MAXWELL

K nown as an excellent "actor's director," Ronald Maxwell studied acting and filmmaking at New York University's College of Arts & Sciences and the NYU Graduate School of the Arts, Institute of Film.

After serving as Assistant Director on *Antony and Cleopatra* (1971), Maxwell served as Artistic Director of the Educational Theater Company of New Jersey and became a producer/director for PBS-WNET's *Theater in America* and *Great Performances* television series, making his directorial debut with *Sea Marks* (1976), which he also produced. His next directorial effort was *Verna: USO Girl* (1978), which earned him an Emmy nomination for Best Direction and brought his work to the attention of the film industry, resulting in his first feature film directing assignment, Paramount's *Little Darlings* (1980), which was followed by *The Night the Lights Went Out in Georgia* (1981), *Kidco* (1984), and the Disney Sunday Night Movie *Parent Trap II* (1987).

Maxwell purchased the rights to the Civil War novel *The Killer Angels* and wrote a screenplay based on it, which, after an epic fifteen-year struggle to get it made, became a reality when he was given the green light to shoot the four-hour feature *Gettysburg* (1993) with a star-studded cast. A year later, it was broadcast on the Turner Television Network as a mini-series, capturing the network its highest rating for a mini-series.

At the time of this writing, Maxwell has written the screenplay for a four-hour feature film based on the life of Joan of Arc, which he is trying to bring to the screen.

The following interview took place May 9, 1996.

• • • • •

You started out as an actor. How and why did you become a director?

I was acting, writing, and directing simultaneously in my youth. I was doing plays, which included building the scenery and selling the tickets. By the time I could write, I was into writing plays. It all evolved in a seamless way, so that by the time I was in junior high school, I had my own theater company.

Was your goal to be an actor at the time?

I always thought I would act. It was not just a goal, I was doing it. As an undergraduate, I did a lot of Shakespeare and Molière and other classic plays. During my junior year at NYU, I played Hamlet. By the time I graduated film school in 1970, I had done a few small parts in films, but my focus was centered on directing.

Do you think it's a natural progression for an actor to become a director?

An actor who becomes a director has a wonderful insight into a huge part of the storytelling process, because he understands the process of acting, what it takes to develop a performance.

What's your definition of the director's job?

The director is a storyteller. If you strip away the technology, he's the same as the storyteller who sat around the campfire three and four millennia ago.

You're telling a compelling story, and through your conviction and artistry, allowing the listener to become as involved in the story as you are. It begins with your heart, your desire to tell a story, and then that desire is shared with an audience through your ability to tell the tale, so that the audience ends up owning it, ends up being as attached to it as you are in need of telling it.

I think that the best filmmakers I've seen work are those who tell the story that they feel a compulsion to tell. They invest themselves in it, and as a result, more often than not, the audience, or the listener, feels compelled to listen, to engage themselves in it.

Often, as we know, stories are not told that way. A director is asked to tell someone else's story, and so he has to find a way into it, or find a way to connect with it, which is probably more often the case. And if the director can find his way into the story, so that it becomes his own, and if he is one hundred percent invested in it as a story he must tell, then he has the opportunity of making a film that others will care about. If, however, it doesn't become his or her own and just remains some kind of an exercise, then to the extent that the filmmaker doesn't care about it, obviously neither will the audience.

How do you personalize a story that you didn't initiate?

If I don't feel it at the first read, I know it's not for me, and there's no sense in trying to rationalize it or justify it. There are a lot of wonderful reasons to make a movie you don't believe in—to pay the rent, support children, etc. But those are all the wrong reasons, as far as being a storyteller is concerned. So if I don't feel that it's a story that I can share in the telling of, I know it's not for me, which doesn't mean it won't make a great film in someone else's hands.

Is it easy for you to visualize someone else's words and images, as opposed to material that you've created?

Oh absolutely. I've read a number of screenplays over the years that have thrilled me, that I've wanted to make. At other times, just the nature of a subject will appeal to me, so I will write the screenplay, as I did with *Joan of Arc*. And there's the case where I read a book that got under my skin, *The Killer Angels*, and then did the adaptation, which became the basis for *Gettysburg*. It started with someone else's vision and became something that I could invest myself in. It's making a connection with the material in a profound way that allows you to make it your own.

You've stated that if a project isn't worth investing a lifetime in it, then don't do it.

I'm not projecting this on anyone else. That's just what I've learned about myself and how I work, how I live really, because it's impossible to extricate your work from your life when you're a filmmaker. It's all one. If I feel that the subject isn't worthy of that kind of commitment, I won't spend a day on it.

Can you tell me a little bit about your directorial debut? What was your first film?

My first film was a Super-8 film that mom and dad and my neighbors saw. The first long narrative film I did was my graduate thesis at NYU film school. From 1971 through 1973 I made documentary films. In 1974 I started working as a producer for Public Television, and in 1976, I directed *Sea Marks*, which was an adaptation of a play for *Theater in America*.

Prior to *Sea Marks*, those *Theater in America* programs were all done on videotape. I argued that some of these plays should be reconceived for one-camera film, to present them as plays, but to use them in a cinematic way. So when the decision was made to do *Sea Marks*, it was decided to do it on film. We shot the two-hour film on location in Ireland, 16mm, on a budget of $95,000. The following year, I did *Verna: USO Girl*, which was initiated and developed by me, based on a short story. A year later, I did *Little Darlings*, my first feature film for Paramount.

How did you get *Verna* made?

We were doing a series called *Great Performances*, and under the umbrella of *Great Performances* we did a series of four films called *The Lives of Show Business People*. These were four distinct films on people in various aspects of show business. We had a mandate to look for material, and I came across *Verna*, which I connected with. And the funding for the show was in place before I actually found the subject matter, which was then immediately developed and filmed.

Tell me about casting Sissy Spacek and William Hurt.

Sissy had already done *Carrie* and *Three Women*, and I thought she'd be perfect for *Verna*. We sent her the script, and she loved it. It was William Hurt's first film; he was right out of Juilliard's acting program.

How did *Little Darlings* come about?

Verna: USO Girl received numerous Emmy nominations, including nominations for script and direction. As a result of that, I started getting a lot of industry attention in Los Angeles. I was asked to come out there from New York, where I was living at the time, to "take a meeting," which was the first time I'd heard that expression. Scripts were offered to me, and a few months later I started working with Paramount on *Little Darlings*.

Was the screenplay already finished, or were you involved in its development?

There was a draft which interested me enough to get involved, and then Dalene Young was brought in and the script was greatly rewritten and reshaped.

How closely do you work with your writers?

I have very intense conversations, brainstorming with the writer, and we usually arrive at a way to proceed and an idea about what we want to do. But once the writing starts, I like to leave the writer alone, although I'm available to the writer twenty-four hours a day. I just don't like to be breathing down the writer's neck. And I don't need to see pages every day, or every third day. I say, "Do the draft. If you want to show me pages, great, but you don't have to."

I like to give the writer freedom to do his or her thing. Now on a rewrite, it's different, because unless you're going to throw away the existing text completely, you're going to have to build on it. So you have to sit down and do an outline, give detailed notes, and go scene by scene by scene and decide how you want the rewrite to proceed. But again, once the rewrite proceeds, I like to leave the writer alone.

Are your notes specific or broad?

I'm very specific with what I want to achieve. I write my notes right on my copy of the script. In the margins or on the opposite page. I might type something up separately, but it'll be on the script, too.

Then you've got to sit down with the writer, one on one. You can't just send somebody notes on the fax machine. You've got to discuss it, point by point, even going as far as discussing dialogue. I find that the more specific I get, the more ideas it sparks in the writer.

How was your first day as a director on *Little Darlings*?

I must admit, I felt enormous pressure on my first day on *Little Darlings*, both in production terms and on a personal level.

Were you trying to prove yourself?

Yeah, but I tried to put the idea of proving myself out of my mind. The idea that you've got to prove yourself, either to yourself or to some studio executive, just gets in the way of the work, because what you should be concentrating on is telling the story cinematically. Anything else is just an intrusion, a diversion.

Some directors feel they've got to pull out all the stops on the first day of their first feature. And often, it's not just manifested on their first day, but over the whole picture. They feel they've got to establish their identity completely, finally, absolutely, and unequivocally with their first film. And so there's a temptation to be overly clever and flamboyant.

And again, I think this gets in the way of the work, because some sto-ries require flamboyance and others don't.

The filmmaker should always serve the story. Maybe the first day of shooting is just a close-up, but you're afraid that when you send it back to the executives, they're going to say, "Well, what's this?" You've got to rise above that fear. You've got to just do what's required by the script and not allow yourself to be distracted by what other people think of you and what you're doing. Because, ultimately, when they're sitting in the dailies, they really have no idea what you're doing, be-cause you, the director, have the vision, the big picture, in your head. So I never allow myself to be intimidated by other people's judgments and opinions. I have to be true to myself. And if I am true to myself, that will express itself in my work.

On your first day on *Little Darlings*, did you bring in an exten-sive shot list?

On the first day of *Little Darlings*, I succumbed to the temptation and designed a very elaborate crane shot.

Beforehand?

Yes. I design every shot beforehand, with the idea of serving the script, not serving myself. But in this particular case, which is why I know this temptation, I figured I had to do something spectacular on my first day. And it was spectacular. And it did work. But the joke was on me, because the focus puller gave me a "thumbs up" when the shot was actually out of focus and not framed correctly. We ended up having to reshoot it three days later.

Do you feel that the director sets the tone and the pace on the set? And what kind of atmosphere do you try to establish?

Unquestionably that's the case. The director sets the tone, so the director has to be physically fit and mentally prepared in order to guide everyone else. If the director is dragging his butt, everyone else will, too.

It's a physically demanding job, and it can be emotionally draining since you are fielding everybody's questions, dealing with your actors, and working with your technical crew to tell your story. It involves long hours, and your day is not over when you wrap: You still have to see dailies, and you still have to discuss the next day's schedule and think creatively about what you have to do the next day. You can be working on an average of three to four hours of sleep a night, but you have to be fresh, on your feet, the following morning.

As far as the atmosphere goes, it should be professional. I like a quiet set, even it there are a hundred people working. I like to think that the people are working in whispers.

A set has concentric rings. There's the outer ring, where maybe you have some visitors that day. There's the ring where hair, makeup, and props have staging areas. There's the actual set, where the grips and electricians are working. And then you have the inner-most circle, which is where the director is working with the actors, and perhaps the DP and the script supervisor. As you get closer to the center, it gets quieter and quieter, so in that space in front of the lens you're able to create the world that you want to create, without intrusions. I expect the crew and the cast to respect that space where this kind of soulful work can be done, where the craftsmen and the artists work together to create something that's going to move or enter an audience's soul.

You're not one of those directors who thrives on chaos?

No, absolutely not. I like to be prepared. I like to know that my actors and my crew are prepared. You couldn't make a film like *Gettysburg* in chaos. You wouldn't get through the first week.

There has to be the sense of a well-oiled machine, a team that's functioning, and a working chain of command. It's a matter of mutual respect, where people can exchange ideas.

Contributions can come from anywhere, and these ideas have to be acknowledged, considered, and encouraged so that people can do their work with a sense of inspiration. Otherwise, if you don't create an atmosphere where actors can dare, where actors can be willing to take a chance, where actors can be willing to make fools of themselves, all you're going to get is actors delivering what I call a "bag of tricks." By "bag of tricks" I mean that an actor, working under extremely adverse conditions—adverse moods on the set—can deliver a performance because he or she is a professional, but that performance is artificial. The actor goes for the result without going through the process the character is going through. The actor falls back on clichés that belong to something else they've done in the past, and which does not come out of the character they're playing now. So you're going to get something that is less than excellent, something superficial.

Why get wonderful actors together and just have them resort to their bag of tricks and have your whole film limited in that way? Actors can do wonderful things, but they need a space, a climate, an atmosphere where they are protected—protected from judgment, protected from pressure, protected from any kind of hostility or abuse—so that they are free to create.

Let's face it, the actors are the most exposed people on the film. They're dealing with their emotions, their feelings. For example, actors know if the picture is or isn't on schedule, the same as directors do, so they don't need to be reminded about that every five minutes.

They don't need to have it in their face any more than a director needs to have it in his face from the studio executive.

A director knows what it takes to get the day's work done. He knows the pressure. He doesn't need to be reminded in a crass or coarse or redundant way about what needs to be done. The director needs support to do his work. And the actors need support to do their work. The director needs to protect the actors and protect their space on the set. And in the same way, producers should protect the director from extraneous pressures that divert him from his work.

Do you find that producers sometimes forget that when they're under pressure, falling behind, exceeding the budget?

Good producers are a rare breed. There are few producers who understand the importance of supporting and protecting the director in the same way the director protects the actors.

Again, the professional director, the veteran director, will understand intuitively the demands of the schedule, so having somebody harp about this is not helpful. The director needs the producer to help solve problems, as a partner, and to protect him or her from that incessant reminder about what the schedule is. After all, the schedule and the budget have all been devised to support the making of the movie. The making of the movie is what everybody's there for.

Ideally, the director and the producer should have total open communication, be able to say anything with mutual respect. Ideally, the producer, the director, the DP, the editor, and the actors should all be like the fingers on one hand.

I think you have to choose your producer as carefully as you choose your cast.

That's if you've initiated the project.

Yes. If you're being hired, when you're being interviewed and considered by the producer, you have to do your homework about the producer. You have to call other directors who worked with that producer. You've got to call people you know in the business—studio executives, other producers.

You can't think, "Well, I need the job." Believe me, you don't need the job that badly if you're with the wrong producer. The wrong producer will make your life misery, because if you don't have a meeting of the minds, you won't be able to make the film you want to make. I'm not saying that you must fall in love, but it's very important that there's a profound mutual respect and some kind of common aesthetic. A shared aesthetic and a close collaboration between the producer and the director is conducive to the making of a better film. Anything less than that is destructive, and misery ensues, which not only affects the outcome of your film, but affects the outcome of your health.

Has your shooting technique changed since your first studio film?

I would say yes and no. It hasn't changed in the sense that I've always been interested in a kind of classical filmmaking. The filmmakers I admire most work in that genre. For example, Stanley Kubrick, David Lean, Akira Kurosawa are great artists who have different styles, different personalities, but all work in a classical genre, which means that they serve the story, not ever drawing attention to themselves. They surrender to the story, and they tell the story within a classical tradition. And that has nothing to do with moving the camera, for instance, for the sake of moving the camera or being clever for the sake of being clever, which is an approach to filmmaking that just does not interest me. It's superficial. It doesn't go to the heart of things. It has nothing to do with life and soul.

So in the sense that I was interested in classical filmmaking even in film school, I still am. That hasn't changed. What has changed is a certain facility with the medium. I am more confident and more fluid and more relaxed, much less rigid, with what I do on a set.

And you obviously know a lot more shortcuts.

Well, one learns when not to shoot, for instance.

For example.

The only way you learn that is by spending lots and lots of time in the editing room, where you see what ends up on the floor. For instance, a gross example of what I'm talking about is people getting in and out of cars, or going in and out of doors. That's the kind of stuff that never ends up with a cut, unless there's something significant about the way they're getting in and out of the cars or going in and out of the doors. That's something I would never shoot.

By the time I got to *Gettysburg*, I was able to shoot with greater fluidity. And I'm shooting more and more in one. Not so much to stay ahead of the production schedule, and certainly not, I hope, to show how clever I can be with the camera, which is a futile exercise in vanity, but because it is the most fluid, organic, and appropriate way to tell the story. So in that sense, I think there's been an evolution in how I use the camera, and how I shoot a film.

Are you saying that you like to work more with masters and move your camera according to the needs of the story or the

scene, that you're not really concerned anymore about basic coverage?

Yes, I think you could say that, although that's somewhat of an over-simplification, because mastering implies that you're going to do coverage as well. There's an implication, maybe an erroneous one, that the master shot is the whole scene, which now you've got to go in and cover. And that's not what I'm talking about.

I'm talking about a way to shoot a page, or two or three pages, in one shot. You don't cover it. It just works as one shot. And only to serve that particular scene, because some scenes lend themselves to this style of shooting while others may have to be more static, may require a more extensive kind of coverage.

I find that, while you may have an overall vision, thinking out the style of shooting requires a certain flexibility and a knowledge of what works under what circumstances, which then you adjust for the requirement of the moment, logistically, and most importantly, for what works and serves best the emotional key of a particular scene within the overall scheme of things.

How do you plan the shooting of a scene? Does your plan emerge from watching a rehearsal on the set? Or is this something that's preconceived before you get to the set?

In some cases it's preconceived. For example, as I wrote *Joan of Arc*, I already saw the whole camera move. On other ones, I don't see a shot list quite that clearly, so I'm going to be influenced by the location, the set, the actors, the director of photography, and the production designer, who are all different intellects who may see things that I may not have envisioned. I try to stay open to that.

I like to rehearse on the location where I'm going to film. Rehearsing in a room is good for getting the drama points and the character points, and for breaking down the scenes in actors' terms. But as far as how you're going to shoot the scene, you've got to do that on the location, because that's where it becomes evident if your preconceived ideas are going to work. And little things, like how cold it is outside, are going to affect everything—the actor's performance, for example, and what you do with the camera. So that rehearsal, for me, is essential. I do that rehearsal with the actors first, then I bring in the DP and the continuity clerk and we devise the shot list before we get on the set.

How do you choose your projects? Do you initiate them?

I'm in a place now where I'm originating my own projects, but it doesn't always need to be that way. In the last year and a half, I've had three or four outstanding scripts sent to me that I would direct in a second if I was available. So I'm open to both.

How involved do you get with packaging, financing, and marketing your films?

I get involved with all areas, because I think it's incumbent upon the filmmaker to be involved. Ultimately, no one cares as much about that particular film as you do. Not even the people who've got their money in it, because they also have their money in six or seven other films. Yes, they care a lot, and they want to maximize their return, but they're not focusing on just that one movie. The filmmaker is the only one who's focusing only on this one project. So the filmmaker can therefore catch things, or bring attention to things that might otherwise go unnoticed.

I think there's a big contribution the filmmaker can make to marketing, distribution, advertising, and public relations—all of those things that have to do with selling the film and delivering the film so that the film finds an audience and an audience finds the film. I'm not talking about being a pain in the ass. I'm talking about offering advice, comments, and suggestions. And I found, certainly in the case of *Gettysburg*, that it was appreciated. Whenever I talked to somebody at Turner Pictures or New Line, or in marketing or advertising, my contributions were always taken seriously and appreciated.

Did you have approval on the *Gettysburg* poster?

No, I did not have approval, but I had input. And I loved the design New Line came up with. It was just outstanding—that blue sky with the Confederate and Yankee forces facing each other on the lower part of the poster. I thought that visual was very simple and striking, and the byline, "Same land, same God, different dreams," was just right on the money. It got to the heart of the film.

We've all seen posters or ad campaigns that misrepresent movies. But this one really captured the essence of the film.

You had a lot to do with the packaging and the financing of *Gettysburg*. You were actually functioning as a producer. Is this something that you do generally?

No question about it. In *Gettysburg*, I was really a silent, uncredited producer. But of course, I was involved because it was my project. I had optioned the rights years before. If it's a project I've initiated, I obviously get involved with all aspects of the financing and distribution.

Do you believe that casting is the heart of any film you make?

Totally. It gets back to what I said about the match between the producer and the director and the match between the director and the DP. If you share an aesthetic universe, you can almost learn to talk in shorthand. If you don't share that, your life's going to be much more difficult.

It's the same thing with actors. You choose actors who are not only right for the role, but who you can feel an artistic rapport with. Miscasting someone is a nightmare. I certainly won't mention any names, but there have been cases where I've had actors imposed on me by the "system." But I've had nothing but the most marvelous, exhilarating experience with every actor who I've chosen. When they weren't my choice, and I'm talking about only one or two examples in a lifetime of making movies, the work was very limited.

How do you know that a particular actor is right for your film?

There are no set rules. I think you know it the same way you know when you meet your future spouse. You know it intuitively, supported by years of experience.

But what about in the beginning of your career?

Less experience, more instinct. But remember, I had been working in theater since my youth, so I know actors. I'm comfortable with actors. I know what makes an actor tick. I know the process. I know what an actor has to do to create a role.

Knowing acting and knowing actors is an enormous help in cast-

ing. And not only in casting, but in the process of working with actors. For me, working with an actor to create a role is one of the most
exhilarating parts of filmmaking.

I like it when they do their homework, like all the actors on
Gettysburg. Every single one of them came on the set having read the
biographies and/or the regimental histories of their characters. And of
course, I had read all that stuff, too. So we could work on a very fine
level.

**When you write a script like *Gettysburg*, do you visualize your
lead stars as you're writing it, and then go after them?**

Generally speaking, no. I visualize the character without any actor in
mind. That's been the case in every film I've worked on, but it's especially true in a historical film. I didn't want any contemporary references
to cloud the clear view that I was trying to get, looking into the past.

Having said that, there have been exceptions. For instance, when I
was writing the role of Armistead in *Gettysburg*, I knew from the beginning that I was writing that role for Richard Jordan, who was one
of my very best friends and an actor I'd always admired. That role was
tailor-made for him.

What about Robert E. Lee?

Yes, there were different actors who were considered who could have
played Robert E. Lee before his final incarnation as Martin Sheen. And
there were different actors who could have played Joshua Chamberlain
before his final incarnation as Jeff Daniels. But that was all after the
script was written. That's just the normal convolutions of casting a picture. I was not influenced by that when I was writing the script.

I believe that casting is a process like writing, like editing, like shooting. It's not black and white. There's a road you have to travel, and you're not sure where the road is going to go. You have an idea, but that idea is influenced by the people you meet. That's certainly the case in the, let's say, secondary roles, where you might see ten or twenty actors for a role. You have an open mind, even though you have an idea of what the character looks like.

In my mind's eye, I know the character, and then an actor walks in and I feel, "Oh, this is the actor." But the actor brings so much of his own persona and humanity that it's going to shift your take on the character.

If you're talking about the leading roles, where you need "names" for financing reasons and for marquee reasons, you're restricted to a very short list. In that case, it's a different kind of discovery process, but it's a discovery process nonetheless.

You might not end up with the first choice on your wish list, but you will end up with your best choice. Your first choice may not have been the best choice, because when you finally cast the picture, you have to believe one hundred percent in your cast. And so, for instance, Martin Sheen came on the picture at the eleventh hour. He knew that other people had been offered the role and couldn't do it for various reasons—timing, availability, whatnot. But once I thought he was the actor, he was the actor. I wouldn't have traded him for any actor in the world, because, to me, he became Robert E. Lee, just like Jeff Daniels became Joshua Chamberlain. I couldn't imagine, in hindsight, any other actors playing those roles, because Marty and Jeff owned those roles.

Who has control over casting your pictures? Is it a very collaborative process with you and the producers and the studio?

As we all know, it is a collaborative process. And unless you have the final determination of such things in your contract, usually the studio and the producers and you, the director, have to agree. If there's no agreement, something has to give. That's the way the business is set up. If there's no agreement, usually the director takes a walk.

I believe that a worse alternative is to do the picture, compromising yourself in terms of casting, just because you don't want to lose it. And I'm not talking about coming to a common agreement. I'm talking about when you really feel compromised, when you know an actor is wrong. That's the time to disassociate yourself from the project, because there's probably no more fundamental choice you make, after the choice of the script, than the choice of casting. As a director, you have to absolutely believe in your casting, every single role, or it's virtually impossible to go forward.

Did you compromise any of your visions in *Gettysburg* to please the studio?

No, I did not have to compromise. But I have to qualify that, because sometimes you have to compromise things because of the limitations of the budget or the limitations of time, not because somebody dictated that you compromise.

Those kinds of compromises certainly happened on *Gettysburg*. For instance, I had to give up a location that I thought was very important. And, although some people may laugh, because *Gettysburg* is one of the longest movies in American history, I had to give up filming certain scenes, which I don't really miss in hindsight, but which, at the time, were tough decisions.

So, yes, there were compromises made in the interest of achieving the whole. But the integrity of the piece was not compromised at all.

And nobody asked me to compromise my vision in a specifically artistic way. There were some differences over the cuts, but things were debated in an open manner. There was give and take on the part of the executives, and on my part. Basically, I can say that I'm ninety-nine point nine, nine, nine, nine, nine percent pleased with the integrity of that film.

How important is your relationship with your casting director in terms of finding the best actors for your film?

Just like the other key people on the crew, you want a casting director who can, in a sense, crawl inside your mind and see the picture through your eyes. That doesn't mean the person surrenders his or her own artistic vision or integrity any more than the DP or the editor does. You want people to be themselves but, at the same time, share your vision. I think this is an accepted understanding about those roles.

In the case of the casting director, you want somebody who understands what you want, yet can, at the same time, make their own suggestions. I welcome casting directors who bring things up from left field, or things that are maybe not at all in alignment with what I initially had in mind.

They should provide you with alternatives. They should have their ear to the ground. They should know who's working off-off-Broadway or whatever the equivalent of that is in Los Angeles. They should know the up-and-coming people who've done independent films. They should know where the new talent, young or middle-aged or old, is coming from. They should remind you about people you may have forgotten, people who are not the flavor of the month. They should have their finger on the pulse of what is going on, so they can bring you a wide variety of people for a role, but they should not waste your time and bring you too many people. They've got to screen people, be very selective, so that you end up meeting the best of the crop. And to do that, there has to be a great degree of trust between the director and the casting director. The director has to trust the taste and vision of his or her casting director. It's all about communication.

I like my casting director to be an agreeable, experienced person who's totally confident in their choices. Furthermore, they should clearly have good relationships with agents and managers, so that they can facilitate getting the script to actors who the director may find it difficult to get to.

Another thing that's very important is that your casting director be somebody who treats actors with respect. I try to respect not only actors but everybody on the crew. And I like to know that when actors come in to read for one of my films, they've had a positive experience, and I've had a positive experience. I'm meeting a lot of people, and I'd like to give myself and them the opportunity for a positive, productive experience, which is also the best way to find the best person for a role. So I like a casting director who creates a positive, productive atmosphere, and who treats actors and their managers and their agents with a degree of respect.

When you cast newcomers, what qualities do you look for?

I look for their gift, or their talent—whatever word you want to put on it. I look for how close they are to my vision of the role or whether they can bring something so startling that they alter my vision of the role, so I come closer to their position. I also look for a sense of commitment, for a sense of enthusiasm, and dedication to their craft, to their work, to their life as an actor. I take what they do seriously, and I certainly expect them to take what they do seriously. I like to see that they want the role, because if I don't see that in an interview or a reading, I ask myself, "How on earth are they going to deliver the stamina and dedication needed to get through a motion picture shoot?"

I'm willing to see past a bad reading. Sometimes brilliant actors who I've seen work on stage or in movies are not good at cold readings. So I often try to give an actor an opportunity to see the pages, if not the whole script, the day before, so it's not a totally cold reading. When I shoot the film, it's not a cold reading. Why should I subject an actor to that? When I shoot a scene, we've talked about it, we've considered it, we've rehearsed it and blocked it. So I like to give an actor an opportunity to prepare for a reading. And if they have an off day, I don't hold it against them. If I'm interested in them, I might say, "Come back in tomorrow, or at the end of the week." And it's not to do them a favor, it's to give myself the benefit of the doubt.

So let's say a new actor comes in and brings you a reel. What do you look for when you look at a reel? Do you look to see if the camera loves the character?

I have the theory that what we call the camera loving the actor is really the actor loving the camera. It's really the actor loving the audience. Because the camera is just a window to the audience. And that is a quality that some actors have and some don't.

What sort of quality it is?

It's a desire to connect with an audience, a desire to love the audience and be loved by the audience. And it may not even be a conscious thing on the part of the actor. You may feel this quality in an actor who says, "I'm the last person in the world who needs to be loved by the audience."

When the camera loves an actor, we feel a great empathy for that actor. We root for that actor. We care about that actor. We want to go where that actor goes.

Then there's charisma, which is a difficult quality to explain, but we use the term and apply it to certain people, whether or not they're actors. And charisma has a certain attraction on a screen. Sometimes we say that a charismatic actor "jumps off the screen." Now charisma may or may not work in conjunction with this quality that I call empathy, or the camera loving an actor, but when both qualities are there—when an actor has both this empathy and this charisma—you have something very potent on the screen.

But these are things that are part of the actor's persona, and have nothing to do with the craft and the skill of the actor. You could find empathy and charisma in an eight-year-old or you could find them in a more mature actor. They make up what we call star quality. Some movie stars may not be the greatest actors in the world, but they connect with the audience, and the audience responds to them. And often you have a great actor who lacks that special star quality, who'll always be a great character actor but never a star.

Once you find an actor who has star quality complimented by technique, experience, and good instincts, you must have the ingredients for a great performance.

I'd say the potential for a captivating performance. Obviously there are some roles for which you may not want that much charisma, where you may want a flatter, duller hue. You wouldn't want a movie where every single person in the cast was charismatic. That would be like an overly-sweet dessert.

So there is room for all types of actors, which is why I think there are very few stars. They're special and deservedly so. Star quality is something you're born with, and the other qualities can be cultivated.

Will you hire new actors without seeing them on film?

Yes. Most directors like to get as much information as possible on an actor. If they're in a play, I want to see the play. If they've done twenty movies, I want to see the twenty movies. If they can come in, I want to have an interview, I want them to read. The more information I can get, the better. Even if I have a "love at first sight" response to them, I want to be as informed as possible. Also, actors look different on film than they do on their eight-by-tens or in real life. But because I've done a couple of pictures where I've had to utilize child actors who in many cases had no film, only an eight-by-ten and a reading, I've just gone on what I had to go on. I feel comfortable knowing that, when the right person comes along, I will have a gut reaction that I cannot rationalize. It's all about instinct.

How are you able to visualize the transformation of an actor, like a Martin Sheen, for example, into Robert E. Lee?

In the case of *Gettysburg*, it was easier to visualize because we had photographs of the real characters.

When Martin Sheen or the others came in, I just looked into their eyes, into their inner life. Assuming that you're in the right racial category, for starters, because some broad strokes you've got to get right—if you're doing Malcolm X, you'd better cast a black actor—then it's a question of their inner life, what they project through their eyes. And then from that, secondarily, how much the actor looks like the character.

I was somewhat influenced by how much the actors looked like the characters in a few cases in the *Gettysburg* cast. Cases where, once the actors were made up, they looked almost identical to the characters they portrayed.

But the most important thing to me is the inner life. The best example of that I've seen in recent years is Anthony Hopkins in *Nixon*. He doesn't look like Nixon, but five minutes into the movie, you're with Nixon. Sometimes, especially when it comes to playing real-life characters, the inner life supersedes the look. Get the inner life, and then work on the hair and makeup after that. If you don't have that inner life, you don't have anything, you have a wax museum.

So in the case of Sheen and *Gettysburg*, how did he prepare for that kind of a role? How did you work with him? What did you tell him to do?

Not just Marty, but everybody in the cast, was given the biographies, and in some cases the autobiographies or diaries of their characters, so they had a lot of reading material and a lot of photographs.

Everybody was counseled to slow down their speech. We talk fast now because we're in an electronic age, and are bombarded with television. We live in big cities now, but in the nineteenth century, there was a different sense of time. Time had to do with solar time, with day and night. The battles were fought mostly during the day. Distances were perceived differently. You had to go by horseback, there were no airplanes, everything proceeded at a slower pace. And we have a clue into that when we go to the South today, not the new South but the old South. The Southern drawl is not the accent alone. It's also the slower speed of speaking. If you listen to the film, scrutinize the film, you'll see that everybody, including Martin Sheen, talks slower than we do now.

Did you have a dialogue coach help you with this?

We had eight different regional dialects in the film—three Yankee, three Confederate, Irish, and British—so we had dialogue coaches working with everybody. Robert E. Lee's dialect was Virginian—educated, aristocratic Virginian. Marty had a week of rehearsal, and he also did a lot of work with Tom Berenger, who is a Civil War aficionado. We were able to bring Marty up to speed in a shorter amount of time than anybody else.

We also had to have all of the actors forget about the intervening years, the years between 1863 and now.

Why?

Because that had nothing to do with their roles. Martin Sheen, for example, had to erase from his mind that Robert E. Lee was a hero or a mythic figure. It's irrelevant to playing the role. Lee's a man in a tight spot.

We had to erase, to the best of our ability, not only what these historical figures became in our mythic understanding but all the knowledge we've accumulated in the intervening years: We had to erase the theory of relativity. We had to erase Sigmund Freud and psychotherapy. We had to go back to a pre-twentieth-century world.

Did you know that Tom Berenger was a Civil War aficionado before you cast him?

Yes. While he was shooting *Someone to Watch Over Me*, there was an interview with him in one of the New York papers. They asked him, "What's your favorite book?" And he mentioned *The Killer Angels*. The next day there was a script in his hotel suite. And the same day there was a call on my service from Tom Berenger.

What about the casting of Stephen Lang as General Pickett?

I was considering Bill Campbell as a possible candidate for Joshua Chamberlain. At the time, Bill was playing Laertes in a production of *Hamlet* on Broadway, and Hamlet was being played by Stephen Lang. After the performance, Bill introduced me to Stephen Lang as the director of *Killer Angels*, as *Gettysburg* was originally called. It turned out that Stephen Lang had read the book and was also a Civil War buff. The first thing out of his mouth was, "I am Pickett." Not, "I want to play Pickett," not "Hello, I'm an actor . . ." "I AM PICKETT." And he said it so convincingly that a couple of days later we met for breakfast, and a week or so later he was cast as Pickett.

What about Jeff Daniels? Was he your first choice?

The original concept was William Hurt, but he was unavailable. We considered a few other people, and Jeff Daniels' name came up. I had seen a few of his films and thought, "Wow, that's a stretch." Then I went back and saw every film he ever made, but was still ambivalent.

A meeting was arranged. Everything depended on the meeting. He had read the script and was interested in it, and by this time I was somewhat interested in him. After we got through the pleasantries, I told him that I'd seen all his film work and knew he had done a mammoth amount of stage work and had worked for some of the best directors of our day. I'd seen his skill, craft, humanity, humor, intelligence—all sorts of wonderful qualities that were very important to the role of Joshua Chamberlain—but in none of his movies did I see a sense of that quality of steel, that deathly commitment, that willingness to take life in a kind of zealot way for a cause. He had never played a role like that, so I said, "This is a dimension of this guy that you haven't demonstrated in any movie. That doesn't mean that it's not there, but I just have to hear from you that it is there." And he fixed this cold look on me and said with as much conviction as I've ever heard in my life, "I'll give you the fucking steel." And did he ever. He also said, "Will you give me the fucking steel? Will you commit yourself to this movie and really do the movie you have on the page?" So we exchanged commitments that night, one of those male-bonding episodes, you might say.

I can certainly say, looking back on the experience, that he sure delivered. And many a critic and many an audience member have told me, and I'm sure they've told him, too, that they saw a completely new side of Jeff Daniels in this role.

What sort of direction did you give him? What do you mean when you say "steel"? How did you make him interpret that?

That's what actors and directors call a "result," and I don't talk in terms of results on the set. This was a conversation hundreds of miles away, months before the shoot, trying to get down to results.

When I'm on the set, I almost never use those kinds of terms, because I talk more in terms of actions that will get the result I'm looking for, the result the actor's looking for. In the case of *Gettysburg*, the actors were all professional, experienced, accomplished veterans of stage and screen, all very advanced in their craft. So they did not need to be pushed around. They certainly did not need to be talked with in a result-oriented dialogue. I just gave them hints to help them with their specific actions in a given scene. And then, having given them hints, it was just a matter of tuning them in. And in simplistic terms, "tuning them in" is "less"/"more," "bigger"/"smaller."

Take, for example, the first filming of the 2nd Maine deserters scene. We had a two-hour window to get that and it had to be shot at the end of the day, the magic hour, when the light was low and warm and the shadows were long. We had enough time for two or maybe three takes. It's a long piece, and I rolled the camera in a medium shot, then the whole thing in a close-up.

I didn't want to interrupt Jeff Daniels. We had talked about it. We had rehearsed it. And we talked in between the shots. He's an actor who's never going to do bad work. And he was very good—very close, very close. But it just wasn't there. He knew it and I knew it. When we walked away from the set that day, I took him aside and said, "We came very close, but there's more. We didn't get the heart of it." And he looked at me with great relief and agreement and said, "I'm so relieved, because I really want another crack at this." And I said, "Absolutely." It's one of the most important moments in the film. I couldn't walk away with ninety percent of it, I needed to nail it. I needed to get one hundred percent of that scene.

We were on a very tight schedule, but I told the producers and the studio that we had to reshoot the scene. They said, "Why don't you wait for the dailies?" And I said, "I was there. I don't have to wait for the dailies." Then the producers played back the audio tapes and said, "It sounds good to us." And I said, "This is not a matter of 'good' to you. As the filmmaker, I'm telling you we didn't get it." They said, "Well, we want to call Jeff Daniels." And I said, "You're free to call Jeff Daniels. We're not running a secret society here. But I'm telling you we've got to go back." They played the tapes over and over again and said, "It's perfect. It's an Academy Award-winning performance. How could you want to improve this? You're a perfectionist." I said, "Call me what you want. We didn't get it, we're going back."

Happily for me, the studio executive on the scene, Nick Lombardo, said, "If Ron feels we got to reshoot it, we reshoot it." Now I think that was because, by that point, there was mutual respect, there was confidence in me. They knew I wasn't saying that every day, so if I said I needed to reshoot, there must be a good reason.

We went back to the location at the same time on the very next day with all the extras, all the troops. Jeff and I talked a little bit about where we wanted it to go, but it wasn't so much a question of my conversations with him as him just achieving it. He knew where he had to go.

I told him over the course of the two days, "Keep it conversational." I said, "The first take, even though you would be impressed by it, was a little too oratorical. It was a little bit too Marc Antony in front of the Senate." It had to be as if he was talking to one soldier, not fifty. And at one point in the middle of that, he sees it.

I remember saying to him, "Jeff, you're talking about an America that doesn't exist yet. You're talking about a country that is torn apart, in the middle of a Civil War, but you see through this hell, through these broken people. You see this vision, this dream called America. Here we are now, 1992, still not in the citadel. Maybe we never will be, maybe no people on Earth can be in that place, in harmony. But idealistic Americans want to get there, and Chamberlain was one of the most idealistic Americans who ever lived. He could see it, and that was his motivation, that was his life. That's why he was willing not only to risk his own life, but to take life. That's a big step: from risking your own life to taking life. This film was called *The Killer Angels*, because they were all killers, they were willing to kill in their angelic quests."

I said, "Jeff, you see these people, but at some point, you've got to see the nation. You've got to see that these men are living, breathing figures a hundred years later. You're looking into the future when you say your speech. You're there, but you're looking into the future. And so it's got to be intimate, but with a long view."

And finally, in the first take of the second day, Jeff was so calm, so gentle, so personal, and so intimate that his performance achieved an enormous power. It really was an example of "less is more." And I don't mean less delivery, because it's full of intelligence, it's full of dreams, it's full of compassion. That's why it's such a riveting moment in the film.

After that scene I was able to go to him and take him by the hand, and I didn't have to say a word. He knew and I knew that he'd nailed it. And when at the end of the day I told the producers and the studio executives, "We got it," they knew I wasn't kidding. And had we not gotten it that second day, I would have gone back a third day, a fourth day, and a fifth day. But of course, that's not necessary if you're dealing with professionals. And when you're dealing with professionals as good as Jeff Daniels, you don't have to spend that much time.

To my way of thinking, you've got to work with actors who are as demanding as you are, because they know as well as you do when they've achieved excellence. Sometimes I've had actors on different films say to me, even when I was satisfied, "Let me take another shot at it, " and I've never said no, because they know, and you'd better follow their instincts. So it's not about rules, it's about feelings, instincts, and patience. Actors can bring something different, a nuance, or maybe a moment that I'm glad to have. So I've never said no to an actor, even under the most intense time pressures, even when I thought I had it and wanted to move to the next setup, if they come to me and say, "I want another shot at it," I give it to them. That's the least you can do for an actor.

When you're casting, how important is it for you to actually read the actors? Do you ever just sit around and talk?

I like to read actors. By putting the character's words in their mouth, they become the character in that moment. When you're talking to somebody, they're not the character.

I'm talking to you, you're Jon Stevens. You're seeing me because you want to play Laertes. You're not Laertes. You're Jon Stevens at the end of the twentieth century. When I give you the script, you're back in the eleventh or twelfth century. That's a different body language, that's a different look. Right away I can see your skill as an actor. Instantly! I can see your craft. If you keep slouching like you're in the late twentieth century, I'll know you haven't taken a day of acting classes anywhere; I'm going to have to build your performance from scratch. I'll give you an example of this.

Royal Dano, who just passed away, may he rest in peace, was in John Huston's *Red Badge of Courage*. During the casting process for *Gettysburg*, we heard that he was interested in being in our film, and we thought it would be fun to have one of the original cast members of the *Red Badge of Courage* in *Gettysburg*. And there was one part for a man in his mid-sixties. So he came in to read, because even though I knew he was a great actor who had done a million movies, I wondered whether he could still, at his age, pull it off.

He didn't have any ego problems, he didn't have any attitude problems. He had worked with legendary directors on legendary films. He came in like a working actor. We had a conversation, and he was just Royal Dano sitting in a casting office in 1992, an elderly gentlemen, kind of stooped, with a cane. But when the time came to read, he dropped the cane, went into this erect posture like a soldier, and became the living embodiment of a nineteenth-century Civil War soldier in the field. We were in tears.

I ended up casting Morgan Sheppard to play the role, because I thought Morgan was just closer to what I wanted, and Morgan was brilliant in it. But that doesn't diminish the achievement of Royal Dano coming in that day and reading. Had I just met with him, teetering on his cane, I wouldn't know that he could do that. But I saw in that moment that, yes, he could handle it.

I've seen actors become their characters so many times that I always prefer reading them. You get so much more information. Why not be informed? Why not read them? Because you don't want to embarrass them? Because you think they can't do it? I say, inform yourself. And in that process, you'll learn about the script and you'll learn about the character after seeing ten or twenty or thirty actors read for it.

How many actors do you see before you make a final decision? If you think the first actor you see you is right, will you still see other people?

In the casting process, you're really selecting people to inhabit your imagination. It's not too dissimilar from selecting a person to inhabit your life. What it boils down to is knowing your mate—your wife, your husband, your girlfriend. You can look back and say, "Well, there was that moment when I knew." You may go through a courtship for months, but you had a gut feeling in that moment. That's how it is with casting. It can be the first person through the door. Or you may see a hundred people and still not find him. And until you find him, you've got to keep looking. That's just the way it is.

Who can tell you? No one knows but you. Just like only you know who you can get in bed with. It's totally personal. And the act of making a movie ultimately is a totally personal act.

For the director, casting carries enormous responsibility: It's the making or the breaking of a film. If the performances shine, you've done your job as a director. So your casting had better be perfect. The color or the exposures or the sound of your film may be off, but you can fix those in post-production.

Casting is one specific area of filmmaking where you want to be as meticulous as possible, and it calls for a great deal of perseverance and patience as you wade through the hundreds and maybe even thousands of possible options, while being harassed and pressured by agents and managers who think their clients are best for the role. And you're dealing with the stress of needing to meet scheduling deadlines. Your producers, the studio, everybody is pushing you to make decisions, and many times people are second-guessing your judgment, so you've got to keep your cool.

Casting is not the place to compromise your vision. Sure, you're open to other people's creative input and constructive suggestions and opinions, but ultimately the performance of your actors is your artistic signature on your film. You want that expression to be the best that it can be. And achieving that high level of excellence requires courage, determination, and conviction that your vision is true.

It would seems to me that this would also apply to your selection of your key creative department heads.

Less so than actors. There is an element in selecting the crew where, of course, there has to be a rapport, but it's different than casting. The actors are the physical embodiments of the figments of your imagination. So casting has to be visceral. And you don't even have to like the actor as a person if they're perfect for the character.

That's not the case with the crew. I want to like everybody in the crew. I think you've got to get along. You must have an aesthetic rapport. You must share a deep aesthetic. Once you share an aesthetic, you're free to disagree. Unless you share that, every little disagreement undermines you. When you both look at a Rembrandt, you must both get it. You both listen to Mozart, you must both get it. You both read Herman Hesse, you must both get it. If you're not sharing a certain aesthetic, you can't work together. Well, you can work together, but it's going to be misery, and you're not going to do interesting work.

In the case of *Gettysburg*, the director of photography and I shared an aesthetic. We got to a point where I looked at the dailies and the shots were as if I was operating the camera.

How did you select your director of photography? And how did you establish an aesthetic rapport with him?

I looked at every movie he ever shot, projected on the screen. You can't select a cameraman from videotape, because you can't tell skin tones, you can't tell lighting on videotape. It's okay for performances. But not for a cameraman. To see a cameraman's aesthetic, you've got to at least see his film projected in a dark theater.

I talk about art with them. I talk about movies. I talk about painting, music, literature, poetry. We're two different people; we're not going to agree on everything. But unless I feel an aesthetic rapport, he's the wrong guy for me. I don't care how good a technician he is, I must have an aesthetic rapport. Then we can disagree, and we did have our disagreements. Thank God we did, because that way you get the best results.

When you're casting your leads, do you try to match people up, bring actors in together?

Definitely. The sense of ensemble is very, very important. Whenever I can, whenever it's physically possible and the agents allow it, I like to get people together. It's usually more possible with the secondary roles than with the leads. Leads have an established reputation.

Did you use any non-actors in *Gettysburg* or in any of your other films?

Yes. In *Gettysburg*, we used a number of non-actors for bit parts or silent bits, where it was appropriate to do so.

General Barksdale had one line. He was portrayed by an Episcopal minister and a talk-show radio host in Maryland who is a direct descendant of General Barksdale.

Let's say you start with a concept of a character looking a certain way, then, for one reason or another, you cast an actor who looks totally different. Do you ever rewrite the character to fit the actor?

No. I've never rewritten a character. I may give the actor some liberty to play with the dialogue a little bit, but not that much.

Gettysburg, and my next film, *Joan of Arc*, are not extemporaneous, ad lib, improvisational kinds of movies. They have honed texts, dialogue that aspires to be poetic. And this dialogue has been worked on assiduously; there's a sense of rhythm and a sense of musicality to it, as there is in classical plays.

In *Gettysburg*, the actors didn't stray; they understood that while the text looked very formal, it had to sound conversational. And it didn't come across sounding formal, even though the language is somewhat complex, more complex than a typical dialogue scene in a contemporary movie. The guys in *Gettysburg* were all educated, officer-class, highly educated people who read a lot and wrote a lot. They had language at their disposal.

As a filmmaker, I am not afraid of language. I think language shows a purpose. The trick is not to get oratorical, but to be conversational. And that's the same challenge I'm facing in *Joan of Arc*. So I like actors who learn the words and say the words as written, unless they can improve them. And I'm always open to hearing their improvements.

What do you think is the process of creating a role?

[Laughter] How many pages you got for this?

I believe it starts in the inside, but then you've got to do a lot of homework if you're doing a period piece, you've got to study the period, the manners of the time, the mores of the time, what people wore, how they moved. But most important is the inner life—getting into the character as written in the text, understanding the actions and the motivations of the character, where the character wants to get to, the dilemmas of the character—getting into what I call the moral universe of the character.

The moral universe of the people in the fifteenth century was different than it was in the nineteenth century, which was different from where we are now. Some period pictures, to my view, just utterly fail because they fail to leave the twentieth century. So you really don't have a period film, you really don't have a historical film. You have a film parading as a historical film, a film pretending to be a historical film. But there are historical films that achieve excellence, and among those I certainly can cite *Braveheart*, *Dangerous Liaisons*, and *Restoration*. Those films became immersed in a foreign, alien moral universe, and part of the reason those films succeeded in recreating a sense of the period is that all the actors in them did their homework in creating their characters, therefore creating the world.

Some directors dislike rehearsals prior to shooting, saying that the performances lose freshness. What's your philosophy?

I find that view to be utter nonsense. I find that the only way that you can achieve spontaneity, surprise, invention, and excitement—the only way to give yourself that freedom when you're shooting—is to have it meticulously prepared in rehearsals. So that when you get on the set, it's not a free-for-all. You've already tried it out in the rehearsal process. You've explored different avenues. You've got it honed down to a very finite area. And within that area, you can create a universe encompassed in subtlety. As a director, as an actor, you go on the set and you're confident. You know exactly what you have to work with. And your confidence stems from the knowledge that you're not starting from scratch.

I don't believe in that whole improvisation school, though some great filmmakers do it and make great films. It's not for me. I like preparation and rehearsal. And again, that's assuming I'm working with professional actors. If you're not working with a professional actor, you can't get to that place through rehearsal. But again, there are exceptions to that. Maybe I sound like I'm contradicting myself, but there are always exceptions to the rule.

What do you focus on when you do a rehearsal? Do you do a lot of blocking?

Yes. By the time I get to the shooting set, the entire movie has been blocked on the location if possible.

What if it's not possible?

If it's not possible to block on location, you can't block the scene. It's a futile exercise: Where's the rock? Where's the light? Where's the sun? Where's the tree? Where's the water? You can only block a scene on location or on the set. But blocking is the last phase.

When I start the rehearsal process, the first thing we do is read through the script. Read through the whole thing, even if the actor's not in the scene. Then I get the actors in individual scenes and start to work on them. And when I work on them the first time, I let the actors do whatever they want. I want to see what they bring to it. I don't impose myself on them. I selected these people through an arduous casting process, because I have confidence in them as actors—in their talent, their gift, their charisma—so I let 'em go. I let 'em stand on their heads if they want to. The more crazy, wacky, inventive they get, the more I like it. They bring ideas, I get influenced, we break down the scene, like you do in an acting class: What is this scene about? Why is this scene in the movie? What are you doing in this scene? What do you want to do in this scene? We define all those things. We define the emotional key of the scene, and then we decide what every line is about: Why are you saying this line? I'm not saying that we necessarily have to articulate that, but if I look at the actor and don't understand why he's saying his line, I want to analyze it. Either the actor hasn't achieved it or I don't need the line. I'll change the script at that point. All that comes out of the rehearsal process. And that's different than doing it on the set. If you're doing it on the set, you're ad-libbing the whole movie. Again, some great filmmakers work that way, but improvisation is not for me.

So we get the scene in shape emotionally, the beats, which has nothing to do with blocking. I do that with all the scenes, all the actors. And I try to do that in the first week. If I have a second week, then I go on location. If I don't have the second week, I do that for the first two or three days and then, during the next three or four days, I take everybody out to all the different locations and we block it. We've already worked on the emotional beats of the scene in a room somewhere, now we're influenced by the physical conditions and challenges of the set. We're influenced by the sky, the wind, the birds. We're influenced by everything. And we block it so that when we leave that set, that's a lock on what the actors and the crew are doing. The whole movie is nailed down before the first day of shooting.

When we go to the set, we have it blocked, and we have a shot list. The cameraman has a shot list. The first AD has a shot list. The continuity clerk has a shot list. And the actors know it. They all know it's going to be six setups or ten setups or one setup or whatever it's going to be. Now on the day of shooting, I may change it. That's the upside of preparation and rehearsal, because I can say on that day, "Oh wow, there's a better way to shoot this scene," and we can change it. But nobody goes into a panic, because we're so prepared we know we're going to change it within a certain context. And then everybody can readjust.

When you're doing the preliminary part of the rehearsals, do you also have your script supervisor there to keep track of the notes and changes?

Yes. And no one else at that point. To have more people in rehearsal is utterly counterproductive. You want actors to be free, loose, and open. Once I get to the set rehearsals, it's the script supervisor and the cameraman, and maybe the soundman if he's already there.

What about your first AD?

Not necessarily. The first AD, at that point, is usually so busy doing all the other things to get ready for the shoot that he can't be there. If he can, it's a plus. But he must stay a little back; he can't stay on top of the actors. I'm still working with the actors, because the emotionality of the scenes is going to be influenced by the location, too. It's not just blocking. It's also what the scene is about. The actors are still in a place where they're somewhat free to try things out, so that when we get to the shooting of the scene, we've already had all our bright ideas, and now it's about execution.

The problem if you don't rehearse is that you've got to compress everything in that shooting day. You've got to compress trial and error, experimentation, and execution, and that deprives you of doing your best. It removes the craft and makes everything depend on the genius of the moment. Maybe you can't be a genius a hundred percent of the time on every setup in a sixty-five day schedule. By rehearsing, you rely more on craft. And time is a big ingredient, too, because in the rehearsal period, you have time to reflect, to mull things over, which is a luxury you don't have when you're shooting. That's why I find rehearsal so essential. To not have rehearsal on a movie is counterproductive, counter to the organic process of filmmaking.

Do you videotape your rehearsals?

There was a time when I did. But I wouldn't now, because it pushes the process too far too fast. Wait until you have the film and the camera. You can work on something and drive it into the ground, so that when you get there on the shooting day, everybody feels that they've been there, done that, and it's hard to bring the spontaneity back.

So how do you find a balance between being prepared and not being overprepared?

Intuition. You just got to know it.

I only go to a certain point when I'm in rehearsal. For instance, I don't expect to elicit the kind of performance that I got from Jeff Daniels, which I discussed before. I expect him to get to where I can say, "I know where he wants to go. I know where he's moving. He knows where I want him to go. We understand what the scene is about." I don't want the big, emotional breakdown in the rehearsal. The last mile, emotionally, I save for the camera.

When you shoot an emotional scene, do you do the close-ups of the actor first?

The traditional way to shoot a scene, as we all know, is to go wide first, and then go close. But I've done it both ways, and find that there's only one reason to do a close-up first. And that's if you know that close-up is going to constitute one of the big emotional scenes in the movie, so you don't want the actors to shoot their wads, be completely emotional, in the wide shot.

Let's say you start shooting a scene, and the actors are hitting their emotional keys. But suddenly there's a problem in the camera. Do you let the actors continue or do you cut?

In most cases, I would cut, because it's not fair to the actors to let them continue. They'll get up and hit you.

Do the DP and the sound people ever have the right to cut?

No. Never. Never. Never. They have to communicate to me somehow that there's a problem, and it's my discretion whether I want to cut or not. There may be a reason why I don't want to cut. Let's say it's a big, intimate dialogue scene, and we're thirty seconds away from the end of it when the film runs out, which almost never happens with a professional film crew. Now, am I going to say "Cut" thirty seconds before the end of the scene? No, that would demoralize the actor, so I let them finish it. I never have to tell them that we didn't get the last thirty seconds. They'll never know it. I just say, "You know what? We need another take." He'll say, "Why?" I'll say, "Give me another color." But if the problems happens at the beginning of the take, for heaven's sake stop. Don't let the actor waste his energy.

Do you choreograph your actors when you set up a scene? Do you give them the freedom to choreograph themselves?

It's an organic process, a process founded on the emotional life of the scene. I give the actors total freedom to move and do whatever they want. I watch it, and then I start to tune things, move things, shape things, based on the clay that they have provided me with, and visualize it for the camera. And then we start to lock things down, so that by the time we get to the final rehearsal with the crew, the actors can actually hit marks and have eye lines established.

Do you film your on-set rehearsals?

That's usually a bizarre choice. However, sometimes, for who knows what extraneous reasons that come up on the moment, you may want to film the rehearsal. Maybe the light is waning.

In some situations, you may be looking for something where you don't want the actors to know you're rolling film. Personally, I don't like to do that, because I find it dishonest. It shows a director's lack of trust in the actors. And if you do it once, they'll say, "Will he do it again? When will he do it again?" It also involves the crew in a kind of complicity. So I am not one who likes to roll the camera without telling the actors. However, I can visualize certain situations where a director might want to do that to capture some kind of unique situation.

Maybe something extraordinary is happening in that moment. You didn't plan to shoot it, but you tell the cameraman and sound crew to roll. In that case, it is not manipulative, it is not dishonest to the actors, you're just being spontaneous and scrambling to capture something extraordinary in a rehearsal. And I have done that on nearly every picture I've worked on, sometimes capturing wonderful results.

But, as a rule, I think that if you tell a seasoned actor that something is a rehearsal, he's is going to save something for take one. He's not going to throw it all away, especially in an emotional scene, where there are limits. There are inherent, organic, physical limitations to how emotional somebody can get, or how many tears an actor can shed. So I like to save the actual extraordinary thing we call "the performance" for take one.

If you thought your first take was perfect, would you do another take?

Absolutely, yes. I always do a second take, because it's an insurance policy against the unforeseen. Even though when you say "print" the operator checks the camera gate for hair, and even though when you say "print" the soundman replays the tape to make sure the sound is good, things can happen after the fact. Things can happen when the film is taken out of the camera. Things can happen when the film is shipped. Things can happen in the lab. So, for my own peace of mind, I always insist on having two circled takes, and I'll mark which of my takes is the preferred one.

I also like to give detailed notes, which become essential when you're in the editing process, to the continuity clerk: "I prefer number one overall, but take three has a moment that was not on any other take, and it's this moment I want to take from take three."

Do you light everything in one direction, shoot everything in that direction, and then go into your reverses, which require hours of relighting?

As a rule, yes, you want to finish everything in that direction before you turn around. But there always can be an exception: Maybe an actor's got to leave that day, maybe the weather is deteriorating.

When you work with your actors on the set, do you ever give them line readings? And do you ever speak to them while the camera is rolling?

I don't think I've given a line reading to an actor in my entire life, and I hope I never will, because actors are there to bring their own humanity, their own craft, their own artistry to the process of character creation. As soon as you give someone a line reading, you are putting them, as it were, in a certain kind of limitation. You're giving them a certain arbitrariness. I'd rather have an actor give me something that's authentic but not exactly the way that I'm hearing the line in my mind to start with, because usually, if you give actors the right direction, they end up giving a line reading that's exactly what you wanted, or very close, anyway.

Who chooses your angles and framing, you or your DP? Do you just focus on your actors and let the DP set it all up?

No, I'm totally, one hundred percent, involved in the visual storytelling of the film. I see it in the beginning of the process when I work on the screenplay. Of course, it's going to change, it's going to be influenced, it's going to go through a metamorphosis, but that metamorphosis takes place in my mind.

When the DP arrives on the scene and we start to rehearse the picture with the actors, then the DP and I start to visualize it together, so that the DP finds a way to understand and share the visual comprehension of the director.

In the case of *Gettysburg*, for example, I had a very specific visual style in mind, a very specific way I wanted to tell the story, which comes right down to lenses and camera moves. And the DP became intimately involved in that process. We would discuss everything. And on many occasions he would offer an alternate way of doing something. And on many occasions I would leap to his suggestion, because it suited the scene better than my original idea.

In the best scenario, there's a free exchange and a total collaboration between a DP and a director. Although, as we know, there are some DPs who don't even want to look through the eyepiece, they're only concerned with lighting. And some of the greatest DPs I can think of rarely if ever look through an eyepiece. And there are some directors, conversely, who don't have a strong sense of visual storytelling, their strengths lie more in getting performances from actors, and who have to rely more on the DP for that.

There are all sorts of working relationships. But for this director, knowing precisely how I want to tell the story visually is something that I'm very much involved with.

Have you ever had a person on the set who would second-guess you? If so, how did you deal with it?

That happens now and then. But with less and less frequency, I think, because people are a little more careless and flippant and arrogant when you are a director at the beginning of your career, and a little more circumspect and respectful as you survive through the years.

I can recall a situation like that when I was shooting *Little Darlings*. I wanted rain and I wanted sunlight at the same time. So I waited for the cloud cover to move, and finally the sun came through the cloud, Jacob's ladder, and I said, "Let's do the shot," and I had the rain effect come in. It was exactly what I wanted; I was very pleased with it. And then someone on the crew in a very loud voice said, "Whoever heard of the rain falling and the sun shining at the same time?" in a very sarcastic, smart-ass way. I didn't say anything about it, because I didn't want to have a confrontation. But I thought, "How sad that that person has never seen the sun shining and rain falling at the same time." I felt so sorry for that person. So the way to deal with it was to ignore it. However, there are times when, as a director, you have to put your foot down if you're being challenged in front of the whole crew and cast, and it is disruptive, affecting the work of the crew and cast.

Do you mean people actually arguing with you about what you want to do?

Arguing, no. I haven't had much of that. I did get some resistance from a DP on one of my earlier films. Every time I wanted to do it one way, he wanted to do it another way. He always thought his was the best way, and he had a smugness about it. Ultimately, of course, he had to do it my way, but dealing with his attitude was like dragging somebody through the mud. He was always so reluctant and filled with a disdain that he could barely conceal.

It was a situation early in my career, when the DP had a bigger reputation than I did, and it would have been disruptive in many ways to fire him, so I had to make a decision to grin and bear it. And I got pretty much what I wanted for the film, but it took a toll on me personally.

Do you edit your films in your head?

Yes. By the time I'm done writing the screenplay, I see it, scene by scene. Then it's a matter of bringing it to life physically, embodied by actors and a certain visual presentation for the camera.

It exists in my mind's vision, but of course, that vision will be modified by other influences: by the presence of actors, by the presence of people on the crew, by circumstances on the set, and by the limitations of how much money I have at my disposal. But essentially, I'm trying to make the film that I've seen in my head and now exists as its own entity on the page.

So you try to stay in the moment, open to the changing circumstances?

Yes, it's very important to stay open. I always try to remain open to constructive ideas and circumstances on the set, since many wonderful things can happen on the set—new discoveries and revelations that seem like miracles.

Rigidity doesn't serve anyone. There's a difference between holding onto your vision and having rigidity of vision or inflexibility. And I'm not talking about somebody else trying to get you to compromise, or second-guessing your vision, passing judgment on your working style and on your dailies without ever understanding the fundamental vision you have for the film.

Do you cast your extras and choreograph them, or do you leave that strictly to your AD and your extras coordinator?

The AD and I will have discussions in great detail about every single extra who comes near the lens, and what they do. On the other hand, if the extras are placed where I'm not concerned so much with their faces, I usually leave that entirely to the ADs.

The casting of extras is like any other casting process—it involves the director. But the first screening of extras is done by the ADs. In a film like *Gettysburg*, where we had a distant background, a middle background, and a foreground, we had so many layers of people moving through the shot that it would be initially choreographed by the ADs, and then I would look at it in a rehearsal. So let's say the first rehearsal is just with the actors, and then in the second rehearsal, we start to layer in background, which takes some serious rehearsal, because you don't want your extras bumping into your cast or doing things that take your eye away from where you want the audience's attention. So essentially, the ADs choreograph it and I modify it.

In shooting *Gettysburg*, you had a second unit director and you used multiple cameras. Do you give your second unit director a specific shot list, or do you just tell him what you're trying to accomplish?

I give him a specific shot list. And in the case of *Gettysburg*, even a storyboard. And the cameramen, as well as the directors, have to talk, so that the film looks the same, so that they're shooting with the same lens and sizes, the same depth of field, same lighting conception. The DPs and the directors have to work very, very closely together to coordinate that. Otherwise it'll look like two different films.

You also have to delineate your shot list in detail, so that the first unit and the second unit aren't shooting the same thing, especially if you're talking about action sequences. The first unit on *Gettysburg* shot an enormous amount of action—nearly all the action involving a principal actor. And it had to be integrated seamlessly with all the action filmed by the second unit.

We had to have a detailed shooting plan, so that we would not be shooting into each other's shots, because, let's say in the case of Pickett's charge, it was the same battlefield on the same few days. And also we had to know where explosives would be placed, for safety reasons. It was a great logistical challenge. But having said that, the nice thing about being as well prepared as possible is that the second unit director, as well as myself, the first unit director, could therefore be afforded some room for spontaneity and flexibility.

The working relationship I had with my second unit director was excellent. I would say, "This is the shot list, go for it, but if something is extraordinary, go for it, too." And as far as the choreography of his shots—how he would shoot something—once he had the shot list, it was up to his imagination and his abilities. And in this case, he rose to the occasion and used great imagination in the second unit's photography.

When you're shooting a scene, do you primarily listen for the performance, or do you keep an eye on all the other details as well?

My main focus is on the actors right near the lens, on what they're doing if it's a scene about performance. But there's another consciousness and another view around and behind them, so that if there's a scene going on in front of me and, let's say, 500 yards behind me a horse falls over, I know I've got to do another take, because the audience's going to laugh at the horse falling over.

Don't you depend on your script supervisor for that?

I do rely on my script supervisor, but not a hundred percent. The script supervisor is already overwhelmed. The script supervisor is looking for continuity details, like what hand held the eyeglasses. I'm looking at the emotional life, the performances, the subtlety. But I also must have an awareness of the totality, because if I'm just looking for a great performance, and I come back to dailies and some extra is sleeping, or scratching his nose, that's a ruined take. So even though you're focused on the performance of the actors, and you cannot risk total dependency on someone else, because as the director, the final responsibility sits on your shoulders if you have to reshoot.

What constitutes a great actor?

First of all I think there is a quality of soul, a quality of humanity that is important to the characters in the films that I want to make. I'm not interested, for instance, in making films about serial killers. As a matter of fact, I'm not interested in watching films about serial killers. I leave that to others, because perhaps if you wanted an actor to play a serial killer, you might find somebody with a dead soul, or no soul. And while that may be very interesting to some, it doesn't interest me.

What interests me is the soulfulness of humanity. What interests me is the largess of humanity that can perhaps, in certain circumstances, be corrupted or diminished. So I have to start out with actors who have that quality of soul, that warmth, if you will. And I don't think that's something you can pretend. I don't think that's something you can draw on if it isn't there.

Beyond that, I would say that there is a quality that we call charisma. And I'm not talking about heroic people necessarily, or good people necessarily, but a character who has this potential, this life force in them. An actor has to have that to start with. Then it's a question of craft and a question of talent, which are ephemeral concepts, but you know them when you're in their presence.

Not everybody could play Joan of Arc, which is a role I'm casting now. Many actresses with great talent, actresses with great craft, could not play this role, because this role requires a profundity of depth, a presence and persona which turned the minds of the greatest thinkers, military men, and political men of her day. So there had to have been a powerful force in that person, which is not something you can just play as an actor. You have to have it in your makeup to start with. Even though you don't go around in your daily life that way, you have to have it to draw on. And I think the actors who have that depth are the actors who rise to greatness. And we know who they are: Vanessa Redgrave, Albert Finney, Anthony Hopkins, Meryl Streep, just to name a few.

To no lesser extent, we can think of other actors, whom we remember because of their persona. Given that, there's a whole range of acting styles: You can say, this is an actor's actor, or an actor who loses himself in the role and from one movie to the next, you hardly know it's the same actor. Robert DeNiro provided a good example of that when he gained forty pounds to play Jake LaMotta. What great actors, regardless of the characters they portray, have in common, and what we as an audience respond to, is a deep humanity and soulfulness.

From the point of view of an actor, what constitutes a great director for you?

I'd say the directors who try very hard to keep their hand invisible. In other words, if you looked at one film by John Huston, you'd be hard-pressed to talk about his sense of style. You'd have to look at ten of Huston's films to discern his filmmaking style, because he was a film-maker who served the story and served the characters.

And then, if I was an actor, I'd want a director who gave me lots of challenges, lots of ideas, lots of direction, and at the same time left me an enormous amount of freedom to create my own role. I'd want a director who gave me an atmosphere in which I could feel free, in which I could create in and not be worried about undue criticism or, even worse, ridicule. And also, someone who would give me enough time to do my work, who would create a situation where I wouldn't feel the pressure of the set.

A director should let the actors know that they have the time they need, and then a director must make himself available to the actors, give them his time, because the performance of the actors is the most important thing.

Finally, I'd want a director who was really exploring the issues at hand, really interested in delving into the great mystery of the human drama, not content with merely exploiting the story and the subject matter. A director who serves the story and serves the characters of the story, and in so doing, serves the interests of the audience.

KEVIN BACON

K evin Bacon left his native Philadelphia to become the youngest
student at Circle in the Square Theatre in New York, where he
studied until he made his film debut in *National Lampoon's Animal House*
(1978). This led to roles in *Diner* (1981) and *Footloose* (1984), which
propelled him to stardom.

Bacon's stage work includes off-Broadway productions of *Album,
Poor Little Lamb* and *Getting Out*. And he won an Obie for his off-
Broadway performance in *Forty Deuce*. He made his Broadway debut
in 1983 with Sean Penn in *Slab Boys*, and went on to star in a production of Joe Orton's highly touted play *Loot*. More recently, Kevin returned to New York to appear in the theatrical comedy *Spike Heels*.

One of the most versatile actors of his generation, Bacon's film
appearances have included *Starting Over* (1979), which earned him a
Golden Globe nomination, *Planes, Trains and Automobiles* (1987), *She's
Having a Baby* (1988), *Criminal Law* (1989), *The Big Picture* (1989), *Trem-
ors* (1990), *Flatliners* (1990), *JFK* (1991), *He Said, She Said* (1991), *A
Few Good Men* (1992), *The River Wild* (1994), *Apollo 13* (1995), the intense and powerful *Murder in the First* (1995), and *Sleepers* (1996).

Having worked with some of the greatest directors in Hollywood,
including Ron Howard, Oliver Stone, and Barry Levinson, Kevin Bacon utilized his vast experience as an actor to elicit wonderful perfor-

mances from his cast in his directorial debut film, *Losing Chase* (1995), starring his wife, Kyra Sedgwick, Beau Bridges, and Helen Mirren.

The following interview took place December 5, 1995.

• • • • •

Before we discuss your work as a director, I'd like to talk a little bit about your career as an actor. What motivated you to become an actor and how did you get started?

I decided that I wanted to be an actor when I was thirteen. I didn't come from a family of actors, but I came from a family that certainly encouraged all different kinds of creative expression, whether it be music or art or dance or whatever. We weren't professionals, we weren't business people. We were an artsy-fartsy kind of family. My motivation grew out of that basic Freudian stuff you've heard about before—wanting the world to look at you and love you and wanting to be the center of attention, especially since I came from a big family and was the youngest of six. I was a performer at a young age.

I was a very driven kid. I had a strong and intense desire to be famous and successful. I wanted do everything on my own, to move away from home and be independent. In any event, by the time I was thirteen, I started taking acting classes and found that acting was something that I was into.

At that point in my life, I was either going to go into rock and roll or acting. From Bobby Sherman to the Beatles to the Monkeys, I had many pop idols, not necessarily actors but singers/actors. I enjoyed watching films and television, but they were a source of frustration for me because I really wanted to be up there. It wasn't enough for me to be in the audience, sitting back and watching. I wanted to be part of it.

When I'd leave the movie theater, I'd immediately go home and try to put together the costume of the person in the movie who most appealed to me.

When I got out of high school, I skipped college and my parents gave me a little money and I set up shop in New York. I worked as a waiter, went to Circle in the Square acting school for about a year, and started pounding the pavement. My career is kind of classic. I went from a short stint in acting school to working in a bar to getting extra work to getting small parts on soap operas, still thinking I was destined for a career in pop music. It wasn't until I discovered the theater and off-Broadway in the 1970s that my whole focus of what I wanted to do with my life shifted to becoming a serious actor.

I started doing a lot of off-Broadway and became a member of that off-Broadway family, doing a lot of different kinds of parts and trying my best to be taken seriously as an actor. It's ironic that when *Footloose* came out and became a big hit in 1992, I was considered a pop star, which was everything I was fighting against, everything that I didn't want to be identified as anymore.

The role of Chip in *National Lampoon's Animal House* was your film acting debut. How did that come about?

I didn't have an agent, but the casting director happened to come to the Circle in the Square and asked if they had any freshmen-types who might work in this crazy movie. I went for an interview and there was little or no dialogue for me to read, but I read what was there. John Landis, the director, said, "Make this kind of face. Now make this kind of face." So I made faces. The next thing I know, the casting director called me at home one night and said that I had gotten the job. I was shocked and amazed.

Tell me about working with John Landis.

I didn't have a very close relationship with him. I felt, in some ways, like an outcast. I had this dumb haircut; I just wasn't cool. The cool guys on the set didn't hang out with me, which gave me an indication of what life can be like working in movies. It can be intensely romantic and sometimes intensely lonely, all wrapped up in one.

By the time I returned to New York, I thought my acting career was set for life. I ended up spending the money that I made on the film in about two weeks, and within a month I was back waiting tables again. In fact, when the movie came out, I had to ask for the night off just to go to the premier. It was a good lesson for me, because I thought it was going to be so easy. It sobered me up. I realized it wasn't going to be any kind of straight shot right to the top—bing, bang, boom, you're a movie star. It was going to be a long road, and it *has* been a long road. 1996 marks twenty years since I moved to New York. People think of me as a young man, and I am a young man. But I started out really young, and there've been a lot of ups and downs.

I would assume it's good to start young?

As long as you're emotionally ready to face failure, heartbreak, frustration, poverty, and loneliness, which all go with the territory. And you must be ready to move to Los Angeles or New York, places that can be very intimidating to live.

How do you deal emotionally with hard times?

I have a very strong sense of self-esteem, which is something I got from my parents. It has carried me through the years when I was at the bottom. I have been able to go into my own emotional cave and really look at myself, pull myself together, and come out ready to do battle again. It's hard, let me tell you, but that's all you can do when you face rejection after rejection. You think you've got the job; they call you back a few times, but someone else gets it. It breaks your heart. I've seen actors get lost to drugs or alcohol or even insanity, but I never allowed myself to go there. I always believed that the struggle was temporary and that I'd win in the end.

You had faith in the mission you had chosen?

In the first place, you have to believe that indeed this is your mission. Unless you really believe that, it's hard to survive the ups and downs and the uncertainties. At times, I've had my doubts: What the hell am I doing with my life? But you've got to have the inner fortitude to wake up in the morning when you cannot see the light at the end of the tunnel and look at yourself and say, "All right. I may not be as good looking as Tom Cruise. I may not be as tall as Magic Johnson. I may not be as good an actor as Laurence Olivier. I may not have a lot of things that a lot of other people have, but I have something that's unique that nobody else has."

So if I go to an audition for a part that calls for a twenty-year-old blue-eyed guy and there are fifteen twenty-year-old blue-eyed guys there, I have to be able to say to myself, "I have something to offer that's so unique that I'll stand out." You just cannot compare yourself to anyone else. That's the most self-destructive thing you can do. You must have inner strength, and be able to anchor yourself in that resource. It's the only resource that kept me going when I was struggling.

How long was it between the time you played Chip in *Animal House* and the time you played Fenwick in *Diner*?

It was five years. I had been doing off-Broadway and had been on soap operas and had done a couple of small parts in movies.

I was one of a group of New York guys who got to audition for *Diner*. After reading the script, I was supposed to pick out two guys who I would be interested in playing. I picked the character that Tim Daly played, Billy, and the character that Mickey Rourke played, Boogie. I picked one character because he was romantic—I thought maybe I'm a romantic guy; that'd be good, I could get the girls. I picked the other character because he was tough and streetwise, and I thought maybe I could do that, too. So, I read them both, and Barry [Levinson] said, "Well, I don't know. Take a look at Fenwick."

The thing about Fenwick was that he was not really a standout part in the script, or at least I didn't see it that way. But I came back, read Fenwick, and did a screen test. I happened to be really sick that day—I had a 104 fever, a horrible flu—but I couldn't get out of it. So, my voice was kind of low, like I was slightly drunk, and that seemed to work for Barry Levinson, that was the character. I got the job.

Diner was interesting because it came at a time when *Animal House* and *Porky's* and *American Graffiti* were hot. *Diner* was, I think, perceived by the studio to be one of those films. In fact, there was some zanier stuff in the screenplay, which Barry eventually lifted out. He made this movie totally different than what I think the studio expected. Of course, when the executives saw the end result, they wanted to shelve the movie. It was a sophisticated film. Although it didn't really do much at the box office, it was very well-appreciated by the critics, and lived its life later on, on video and TV.

You said that when you first read the part of Fenwick, it wasn't that big. Did you work with Levinson to develop it?

I didn't feel that the part would resonate. It was a surprise to me that people found the part so interesting. It still is a surprise to me. There are certain scenes, like the college bowl scene, where basically you just have a guy answering questions that he sees on a TV screen. Everybody loves that scene, but I don't really know what made it so powerful. I guess because you get the sense of the character—you realize that Fenwick is not just a self-destructive drunk, he's also an intellectual, a very bright guy. He was a character I enjoyed playing, because beneath the surface he has depth, he's got something that's hurting and he's not showing it. That's interesting to me.

There was a lot of improvising in the movie. I could maybe call it structured improvising. We would improvise around an idea and then start to get into the coverage and actually kind of do it again. And I'm not very good at improvising, at least I wasn't at that time. I was working with a bunch of very funny guys: Paul Reiser, who was a stand-up comic before he started acting, was hysterically funny. Danny Stearn was very, very funny. Guttenberg was funny. Mickey always had some crazy thing that he was going to try to do. I was, frankly, kind of intimidated by all of this stuff. So I made the choice that maybe Fenwick was a guy who just shut up and listened and was amused by everybody, which sort of worked with who he was, an outsider even when he was in the group.

It came out of your own survival instinct?

To an extent, yes. We all tend to do what we are good at. I realized pretty quickly that I just wasn't going to keep up with the snazzy dialogue, so I tried to stay true to the character while listening and responding to the other actors. Listening and responding is very important to me.

Tell me something about working with Barry Levinson. Does he give you intense suggestions? Is he right on top of you—do this, do that—or does he lay back and let you run with it?

He lays back and lets you run with it, unless he has something specific to contribute. I think that Barry is very, very good at casting films. He often is just so right on the money, even starting with *Diner*, his feature film debut. He casts well, and then he trusts that the actors will bring a lot to the table.

I had a tremendous time working with him recently on *Sleepers*. Here we were, working together again fourteen years after *Diner*, and I think we'd both learned a lot. It was really fun to collaborate on my character. From the beginning he said to me, "I think you'll have an interesting take on this," which said to me that he wanted to know my take on this character. He was not going to just tell me; he was interested in seeing what I came up with. That's a fun way to work. In every scene, we'd look for interesting stuff to do. If it didn't work, he'd tell me. And I like to be told.

You did this in rehearsal?

No, this was in shooting. I didn't rehearse at all.

So he doesn't like to do a lot of rehearsals?

Just in the case of my character in *Sleepers*. On *Diner* we had a couple of weeks of rehearsal.

What did you do during the rehearsals on *Diner*?

It had to do with us bonding. We'd rehearse for an hour or two, working on the scenes—kind of improvising around them—and making some little changes. So by the time we made it to the set, we already had a commonality of language and feeling that was important for the kind of a film *Diner* was.

What kind of character did you play in *Sleepers*, and how did you prepare for it?

I played a juvenile-prison guard who's a child molester and abuser—probably the worst unsavory character I've ever played. This guy had no redeemable qualities whatsoever.

How did I prepare? I had spent time doing prison research for *Murder in the First* and *JFK*, so in this case, I didn't do any more prison research. I did a bio for the character, using whatever information was in the script and in the book. And then I filled in the blanks: Where did the character grow up? How old is he? I even answered mundane questions about the character's favorite color, favorite food, brand of cigarettes, and all that kind of stuff.

What does this do for you?

It helps me develop the character's external attributes—accent, walk, wardrobe, hair, makeup. These are my contributions—what I conceive of the character and the way I'd like to see him.

What I find amazing is that often a costumer will come to me and say, "Oh, no, he wouldn't dress that way." And I say, "Wait a second. How do you know how he would dress? Are you playing the character?" Now that's not to say I'm not open and receptive to ideas. I'm always glad to listen, but don't come to me with an attitude; don't dare tell an actor about his character. The one thing that I constantly tell everybody on the set is, "Listen to what the actors have to say because, believe me, they know a lot more about what's going on with their characters than anybody else."

As a director, do you have your actors do this extensive background research on their character as well?

As a director, I want my actors to go through whatever process they want to go through to find the essence of their characters. Everybody gets there in a different way. What's valid for me is not valid for anybody else.

As a director, do you want to know what your actors' processes are?

No. I don't necessarily want to know what their processes are. I might ask them what they want to do with rehearsals and what they want to do on the set, while telling them what I want to do. But whatever they want to do in terms of their homework—and that's what it is, homework—is really up to them. They can do it or they cannot do it. Nick Nolte lived as a homeless person when he did *Down and Out in Beverly Hills.* I don't know if I would go that far, but that was his homework and it worked for him.

Did any of Levinson's style of work have any impact on you as a director?

I've worked with a lot directors, and the sum of all the experiences that I've had on every single set led up to the moment when I took the reins. Acting is the most fantastic training ground for directing. I've spent more than half my life on movie sets, and I've gotten little things from every director I've worked with. Not just ideas about how to work with actors, but also ideas about making the best use of the camera, the sound, the wardrobe, the production design, and all the elements.

Do you believe that it's a good idea for actors to be invited to dailies?

There's a lot of controversy on that. I almost always find that, as an actor, I've done twice as many movies as the directors I work with. So I think that if I want to see dailies, I should be allowed to. I deserve that respect. I find it incredibly insulting for a director to say to me, "No, you can't handle that." Especially now, at this point in my life and career, when it's my ass that's up on the line more than anybody's.

However, having worked as a director, I can see where it can represent a problem. Actors need a tremendous amount of support, which you try to give them throughout the course of the day. And in dailies, you want to concentrate on what it is that you've done the day before, thinking about what you have and how you are going to edit it. Therefore, to be asked to continue to give the kind of support required by the actors can be very draining, because you've patted them on the back all day.

What's the solution?

The solution is individual. As an actor, if I never see the director when I go to dailies, that's fine. Often, in my case, they are worrying—they want me to come and congratulate them, which is also exhausting. So I think you should have the dailies transferred to tape and let the actors look at them at their own leisure.

But what happens when you, the director, are not there and the actors freak out over something that doesn't look good to them?

I would hope that we'd gotten to a point where there was a trust, but if there wasn't, I'd just say, "Look, you've just got to trust me. If it really sucks, we'll reshoot it, but I think it's good." That was the only thing that was hard about my working relationship with my wife, who starred in my directing debut, *Losing Chase*. She's someone who needs a tremendous amount of support, and there were times when we'd watch the dailies and say, "Oh, I hated what I did in that scene." And I'd say, "Look, it's great. You have to keep in mind that I'm looking at my work, too, as a director. You've got to say to me sometimes, 'Hey, this looks good.' It can't be all about me saying, 'You're great, you're great.' You've got to help me out here, too."

As an actor, what did you learn most from seeing dailies?

I learned that there are things that I think I'm playing which are not coming out the way I think I'm playing them. I also learned camera techniques, ways to look, the kinds of shots that I look good in, the kinds of shots that I don't look good in. If I see a scene in dailies that isn't exactly what I think it could be, it gives me an opportunity to adjust my performance. And that can help a director as well, because I may see things that the director may not have detected.

As an actor, do you appreciate more a director who gives you a lot of specific direction or a director who gives you freedom by limiting his input?

Actors like to be directed. They also like to be told that what they are doing is good and in the right direction. It's a fine line. I've worked with directors who get so specific that you lose any kind of spontaneity, you have no idea what you are playing anymore.

I'm an actor who desperately wants to please the director. I want the support from him, and I want to make sure that what I'm doing is on the right track.

Tell me about working with John Hughes.

He was very open to improvisation. He would come up with some idea for a scene and just say, "Okay, let's just try it." It was great. He always kept the camera rolling before and after the scene in case something came up. He also directed as the camera rolled, which was great.

As a director, do you ever talk to your actors while the camera is running?

I wouldn't mind doing it, but I never have.

Do you think that good directors help actors create their characters?

Sometimes. Directors have different things that they are good at: sometimes it's casting, sometimes it's creating characters, sometimes it's working with the camera, sometimes it's writing. A good director is a director who makes a good movie.

Some actors fall in love with certain directors, and tell you, "Oh, he's so great, you've got to work with him." They simply think that because a director blows a lot of smoke up their ass and tells them how good they are, he's a good director. But that's not what it's about. Oliver Stone is not easy to work with—he's a pain in the ass, very demanding—but he makes good movies and he gets great performances out of his actors.

Who came up with the terrific look for the character that you played in *JFK*?

I went into the makeup trailer and said I'd that done a scene where my hair was longer earlier in the film and now I really wanted to change it. I said, "Cut it off." And the makeup guy said, "Like what?" I said, "Like your hair." And then I had all the tattoos done. I had already picked out the clothes.

It was powerful. That one scene was absolutely a stand-out.

It was a great movie for me because I had this big pop film with *Footloose* and spent the next ten years trying to be taken seriously as an actor. But I was going nowhere: I was doing big movies that were not doing well and I was doing small movies that were not doing well. I was just all over the map and feeling very depressed and hopeless about my career.

I had an agent at the time who said, "We need to do something that will give you an edge. I think of you as an actor with an edge, but I don't think that Hollywood does. And for whatever reason, I don't think that the public does." She also represented Oliver. And one day she said to me, "You know, there's this crazy part—a really small part—in *JFK*, and Oliver wants to see you about it." I went in and he said, "Can you be transformational?" I said, "Yeah." And that one little scene in *JFK* really turned things around for me.

In *Criminal Law* there was the courtroom confrontation scene where you cry. How do you do something like that? Do you use sensory memory to get yourself to cry or do you have another method?

Sometimes I use this stuff they blow in my eyes, and sometimes I don't. The good thing about the stuff in the eyes is that sometimes the physical reaction to it can trigger the emotional reaction, as opposed to vice versa. When you feel your eyes welling up, it can bring up something emotionally. Or it can work the other way around: In *Murder in the First*, I said, "Look, I've got a lot of crying to do, you'd better get that stuff ready." But I never had to use it once, because I was just depressed.

In *The River Wild*, were you intimidated by working with Meryl Streep, America's foremost actress?

Not only is she America's foremost actress, but I aspired to have a similar kind of career, because I think she's unbelievably versatile, remarkably talented, and always believable. She was a real hero. But I realized that I had to roll up my sleeves and work with her, just like I would with any other cast member. You can't stay in awe of somebody.

How did this role come about?

It was a part that was out there. Meryl was already cast, and I had a couple of meetings with the director, Curtis Hanson, who had seen *JFK*. We had a lot of conversations about the role, and he said, "You've got to be nice and bad all at the same time. Can you do it?"

The hardest part about it was that it was in conflict with *Murder in the First*, which was already set to go. So they had to go to Warner

Bros. and ask them if they could hold off on starting *Murder in the First* for a few months, which was not all that easy to do. But my agent at the time really did an amazing juggling job, and I was able to do them both. I went from one right into the other. And it was some pretty rough water there, moving from a tough physical film into a tough physical and emotional film.

How did you and Meryl prepare for your roles, the rafting in particular?

Meryl trained really hard. I trained, too, but remember, I didn't have to pilot the boat. Then we worked intensely on the script for two weeks and made a lot of changes. We had really good, solid rehearsal time. Probably the most intense rehearsal time was on location in Oregon, where we had to be near the river because we were all still training. I'm an outdoorsy kind of person, so for me to be able to work everyday in that kind of astounding area was a joy.

What were your greatest acting challenges in that film?

I think the greatest challenge was keeping the balance between truly being the bad guy, wanting people to hate me, and maintaining the character's charm, so that it was believable that Meryl would become attracted to him, that she would allow herself to be duped by him. Portraying the classic bad guy who'd stab you with a smile.

I think that *Murder in the First* is the high point of all the work you've done. How collaborative was your work with the director on the development of your character? His physical look, his monkey-like walk, his speech patterns, his tormented soul?

Many film directors are concerned about actors who make really broad choices in terms of a look and a walk and a talk, because if it doesn't work, it rings so false when projected on the big screen, it can just really suck. So a lot of times directors are most comfortable casting a person who's really close to a role, then just letting them do their thing that you've seen them do time and time before. What I liked about Marc Rocco was he wasn't afraid to stick his neck out, take risks.

I like actors and directors who take chances. There is nothing more boring to me than actors who are intense and sort of good-looking and mumble through their parts. I can't stand that kind of work. I have respect for people who really go out there and go wild and try stuff. You don't often get a chance to do that as a movie actor because directors are afraid.

I've been lucky enough over the last few years to carve out a position for myself where I'm not labeled, where I can take that risk. And Marc was unusual in that he said, "Go farther. Cut all your hair off. Let's have a scar. Let me see how far this walk will go." I spent a night in a cell and found that instead of stretching out in the space, I clamped myself up to make myself as small as possible. And I thought that after three years of doing that, it's got to take a toll on your body, which would take on this shape. And Marc said, "Take it farther." Everything I did, he was willing to support, which was great.

Did Marc Rocco ever consult with you regarding his style of shooting? Did he ever say, "This is what I want to do, what do you think?"

He'd only say, "Look, we have this shot constructed, and this is the way it's going to work." He wasn't looking for my input. Once in a while, I'll make a little suggestion to a director if I think it's going to better serve something that I'm doing. I'll say, "Listen, I've got something that I want to try that's kind of interesting, but you've got to put the camera over here in order to see it."

What was his method of working with you to get you to do all the emotional stuff you did in that movie?

He didn't have to do that much, because it was so unbelievably unpleasant. I was depressed for real. We went through the earthquake and all its aftershocks. They put live rats on me, and spiders and these tiny little crickets called pinhead crickets that are supposed to look like lice. I was naked, and the hours were unbelievably long, inhuman.

After I had kind of built the character and found out who he was, and met the horrendous physical challenges around me, there wasn't much that Marc needed to say to me. I was emotionally wired and ready to go.

We shot for three months. Marc would do a lot of takes. And often, we'd have to do things over, because when you have low light and use long lenses, which we did a lot, and the camera is constantly moving, which makes for very difficult focus problems, everything becomes so technically complex. It was a tough shoot for many, many reasons.

Was there a lot of research material on the character you were playing?

There wasn't that much. I took what I could, and made a lot of it up for myself. His accent and his way of talking I based on the vocal pattern of a child that was about three years old at the time.

Lets jump to your directorial debut with *Losing Chase*. I was expecting more of a macho action film. I was surprised by

your choice of material, with its female sensibility. Why did you choose to debut with this particular film?

For a long time, I resisted the temptation to direct just for the sake of directing. People had asked me to do things—rock videos or half-hour television segments—under the guise of getting some on-set experience. Well, the one thing I do have is on-set experience. What I really wanted to do was wait until there was a story that I felt was interesting enough to tell. I wanted to read a piece of material that gave me ideas as I read it for what I could do directorially. I wanted to find something unusual that spoke to me.

It's true that *Losing Chase* is a girl's movie, and yet it attracted me with its unusual angle on a relationship between two women. I adore women, and I am fascinated by the relationships that women can have with each other. It's always been interesting to me that they can really, truly open up to each other and really love each other and be physically and emotionally able to connect with each other in a very deep way.

I have four older sisters, so I grew up around a lot of women. When I was a kid my really close friends were girls. I think that men have fewer relationships that have a really deep emotional connection. It's not what being a guy is about. A lot of what being a man is about, to me, is being able to do things on your own, being able to take on the world by yourself and fight the battle in a very singular way. Whereas women are much more willing to take someone—a really deep friend—into their lives. And that this kind of female relationship can also sometimes test the physical and sexual connection was intriguing to me.

I wanted to direct actors and great performances. I wanted to work with two great women, and to make them beautiful both internally and in terms of the pictures that I painted.

At the time that Kyra got this screenplay, which she loved, written by Ann Meredith, she had been very anxious to get to work, but wasn't finding material that she really wanted to do. So she said, "I'm going to produce it." HBO and Showtime and TNT had been asking her to do something, so she took the script to them and said, "Look, this is what I want to do." And she said to me, "What do you think about this?" I read it and immediately started seeing shots and thinking in terms of casting and people who would be good in the parts. So I told her I wanted to direct it, and she agreed.

When did you finally realize that you wanted to direct?

That directing might be something I should try was always in the back of my mind. I think it's a natural extension for an actor, because you spend all this time on a set and get to know intimately the workings of a film. And you often work with directors who have much less movie experience than you do, constantly putting yourself in their hands, trusting that they know what they're doing. So after a while, you say, "Well, maybe I want to be responsible for painting the pictures."

I'm a person who I likes a certain kind of comfort in my life. I live in the country. I like to be at home. I like to have my family around. But there also is a strong part of me that constantly wants to be jumping out of a plane, wants to be challenged. It's no coincidence that in my work I'm going down a river or going up in space or going into a prison for three years with no light. I don't believe in sitting back and letting life take responsibility for what I do. Recently I started performing live music, and at the same time, I said to myself, "While I'm doing that, maybe I should direct a movie." So when *Losing Chase* suddenly surfaced, I felt it was both a challenge and an opportunity for me to find out if directing was really something that I enjoyed. You might say that the timing was perfect.

You wanted to do it, and suddenly the script was there with all the elements.

Right. In the back of my mind, I thought to myself, Are these people really going to make this movie? It kind of surprised me, because it's a human story that has some controversial elements, which obviously is not in keeping with the thrillers and T & A kind of material generally produced by Showtime.

It took us a year and a half to get the thing set up. A lot people liked the material but weren't completely sure about it. And as it got closer and closer, I kept thinking, "Well, maybe they're just being nice to me because they want to develop a relationship in case they want me to act in something."

Well, they made it, which obviously delighted us. And once they committed to do it, they were very supportive.

Did you do a lot of rewrites on the script?

Yeah, we did. And luckily, Ann Meredith is an incredible writer to work with. The thing about Ann is that she's strong with her convictions, but at the same time, she's not defensive about her own material. She understands and is completely willing to change something if it can be enhanced or if it doesn't work. With every rewrite and every pass that the script went through, it just got better and better and better. And then we did a reading with Kyra and Helen Mirren and none of the other cast. That helped me a lot.

Tell me about the challenges of directing your wife, then going back home and being husband and wife. How tough was that? How was the challenge of working with your wife, who is also your boss, the producer?

I was thrilled by the fact that on my first movie I get to simultaneously sleep with the star and the boss! [Laughter] To answer your question, it can be a bit confusing.

As a director, you have to give your cast and crew a sense that you know what the hell you are doing, that you are on top of it, that you are confident that what's going into the can is good. There is nothing worse than having an actor or crew member look over at the director and think, "This fucking guy is terrified. He doesn't know what he's doing." That makes the whole thing come crumbling down. But, of course, I had a tremendous amount of insecurity. Everyday I was walking around going, "It just sucked today. I didn't get what I needed."

In a normal situation, I would be bending my wife's ear about it, but in this situation, where she was the producer and I was her director, it seemed inappropriate to share with her what I was going through. In terms of the daily work on the set, Kyra is the best actress I know. And she's so "there" and so available emotionally. The only thing that was difficult was making her believe that she was doing a good job, because she's so hard on herself. She's incredibly professional.

The only other thing that was really hard about working with my wife, and this was a total surprise to me, was that we didn't feel like we were getting to spend time together. I had thought, Well, this will be great because we'll always be together. But on the set, she was so completely consumed with the movie, playing her incredibly emotional part. So, after the movie was over, we had to hook up again.

Were you more supportive of her than you were of the other members of the cast?

I was as supportive of everybody as I was of her. I believe that you get good performances by being supportive, allowing the actors to feel as though they have the room and the talent to fly.

What do you tell them?

I tell them that they are on the right track, let's do another take, and this time try a different shade or color. They're out there exposed. They need that encouragement. Otherwise, actors get resentful and unwilling to take it further. Criticism rarely has the positive effect of making actors want to go out and literally kick ass with their performances.

Maybe with Oliver Stone it's like that, but he's a very rare, unusual example. When I worked for Oliver, he pissed me off, and then I literally felt as though I was fighting back with my work, like, "I'll show you, you cocksucker!"

But do you feel that by being provoked, maybe you brought an edge to your performance?

Yeah, but you know, I would have been there anyway. I'd rather be told, "Hey, you're doing great, now let's try this" or "try it without that" or whatever. So that's what I tended to do with Kyra and the other actors.

As director making your first film, how confident were you in your ability as a storyteller?

I turned around and there it was. I didn't have time to really stop and say, "Oh, I definitely can do this" or "I can't do this at all." I just plunged in. I didn't know what was going to happen.

With a twenty-day schedule, when you've got eight scenes on the call sheet and you're shooting five, six, seven, eight scenes a day, you just shoot it. I barely had time to watch the dailies. It wasn't until post that I actually sat down and thought, Okay, so this is what I have.

What did you learn from this experience.

I learned that I'll never again do a film in twenty days. It's not that it's not enough time; I can do it, but as a director, I like detail and I like to be able to just stop and think about each scene, because the littlest things end up being so incredibly important. As much as I loved the experience, and as much as I learned about editing, coverage, and directing, I'd rather not do another TV movie in twenty days.

What will you do differently when you step out on the set as the director of your second film? What will you do that's different in terms of your preparation?

I would just give myself more preparation and more rehearsal, and make absolutely clear that nothing needed fixing in the screenplay. People say, "Oh, the script is close enough, let's shoot." But it's very hard to deal with the script while you are shooting.

You'd lock down the script, get more rehearsal with the actors, and step out on the set knowing exactly what is happening ahead of time?

As much is as possible, leaving the window open for the spontaneous creativity that happens on the set when you least suspect it. You can plan it the way you see it in your mind, but when you're on the set, blocking for the camera or rehearsing, you can suddenly see something you haven't thought about before, or an actor can make a suggestion that enhances what's already there on paper. It doesn't matter what sparks it—if you're well-prepared, you're able to respond and capture that moment. So you want to keep chaos to a minimum so that your mind is clear enough to grasp and absorb the sudden creative impulses that could turn into the high moments of your film.

What was your first day of shooting like—stepping on the set, an actor-just-turned-director, challenged by a tight schedule and budget? Did you go for something spectacular to prove yourself?

My first day was my biggest, most massive day in terms of production and extras. The sequence was comprised of a scene in a bar, when my characters arrive at the yacht club, followed by a scene where the boys go sailing. We were shooting on an island in Toronto. And on the ferry that shuttled everybody back and forth, I looked out and suddenly saw all of these people waiting for me to make the big decisions, and all I could think of was, "I don't have to put makeup on."

Did you remember to say, "Action"?

I remembered. [Laughter] We had great weather that first day. I felt good, and at the same time there was dread, like what if the whole thing came crashing down—a camera jam or something—and suddenly we fall behind and can't catch up. And then it all just fell into place, I got what I set out to shoot that day, and I experienced incredible highs and lows.

One of the differences between being an actor and being a director is that an actor can go into his or her trailer and shut down for a while. Personally, I play my guitar and wait until they give me a warning. Then I get it together and go in and work for a short, intense period of time, after which I get to unwind again. As a director, it never stops—from dawn to dusk and into your dreams. But the rush that I get standing next to the camera, watching an actor do something magical, makes me jump up and down. And that will carry me through until the next time I get a chance to do it again.

By the second and third day of shooting, did it get any easier?

I can't really say that it got any easier. There were always complications—things that were working and things that weren't working. But I have a very positive, happy sort of attitude. I would prefer, as an actor and as a director, to have a good time while making a movie. I'm not someone who likes to work. Some people really need to work with a tremendous amount of tension. And while I enjoy seriousness and concentration, I like people to be the best that they can possibly be, to be involved to the best of their ability in making the picture good, and to be having fun doing it. I don't like to look around and see a bunch of people who are pissed off at me, so I try not to yell too much. Maybe once in a while, but I'm not like a screamer.

Director Mark Rydell says that he sits up all night visualizing each moment of the scenes he has to shoot the next day. As a director, what's your inner creative process and preparation once you've gotten a green light? Do you go scene by scene and say, "Okay, what's the story point here?"

I don't draw storyboards, but I do break down the scenes and start thinking about shots, about how I'm going to tell my story. That's the starting point, and I think about every detail right down to "Does she use a cigarette lighter or does she use matches?"

What's the story that I want to tell about? I think if you go back to that question, generally, things will become clear. It's the same with camera moves. As an audience member, I don't like to be distracted by flashy camera moves, unless they're really motivated by the story. And even then they can spoil an actor's performance. Like in *Murder in the First*: I did great work and here are these steel cell bars going across my face. I think that if you always ask, "What's the story I want to tell here?" the answer will tend to tell you where to put the camera. Form following function.

In my case, a couple of months before we were greenlit, I talked to Ron Howard, and he said, "Start going through and thinking about your shots now." So I read the script and started to visualize the shots, which gave me other ideas about where I might shoot things. For instance, if a scene is set in the dining room, and I think, "Okay, I've been in this dining room twice and I know for a fact that it's a real pain in the ass to shoot dining-room scenes because you've got to go all the way around the room with coverage." I ask myself, Where else can they be eating? So I took it outside.

That kind of stuff influenced what happened visually. Then it became a story point, because Elizabeth had come and opened things up for this family. She took them out of the dank, sort of oppressed light and gave them some life, saying, "What the hell are we eating inside for every night? Let's go outside, it's a beautiful night."

Ron Howard also said to me, "If all else fails, shoot a master and shoot overs and singles." That took the pressure off me, because I had been thinking, "Here I am making my directorial debut. I want to think of all these interesting ways to do this scene. I want to be a cutting-edge director." And Ron Howard said to me, "Really, it's about telling the story and having the performances be there." So I stopped thinking camera and started focusing on my actors and how I could get the best performances out of them, which was the most important element of this film. You can have all the beautiful shots in the world, but if the performances suck, it's all over.

Did you say to yourself, "I've only twenty days to shoot this, so let's see which scenes are more important, which scenes do I need to cover more extensively, and which ones do I shoot on one master?"

Absolutely. It's a question of priorities, especially when your schedule is so limited. I thought about cuts, about what I was going to do with the editing, and getting my script in shape. And I read books, like Sidney Lumet's book, *Making Movies*. I read that almost up into our first day of shooting; I found it inspirational.

As an actor-turned-director, do you think you have a special edge in dealing with actors?

Today it seems popular in Hollywood for writers to become directors, right? They write a screenplay, it does well, and with their next screenplay, they say, "I want to direct it." Often it works great, and they turn out to be very good directors. But there is also this thing where you think, "The guy's never set foot on a set!"

For an actor, it's terrifying to put yourself in the hands of someone who really has no experience. Whereas actors often just have so much on-set experience, which can be a really positive thing.

I think that when an actor directs, he will always focus on the performance of the cast, which is why actors make very good directors. All you have to do is look out there. Who are your best directors? Actors like Rob Reiner, Woody Allen, Ron Howard, Penny Marshall, Sydney Pollack, Robert Redford, Jodie Foster, Mel Gibson, Kevin Costner, and on and on. Our biggest directors are actors, or were at one time. If your performances are great, all else is forgiven. John Cassavetes' early films were all grainy, but his actors were magnificent.

That's the moment of truth for a director. And as an actor, you have an edge in communicating with other actors, because actors have their own language.

Tell me about your casting process.

Well, Kyra was in place. Then I set out to find the person to play Chase. Now, Showtime would only make it with certain people, so they gave me a list. The list would sometimes change, and sometimes I'd bring someone to them. It just so happened that on the week that this list was coming together, there was a big article about Helen Mirren in the *New York Times*. She was on Broadway, and was nominated for a Tony. So all of a sudden, she was on the list.

I was thrilled, because she's a phenomenal actress and I had been a great fan of hers. We sent the script to her, and she said she wanted to have a meeting with me. So we had this long meeting in New York, where I tried my best to sell myself as a director. She's a very powerful woman; she really knows her stuff, and she's very direct. As we ended the meeting, she hadn't said whether she'd do the movie. So as I turned around to leave, I said, "If you could just let me know . . ." And she said, "Of course I want to do it. I thought you knew that." It turns out she had already decided to do it, but I thought that I was auditioning for her.

Did you have any pleasant surprises or any disappointments in your casting?

I think the most pleasant surprise was Beau Bridges. He was perfect the in part of Richard, because in the process of developing the script, Richard originally came off as the baddy—an unsympathetic jerk who was responsible for all of Chase's problems. And I thought to myself, I don't want to make this a man-bashing movie. So, I worked hard to try to make Richard a two-dimensional character—to explain a little bit of his struggle and show some of his frustration at being married to this wacko woman. So I needed an actor who was inherently charming, which Beau is, to portray Richard. Just look at Beau's face and you want to love him. And he's an actor that comes to the table with all kinds of ideas about his character and subtext.

Tell me about casting the children.

I saw kids in Canada and in New York, and a few tapes on top of that. It was a long process. I thought working with the kids would be difficult, but they were amazing. I loved working with them.

A really strange thing happened with the audition of little Lucas [Denton], the younger boy. I had it down to two kids, and when he came into the audition, he was really scattered, completely unfocused. It never seemed like he really wanted to be there, and I said to myself, "It's just going to be too much of a nightmare to work with someone like this. He's really a sweet kid, but he doesn't want to be doing this, so why force him?" But I got a video camera and shot a scene, and his performance was so good and so natural that I had to hire him. Later I learned that he just hated to audition.

What did you learn from this casting?

That you have to keep an open mind.

What do you think is the key to successful casting?

Oh, boy, that's tough. I don't know what the secret to that is. I think that instinct is a lot of it, but I also think that you should not rush into a decision.

The casting of the sister was really interesting because there were so many different ways to go, so many ways to interpret the part, and so many different physical types. There were just tons of really good people, and we made them come back a couple of times. I feel really bad about that because I've been in their shoes.

There have been times when I've been auditioning for things where I do the scene once and the director says, "Okay, good. Let me see it again." You do it again, and he says, "Let me see it again." And I say, "You're seeing me act, how about letting me see you direct a little."

A good thing to do is work with the actor a little bit. You get an idea about what it is that you want out of the character by trying to come up with something to say to change it. And you also get an idea of how well an actor is going to take direction, because you can get into that situation where an actor comes in and does a great audition, but that's all you are going to get. Don't throw a curve ball at them. They are not going to be able to do anything else.

Would you prefer that actors read a scene from your script, bring in something that they're familiar with, or maybe just improvise?

Definitely from the script. I wouldn't ask anybody to improvise.

How did you help your cast to explore and experiment with their characters? Do you feel that as an actor-turned-director you were especially able to help them make the right choices? And what would you do the next time around?

Next time around, I just hope my communication skills continue to increase. I feel very strongly that you have to create a positive atmosphere where you tell the actors that they're doing well and then encourage them to go further or even deeper.

I think that the other thing you have to realize is that there's no one way to direct actors. You have to get a sense of who they are individually and what they need to get wherever it is that they want to go. Every process is different. Just as you, as an actor, have to learn to work with different kinds of directors, as a director, you have to say, "What I do with Kyra may be different than what I do with Helen." It's very individual. You have to have a certain flexibility in terms of your work.

Were you comfortable directing the two women kissing on the beach and the other scenes that had lesbian overtones? What sort of research did you do here?

Specifically, I didn't really do any research. I talked it over with the women and we talked a lot about their relationship and the sexual nature of their relationship. We discussed it ad nauseam. That was the research that was there for me.

What process do you go through in setting up your shots and blocking your actors?

I come to the table with some ideas, then I like to bring the actors in to rehearse. My best of all possible situations is spending some of the rehearsal time blocking in the two weeks before we starting shooting.

What if you can't?

Then I have the actors come in the morning. I prefer to have them do a little rehearsal before they go into makeup. As opposed to some people, who light and have the whole thing blocked when you come on. I clear out people who don't really need to be on the set, then the cinematographer, the actors, and I work for a little while. And they sort of get some ideas about what they're going to do and where they're going to go. Before I let the actors go to makeup, the cinematographer and I will discuss whether there are any huge problems with the blocking that we've come up with in terms of lighting and camera moves. If there aren't any huge problems, I let them go.

Then the cinematographer and I start talking about the shots. Sometimes on the second or third rehearsal, we'll sneak around and start looking at where the camera might be, and then set up the first shot. After that, I get a shot list in my head. Now, I don't necessarily write all the shots down, but sometimes I'll have the script supervisor write them down. I also like to communicate that list to the actors, so they are emotionally ready and really able to budget and let themselves go and let their time work to the best of their ability. The actor can say, "All right, we are going to do this master, and then we are going to do all of my coverage before lunch, so I know that before lunch I'm going to be really busting my ass and coming up with a big gun. Then after lunch, I'll have to be there, off camera, for the other person, but my coverage is done."

What do you do to stimulate the actors to tap their emotions and give you what you need?

I do whatever I can at the time. That's always a really big question. That's one of those questions that has to do with knowing each individual actor.

What was the most difficult scene to shoot in *Losing Chase*?

I think the scene on the beach was the most difficult. It was difficult to shoot on the beach because of the noise factor, and there was a nuclear power plant in the background, which I was trying to frame out. It was a hard day for everybody.

How did you work with your director of photography?

I would talk about ideas that I had for different shots and different lenses and I'd look through the camera and decide if this is what we were going for.

I certainly want a DP who will ultimately defer to my opinion, but at the same time, I want someone who has strong opinions. I had an amazing DP on *Losing Chase* who was extremely supportive and not condescending at all. He was just incredibly collaborative, fast, and very helpful. Often he'd stop and say, "Listen, I really think you are going to need this shot in the editing room" or "I don't think you are going to need this shot in the editing room."

Tell me about your post-production process.

Post was the total mystery for me. When they showed me the first cut, I was just wiped out by it. I felt, "Okay, there it is, that's fine, but I don't know what to do. I don't have a clue. I don't know how to do anything." And they said, "Well, let's start with the first scene." We went into the first scene and I soon said, "Okay, I get it." And then I ended up really, really loving it as a process, because it's your final rewrite. And that's not a cliché, that's the truth.

You can change characters by fine cutting or fix performances by using bits from different takes. What can be done in the editing room to help a film is amazing. You can rearrange your structure, build suspense, create momentum, give it rhythm, pacing, emotion by using different takes and getting out of a scene earlier or holding on to something longer than you expected. You can do a gazillion things.

I think that the new technology, like Avid and Lightworks, is helpful because you have so much right at your fingertips, as opposed to conventional cutting where it's such a time-consuming process to get the alternate takes up. If you can quickly run through four takes of one line, you can quickly become aware of which take is the best to use. It's tremendously helpful creatively.

Any key bits of wisdom about getting a great performance from an actor?

Well, I have to say I don't think I'm really in a position yet to impart pearls of wisdom. I'm a novice director. All I can say is cast well and carefully and respect and support your actors, because you are dead in the water without them. Make them respect you and they will deliver the goods for you.

From an actor's point of view, who's the ideal director?

The ideal director is the guy who makes the good movie. That's all that matters in the long run. I've had directors who are really fun, who I had a great time with, but turned out shitty movies. To me, the ideal director is the director who puts me in a movie that works.

ABOUT THE AUTHOR

Jon Stevens, born in Israel, is a Los Angeles film director and writer and a former member of Brooklyn's tough Italian-American street gang known as the 57th Street Counts. Illiterate in English at the age of sixteen, he rose from the violent city slums to graduate from the American Academy of Dramatic Arts in New York, which transformed him from an aspiring hood into a filmmaker and journalist. He also studied filmmaking at NYU and UCLA and commercial art at the New School for Social Research.

He recently directed *Irish Whiskey*, a feature film that he co-wrote and executive produced. He is also the director of the feature film *Out 2 Lunch* and the writer, producer, and co-director of the feature film *Choices*, which introduced Demi Moore to the screen. A member of the Directors Guild of America, Stevens has served on the Publications Committee of the *DGA Magazine*.

He has worked as a unit manager for ABC Television and a manager of production, non-primetime television, for Twentieth Century-Fox. He has also worked as a production manager and/or line producer on a number of independent films, including *Missing in Action 2*.

Filmed scripts that Stevens has written on assignment have been distributed by New Line Cinema and Imperial Entertainment.